The Prophetic Call

The Prophetic Call

Celebrating Community, Earth, Justice, and Peace

HUGH SANBORN, editor

CHALICE PRESS
ST. LOUIS, MISSOURI

Cover art: Copyright FotoSearch
Cover design: Elizabeth Wright
Interior design: Stet Graphics, Inc.

This book is printed on acid-free, recycled paper.

Visit Chalice Press on the World Wide Web at
www.chalicepress.com

10 9 8 7 6 5 4 3 2 1 04 05 06 07 08 09

Library of Congress Cataloging-in-Publication Data

The prophetic call: celebrating community, Earth, justice, and peace / edited by Hugh Sanborn

p. cm.

ISBN 0-8272-0495-7 (pbk. : alk. paper)

1. Church–Meditations. I. Sanborn, Hugh.

BV600.3.P76 2004

261.8–dc22

2004005330

Printed in the United States of America

Dedicated to
The United Campus Ministry
of Greater Houston

Sponsored by
The Presbyterian Church (U.S.A.)
United Church of Christ
and
Christian Church (Disciples of Christ)

Contents

Preface

In his Foreword to *Celebrating Passages in the Church: Reflections and Resources,* Howard Clinebell wrote: "It is my hope that there will be a sequel dealing with the pressing social and ecological crises of our times. Among these needed rituals of societal transformation are rituals of protest and 'rites of rebellion.'" After giving an example, Clinebell goes on to note: "Many such rituals of protest are much more than social release valves. They are protests against oppression and the privileged groups that cause, and profit from, economic exploitation of the poor" (p. xiv). This book is a response to Clinebell's suggestion. It summons all of us in the church who take growth and nurture in Christian faith seriously to manifest that faith in prophetic witness. In other words, it is an appropriate and necessary sequel in that it attempts to celebrate what faith growth means for being and becoming the prophetic body of Christ.

The fact that this book is written as a sequel to *Celebrating Passages* makes it clear from the outset that no reductionist approach to the ministry of the church is intended or accepted. These two books provide two primary perspectives on the nature of the ministry of the church. The first book maintains that the church is the faith-nurturing body of Christ, while the present study maintains that the church is the prophetic-liberating body of Christ. These are certainly not the only primary perspectives on the church's ministry, but what is being averred here is that they are primary, that is, basic perspectives on what the ministry of the church as the whole body of Christ is and must be if it is to fulfill its mission.

While the use of the term the "restoring" requires little explanation, at first glance it appears strange to connect the prophetic with celebration. Prophecy is rooted in and critical of communal life in which shared meanings, stories, myths, expectations, hopes, values, goals, and visions are in conflict with idolatrizing structures and ways of living. The prophetic message is disturbingly penetrating, judgmental, and confrontational—a call to the radical change entailed in restoration of relationship with God.

Though also communal in nature, celebration seems antithetical to what hearing the prophetic message entails: acknowledgement of our individual and corporate sin (i.e., with our willful and destructive participation in decisions, processes, and systems that alienate us from God), repentance, and radical reform. However, if in fact the prophetic message accomplishes its purpose (overcoming our denial of sin and avoidance of change, loss, remorse, and suffering) and the liberating movement of faith empowerment is experienced, celebration of that life-giving change is a natural response. To be and become the body of Christ is to take the prophetic message seriously, to be transformed and liberated by the empowering source of that truth, and thus to celebrate all that the redeemed life in Christ can mean in and for God's whole creation. In brief, openness and responsiveness to the prophetic message results in pain and confession followed by celebration of what God's living word calls us to enact as the body of Christ in and for the world.

The authors have attempted to stimulate the development of creative forms of liturgy to affirm and celebrate the church's prophetic ministry. As with all liturgy, its use is intended to contribute to as well as celebrate the transforming, liberating mission of prophetic ministry, engaging congregations in ways that promote embodiment of this primary form of ministry.

The premise of this book is that the church cannot fulfill its mission as the body of Christ if it denies its own prophetic tradition, a tradition that was brought to fruition in the life and ministry of Jesus. It is the editor's hope that the chapters that follow will be as illuminating as they are confronting, as convincing as they are disturbing, and as energizing as they are challenging. To the extent that these chapters contribute to understanding, engaging in and celebrating the church's prophetic mission, they will fulfill the purpose of this book.

The editor is indebted to a number of persons, especially the authors, for the contributions they have made to this book. Their openness and willingness to subject their chapters to modifications suggested by the editor are deeply appreciated. I am also indebted to Martha Brooke, my secretary, and David Polk, former Chalice Press editor-in-chief, for their patience, care, and dedication in preparing the manuscript for publication. Their thoughtful and caring assistance has been invaluable.

Finally, I also want to thank the authors for agreeing to contribute all income generated by the sale of the book to the United Campus Ministry of Greater Houston, the ecumenical campus ministry agency in Houston to which the book is dedicated. This makes their work a double contribution, and I know the authors all join me in the hope that many will participate in celebrating both of these contributions.

Cynthia Bowman holds degrees in accounting, management, and entrepreneurship from the University of Illinois in Chicago. She is also a graduate of North Park University, where she received her master's degree in community development. Her thesis, entitled "A New Model for

Faith-Based Community Development," integrates the traditional models of community development with historic community development models of the black church. She is a frequent workshop facilitator on the subject of faith-based community development and currently serves as director of community and economic empowerment at Trinity United Church of Christ in Chicago, Illinois.

Ann Bragdon, Ph.D., is a faculty member at Northwest College, anthropology chair for the Houston Community College System, and a cultural anthropologist (Ph.D., M.A.—State University of New York, Buffalo; M.A. Sociology—University of Houston). Her doctoral research in the Middle East studied education and women's lives in mid-1970s Baghdad. Since 1981 she has researched Middle Eastern communities in Houston, studying history, sociology, and theology and engaging in Christian-Muslim dialogue locally, and participated with the National Council of the Churches of Christ of the U.S.A. and the World Council of Churches North American Dialogue. Ann has taught at local universities, including serving as 1990 Visiting Scholar of Religion at the University of Houston. Concerned with cultural pluralism and our transforming world society, she works with the Fellowship of Reconciliation and local groups to "engage the powers."

The Rev. John Bullard, Ph.D., is the Albert C. Outler Professor Emeritus of Religion and chairman of the department of religion at Wofford College in South Carolina. An ordained United Methodist minister, he holds B.A. and M.A. degrees from the University of North Carolina at Chapel Hill and M.Div. and Ph.D. degrees from Yale University. He studied the Hebrew prophets with professors Millar Burrows, B. Davie Napier, and Brevard Childs at Yale. His publications include eighteen signed articles in the *Dictionary of Biblical Interpretation* and seven in the *Encyclopedia of the Ancient World,* plus book reviews in *Interpretation* and other journals.

The Rev. Richard L. Deats, Ph.D., is the editor of *Fellowship,* the magazine of the Fellowship of Reconciliation. A United Methodist minister originally from Texas, Deats received his Ph.D. from Boston University and is the author of *Martin Luther King, Jr.: Spirit-Led Prophet; Nationalism and Christianity in the Philippines;* and *How to Keep Laughing Even Though You've Considered All the Facts.* He taught social ethics at Union Theological Seminary in the Philippines from 1959 to 1972 and since 1972 has worked at the Fellowship of Reconciliation in Nyack, New York.

Ismael Garcia, Ph.D., serves as professor of Christian ethics and associate director of the Hispanic Summer Program at Austin Presbyterian

Theological Seminary. He received his B.A. degree from the University of Puerto Rico and his M.A. and Ph.D. degrees from the University of Chicago. A number of book reviews, numerous articles, and two books, *Justice in Latin American Theology of Liberation* and *Dignidad: Ethics through Hispanic Eyes*, are among his scholarly contributions.

Joseph Gerson, Ph.D., is the director of programs and the director of the Peace and Economic Security program of the American Friends Service Committee in New England. An international authority on U.S. foreign and military policy with considerable experience in the Middle East, he has helped to shape responses to terrorist attacks. He has traveled extensively in the Middle East, Europe, and East Asia and has addressed U.S. foreign and military policy issues across the United States and in Sweden, Japan, and Korea. His article, "The Politics and Geopolitics of Missile Defenses," appeared in the July/August 2002 edition of *Z* magazine. His books include *With Hiroshima Eyes: Atomic War, Nuclear Extortion and Moral Imagination*; *The Deadly Connection: Nuclear War, and U.S. Intervention*; and *The Sun Never Sets*.

The Rev. Dieter T. Hessel, Ph.D., is a Presbyterian minister specializing in social ethics. From 1965 to 1990 he coordinated denominational and ecumenical adult social education and directed social policy studies for the Presbyterian Church (U.S.A.). During this period he helped organize and was the initial cochair of the Eco-Justice Working Committee of the National Council of Churches. Since 1992, he has directed the foundation-supported professional development on Ecology, Justice, and Faith program at Princeton and codirected Theological Education to Meet the Environmental Challenge in partnership with another agency in Washington, D.C. His recent books include *Habitat Earth: Eco-Injustice and the Church's Response* (coedited with Larry Rasmussen); *Christianity and Ecology: Seeking the Well-Being of Earth and Humans* (Religions of the Word and Ecology, Vol. 3; coedited with Rosemary Radford Ruether); *Theology for Earth Community: A Field Guide; After Nature's Revolt: Eco-Justice and Theology;* and *Social Ministry.*

The Rev. Dr. Jay Lintner received an Honorary Doctorate of Divinity from Chicago Divinity School. He retired in 2000 after serving more than fifteen years as director of the Washington, D.C., office for the United Church of Christ's Office for Church in Society. As Washington director, he oversaw the denomination's public policy advocacy on social and political issues. From 1981 to 1985 he served as peace priority coordinator for the denomination and convened the Peace Theology Development

Team, which produced *A Just Peace Church.* In 1985 the United Church of Christ General Synod declared itself to be a just peace church. Dr. Lintner died in January 2003.

Charles McCollough, Ph.D., is a theologian and artist who worked for many years in the Washington, D.C., office of the United Church of Christ on social issues including the environment. He is author of *To Love the Earth,* a curriculum for adults on the environment and ethics. His latest book is *Faith Made Visible,* a book of photos of his sculptures and essays on art, theology, and ethics. He lives in Hopewell, New Jersey, on an old farm where he and his family try to live gently on the Earth.

The Rev. David Randle, Ph.D., holds a doctorate in spiritual disciplines, wellness, and the environment, and directs the WHALE (Wisdom, Health, Adoration, Love, and Eneregy) Center, an interfaith organization affiliated with the United Religions Initiative (URI). As the first ordained environmental minister in the nation, he has successfully coordinated a national campaign to preserve water, wildlife, and wilderness areas; served as political and environmental advisor to John Denver; was selected as one of the five leadoff witnesses for hearings by the U.S. Presidential Commission for a Peace Academy & Conflict Resolution; and helped lead a team of 150 persons at the Earth Summit in Rio de Janeiro, Brazil. More recently he developed the Earth and Faith Leadership Development program in collaboration with UNEP and is currently working to implement the Call to Global Healing endorsed at the URI Global Assembly.

The Rev. Hugh Sanborn, Ph.D., is a graduate of Muhlenberg College (B.A., 1962), Andover Newton Theological School (B.D. and S.T.M., 1966 and 1967), and the University of Iowa (Ph.D., 1975). He served as Houston director of campus ministry for United Campus Ministry from 1980 to 2002, taught psychology of religion at Rice University from 1973 to 2003, and was a pastoral therapist serving two churches from 1978 to 2003. He is author of several articles, a book (*Mental-Spiritual Health Models: An Analysis of the Models of Boisen, Hiltner, and Clinebell*), and editor of *Celebrating Passages in the Church: Reflections and Resources,* for which this book is a sequel.

Sharon G. Thornton, Ph.D., is associate professor of pastoral theology and pastoral care at Andover Newton Theological School. She received her Ph.D. from the Graduate Theological Union in Berkeley. Parish ministry and pastoral work in hospitals, prisons, and urban settings inform her teaching and scholarship. Her recent book, *Broken Yet Beloved: A Pastoral Theology of the Cross,* was published by Chalice Press.

The Rev. Jim Wallis serves as executive director and editor-in-chief of Sojourners and convener of Call to Renewal, a faith-inspired movement to overcome poverty. A graduate of Michigan State University and Trinity Evangelical Divinity School, he has become known internationally as a preacher, activist, and author. His speaking tours have taken him throughout the United States and to England, Germany, and Australia. He has also traveled to Central America, South Africa, the Philippines, Middle East, and the Soviet Union. He has authored many articles and several books, including *The Call to Conversion, Revive Us Again,* and, most recently, *Faith Works.*

Editor's Introduction

Hugh Sanborn

Of all the various roles the church is called to fulfill, its prophetic mission is frequently the most neglected. This is especially true for those conservative churches that primarily understand their mission in terms of saving souls, recruiting new members, providing care and comfort amid life's turmoil, and interpreting prophecy in end-of-the-world messianic terms. It is too often true as well for those liberal churches that refuse to seriously acknowledge and consider their complicity in the systemic evil manifest in the sociopolitical and socioeconomic system of our day, preferring instead to assuage their guilt by throwing money at the symptoms (i.e., resulting problems). Proclaiming and living out the prophetic message disturbs rather than comforts, frightens away more potential new members than it attracts, and risks criticism or even condemnation—for taking a stance that is viewed by many as irrelevant to the religious life, unpopular and/or threatening—rather than status in the community.

Recently a layperson approached a well-known bishop of a mainline Protestant denomination with the old story of the wealthy man who asked a beautiful woman if she would sleep with him for a million dollars. She replied that she would. He then asked her if she would sleep with him for five hundred thousand, one hundred thousand, and so on until the offering price in his question had decreased to one hundred dollars. To the final question, she indignantly retorted: "What do you think I am?" He countered: "What you are has already been established; all we are doing now is bickering over the price." Then the layperson told the bishop that at times it appears that the present church is imperialism's whore, bought and exploited by political power to sanction whatever means are used to maintain control, increase prosperity for the rich and powerful, and extend its hegemony and dominance. The price, exemption from paying taxes and participation in the good life, is quite cheap from imperialism's point of view, but from the perspective of authentic Christian faith, it is an extremely costly proposition. The very life of the Body of Christ is at stake.

For anyone who loves the church as I do, this charge that the church at times functions as imperialism's whore is difficult to hear and consider as having any validity. Yet it raises basic questions that must be asked if the church so many of us love is to fulfill its calling as the Body of Christ. Has the church become so comfortable in this land of affluence that no strong prophetic word cries out with alarm over the abuse of power, economic and social injustice, systemic racism, militarism, exploitation of institutions and persons, and destructiveness of the environment that are so rampant in our day? Is the church so captivated by culture that the victims of systemic evil, the weak and suffering, the poor and hungry, the disenfranchised and marginalized, are either blamed for their condition or are no longer visible? Is all the good that the church is doing minimized by its blind participation in systemic evil? When was the last time the church spoke out fervently against an economic system that depends on the unemployment level remaining at or above 4 percent, curtailment of voting rights, or the suffering-producing restrictions placed on Third World nations by the World Bank? On countless issues, from exploitation of cheap labor to ecological deterioration, from production and use of nuclear weapons to the failure to assure the availability of health care to all who need it, where is our beloved church expressing outrage? Where is it mobilizing its members to peacefully march in mass into the Bosnias, Haitis, or Congos of the world or refusing to buy the products of and mobilizing campaigns against national and international corporations that refuse to follow nonpolluting policies and/or maintain respect for persons and communities?

What is being stated here is not that the church sanctions all that the system does. There are times when the church does speak out on this or that issue. It is rare, however, for the church to take a leadership role in prophetically confronting the destructiveness of the system's structures and processes that perpetuate evil consequences. The church too frequently remains mute about the systemic nature of the evil, fearful of offending the status quo, losing members or being seen as too radical. In such a prosperous time, with so much success and affluence, accepting the cross resulting from meaningfully confronting systemic evil appears to be as foreign to churches as the Holy Spirit is to materialism.

Why bother, then, to focus on the prophetic? Why raise such disturbing questions? The answer is, of course, that we are summoned by Jesus Christ to follow where the Holy Spirit leads. God's unconditional love and truth that calls the church into being and becoming summons us to not only love and care for one another with compassion but also to demonstrate that compassion in ways that confront systemic evil in all its forms.

This book, while affirming all aspects of what being and becoming the Body of Christ means, focuses on that terribly disturbing and yet gloriously liberating form of witness described as the prophetic—that which entails all the threat, pain, rejection, grief, and suffering of the cross as well as transformation. Needless to say, we all prefer Easter—life rather than death, joy rather than sorrow, affirmation rather than rejection, transformation rather than spiritual deprivation and meaninglessness. But lest we forget, the cross precedes the resurrection; the confrontation of evil (both in terms of capacity for and actual manifestations of evil within ourselves, our society, and our world) precedes reception of the liberating and transforming power of the Holy Spirit that creates community rather than divisiveness, peace rather than weapons of war, justice rather than ethical impoverishment, and sound ecology rather than destructive exploitation of garden Earth.

Love of the church, the Body of Christ, in other words, must be sacrificial love rather than selective love. Sacrificial love means spiritually empowered love that is willing to bear whatever cross is required in order to serve as the Body of Christ in this needy world. Selective love, in contrast, is love that is self-serving, less inclusive, and less threatening to social standing in society. The latter is a preference for conserving what the church already has become (including the good it is doing) over confronting the systemic evil in which it and all of us participate. Such a preference entails an unwillingness to embrace the whole Christ who confronted evil with love even unto death.

Well, you have been warned. This book is an affront to the status quo and may be injurious to your peace of mind. It is disturbing to mine, for it not only affirms that we are all sinners in need of God's grace but also probes the deeper meaning of what it means in our day to take up the cross and follow Jesus Christ.

1

Introduction: The Prophets as Challengers of Authority

John M. Bullard

If the Christian church is to maintain its relevance to the world in the new millennium, it must recover its voice. That voice finds its content, words, and thought in communication from God, and the church utters its message with absolute self-assurance and positive strength.

Where does the church find its models for such utterance? For two thousand years Holy Writ and the guidance of the Holy Spirit have been the deep well from which church people desiring divine inspiration have imbibed. What, indeed, inspired the great reformers of Christendom to their brave and fearless challenges to ecclesiastical and secular authority? Copernicus, Jan Hus, Luther, Calvin, Knox, Wesley, Bonhoeffer, Martin Luther King, Jr.: History's champions of truth campaigned against entrenched, stubborn, unyielding human power—like granite.

Emerging from the pages of the Old Testament is an extraordinary succession of peculiar characters—Israel's famous prophets. The situations they faced placed them in a position not unlike that faced by the contemporary church. And, like the church, these prophets sometimes spoke in conflicting, confusing voices. Early in Israel's history the question of authenticity arose: Who speaks for God?

Consider the arresting episode in 1 Kings 22. Micaiah the prophet, son of Imlah, has been summoned to add his voice to that of 400 prophetic advisers to King Ahab of Israel regarding the propriety of an invasion of Syria.

> Then Zedekiah [ringleader of the 400 professional prophets]... came up to Micaiah, slapped him on the cheek, and said, "Which way did the spirit of the LORD pass from me to speak to you?" Micaiah replied, "You will find out on that day when you go in to hide in an inner chamber." The king of Israel then ordered, "Take Micaiah, and return him...and say, 'Thus says the king: Put this fellow in prison, and feed him on reduced rations of bread and water until I come in peace.'" Micaiah said, "If you return in peace, the LORD has not spoken by me." And he said, "Hear, you peoples, all of you!" (vv. 24–28)

Ahab, king of Israel, had proposed a joint military campaign with Jehoshaphat, the weak king of Judah. Jehoshaphat was willing to go along but hoped an oracle from God would render the proposed campaign unnecessary. So Jehoshaphat suggested they "inquire first for the word of the LORD" (v. 5). King Ahab summoned his 400 yes-men who spoke "with one accord" to proclaim God's permission for the campaign. Stalling, Jehoshaphat asked, "Is there no other prophet of the LORD here of whom we may inquire" (v. 7)? There was—Micaiah, son of Imlah. "I hate him," said Ahab, "for he never prophesies anything favorable about me, but only disaster" (v. 8). So the unpopular Micaiah, hated by the king, reviled by his professional peers, offers an unwelcome, negative message: To engage in the proposed military campaign would mean defeat for the armies of Israel and Judah and death to the king of Israel.

Micaiah vowed that "whatever the LORD says to me, that I will speak" (v. 14), even though his utterance was diametrically opposed to the expressed desire of the king and the unanimous voice of the majority of the king's advisers. Micaiah proclaimed God's judgment *against* the king, a prophecy of doom, thus freeing the prophets hereafter from echoing popular nationalism as servants of the political establishment.

What sets Micaiah apart from the other prophets? Alexander Rofé observed that Micaiah himself noted an essential difference between him and the others. He participated in the heavenly council (that divine gathering of Yahweh, Israel's God, with his intimate advisers in heaven, as witnessed, for example, in Job 1). 1 Kings 22:19 states, "I saw the LORD sitting on his throne, with all the host of heaven standing beside him to the right and to the left of him. And the LORD said..." He observed its discussions, and now, with permission of the "chairman" (v. 19, "Then hear the word of the LORD"), he "leaks" some of the proceedings to those who had not been present. The 400, on the other hand, were not privileged to participate. They were merely visited by "the spirit" sent by the council and prophesied through its agency. Zedekiah, when he approached to strike Micaiah, merely confirms that his prophecy came through the spirit (v. 24).[1] Abraham Heschel makes clear that the distinction between false prophets and the genuine spokesmen for God is precisely that true prophets "have stood in the council of the LORD," that is, God's assembly, as was claimed by Micaiah ben Imlah.[2] The "spirit" is discounted as the true source for prophetic inspiration, as the council can send "a lying spirit" if by so doing the purposes of God are furthered, as was the case with Micaiah and the 400. Says Rofé, "The silence of most of the classical prophets regarding the spirit of the LORD...attests to their reservations about enthusiasm as a source of prophetic inspiration."[3] The prophet Jeremiah later resorts to this same distinction in his opposition to false prophets who beset him continually (compare Jeremiah 23:16–22; 27:14–18, 28). In 23:23–32, Jeremiah rejects the value of dreams as a source of veridical prophecy. For him, the proper manner of prophetic inspiration is presence at the council of the LORD.

> Both Jeremiah and Micaiah ben Imlah stand alone when prophesying impending doom, confronting a multitude of other prophets who predict deliverance and victory. Both are ignored. Both are beaten and imprisoned, but refuse to recant. Both clash with false prophets who perform magical-symbolic acts (Zedekiah and Hananiah). Both are assaulted by the false prophets (smiting Micaiah on the cheek, breaking Jeremiah's yoke) but adamantly stand firm and castigate their assailants.[4]

Undoubtedly the most memorable case of prophetic confrontation is described in 2 Samuel 11–12. It is the story of King David, who ruled Israel sometime after 1000 B.C.E., and his affair with the lovely Bathsheba, whose husband Uriah is off across the Jordan fighting in one of David's wars under army commander Joab. When David learns that he has made Bathsheba pregnant ("It happened, late one afternoon..."), he tries to save face by ordering Joab to leave Uriah unprotected in battle so that Uriah is killed in an attack. As soon as the news reaches his ears that his murderous plan has succeeded, David marries Uriah's widow and prepares to live happily ever after. "But the thing that David had done displeased the LORD" (11:27). In situations like that, God calls upon his messenger, the prophet, and equips him with a divine message hot with judgment. In comes David's staff prophet, Nathan, who convicts David by employing a tiny narrative. A rich man grabs a poor neighbor's little pet ewe lamb in order to offer a tasty dinner morsel to an old friend coming to visit. With hot indignation David interrupts Nathan: "As the LORD lives, the man who has done this deserves to die; and he shall restore the lamb fourfold, because he did this thing, and because he had no pity" (2 Samuel 12:5–6). Then, at this heightened moment in the drama, Nathan points his finger in David's face and utters the fateful words, "You are the man" (12:7)! David has convicted himself, responding to a story that Nathan may simply have made up. Prophets use parables. What possible response could David make? A silent admission of guilt is the only one in this situation, and Nathan follows the silence with an articulated curse on the very king of Israel. Yet David is forever after regarded as Israel's greatest king.

In our cool society David's misdeed with Bathsheba and Uriah would ordinarily be condemned. But many would consider Nathan's meddlesome and uncalled-for action, clearly an act of rank insubordination, hateful. Discretion and respectful tact should have restrained any prophet. Does royalty not enjoy certain privileges and immunities? What sort of credentials did Nathan carry? Did Nathan actually imagine he was in a morally superior position to the King David? Dare the Christian church imagine itself morally superior to national governments? We often witness a dangerously cozy relationship between the two.

At the outset of the biblical unfolding of Israel's history, the story of the lawgiver Moses (1250 B.C.E.) is told in Exodus from the standpoint of the later prophets. Exodus 3 portrays Moses receiving God's commission to confront the pharaoh of Egypt and urge him to release the Hebrew peoples to "worship God on this mountain" (Horeb/Sinai; v. 12). Moses argues with God and makes excuses, only one of which convinces God: Moses is not a skilled speaker and must use his brother Aaron as his own mouthpiece (prophet). Their confrontation with the king of Egypt and its plague-filled consequences are well known. But the note of challenge to and from the people and their various rebellious leaders gives the story of Moses special, very human, qualities.

B. S. Childs notes that the story of Moses, told through later prophetic eyes (the school of the Deuteronomists in the seventh century B.C.E.), presents Moses not only as a genuine prophet but also as the prototype by which all later prophets are judged. "A prophet is one 'raised up' by God who is given God's word directly as was Moses at Horeb which he is to speak with authority. The prophet is concerned with covenantal law and must be obeyed."[5] Again the twofold task of the prophet is expressed: (1) discerning the word of God, and (2) announcing it to the world. Succinctly

James L. Crenshaw amplifies this: "Reception of the word of *God in the experience of divine mystery*, and the articulation of that word to *men in all it nuances with persuasive cogency*."[6]

The ninth-century B.C.E. prophet Elijah challenges both Ahab, the king of Israel (1 Kings 18), and the people of the Northern Kingdom: "How long will you go limping with two different opinions" (v. 21)? Canaanite Baalism and Israel's traditional religion of Yahweh constitute the two "opinions," and the prevalent confusion in loyalties was a stark challenge to the faith of Elijah, who in turn sharply confronts king and people with his arranged contest atop Mt. Carmel. The deity who could send down fire from heaven to ignite the sacrifice would obviously be the one true God. Prophets for each deity, Yahweh and Baal, would have a go at coaxing the deities to respond. Significantly, King Ahab addresses Elijah as "you troubler of Israel," the prophet as "troubler" or troublemaker, upsetting the normal state of affairs, insisting, on principle, that religious loyalty matters, that standing in a covenant relationship with a deity imposes demands of one's allegiances. Elijah takes on not only King Ahab and the population of the entire Northern Kingdom but also Ahab's Sidonian queen Jezebel, whose pagan prophets, 450 all told, Elijah puts to death in the name of his God, Yahweh. (Jezebel in her turn persecutes the prophets of Yahweh.)

Again Elijah confronts Ahab over the incident of Naboth's vineyard (1 Kings 21). Ahab wanted to annex the vineyard, situated adjacent to the royal residence, in order to have a vegetable garden. Naboth employs Israelite custom and common law to deny the request. Jezebel retaliates on Ahab's behalf by trotting out the obscure law that two witnesses are sufficient to condemn a man to death by stoning if he has "cursed God and the king." Through royal request, two "scoundrels" are engaged to make the false charge at a big feast, and Naboth, an invited guest, is dragged out and stoned to death without benefit of trial.

"Have you killed and also taken possession?" asks Elijah the prophet (v. 19). "Have you found me, O my enemy?" retorts King Ahab (v. 20), and the confrontation degenerates into a prophetic curse.

When the Christian church becomes the "troubler" of society, an unnerving troublemaker in human affairs, the church is playing its traditional, biblical, prophetic role. But how often has the church, like Elijah, troubled society and paid a price for it!

The classic example of prophetic challenge and confrontation to authority is that of Amos, the eighth-century B.C.E. contemporary of Isaiah, Hosea, and Micah. Though born in the southern kingdom of Judah, he, like Elijah, confronted the people of the northern kingdom, Israel. He was indignant at the entire nation from royal government to institutional religion, embracing also trade and commerce. Using the theme of social exploitation and human insensibility, Amos first attacks Israel's neighbors. Then he hones in on both Judah and Israel for practicing the same injustices as their pagan neighbors. But Amos adds a special emphasis: Israel and Judah have committed crimes that are cloaked in a protective garb of extravagant religious observance[7] and insincere piety. Because they have been given, and have accepted, a covenant from God with clear instructions about social and religious behavior, their crimes are the more heinous; they are committed not out of ignorance but in deliberate disobedience. Amos challenges their smugness and their use of national religion to deflect the wrath of an indignant and righteous God who speaks a blistering word of judgment through his prophet.

Many years ago the Jewish scholar Samuel Sandmel sharpened Amos's challenge to Israel. Anyone, Sandmel states, can notice the fact that human beings can commit reprehensible acts on their fellow human beings and yet be punctilious members of a church or synagogue.

> Amos adds a special note of irony, for the target of his attack is not simply the familiar evil of the disparity between daily conduct and public worship; rather it is the more heinous sin of bringing the gains from improper conduct into the sanctuary. We might paraphrase him in this way: "You cheat and steal from the poor and helpless, and thereby are able to put a stained glass window into the sanctuary."[8]

Ironically, Amos himself is confronted by the royal priest Amaziah (chapter 7). Amos has challenged the king of Israel, Jeroboam II (ca. 750 B.C.E.). "And now the decisive drop has fallen, causing the barrel to overflow: a threat of violent death has been made against the king."[9] The priest Amaziah functioned at the Israelite king's southernmost sanctuary at Bethel, almost on Judah's border. Amaziah changes the tone of Amos when reporting his speech to the people. The whole scene, according to H. Wolff, is concerned with the question of who really instigated rebellion.

> When Amos is put on report as a rebel against Jeroboam, does this not mean the prophet has been totally misunderstood? In actuality it is the priest Amaziah who, in his eagerness to resort to compromise, is exposed as a rebel, specifically as a rebel against YHWH, since he has denied to YHWH's messenger the right to speak at the place designated by YHWH. Thus the accuser is himself condemned, and the accused is the one who announces

> the sentence. In this way both sides come clearly into focus: Amos is a witness for the God of Israel, *not by virtue of office* but rather because of YHWH's hold on him, YHWH's commission, and his own unwavering *obedience.*[10]

Amaziah pictures Amos as a traitor. And Amos confronts Amaziah with an oracle of judgment, the only oracle against a specific individual in the entire book.[11] Indeed, most of the prophets were viewed as traitors. Amos is challenging the official established religion in the name of Israel's God, Yahweh. He is saying that God is not dependent on Israel, any more than God is dependent on the Christian church of today. Amos is challenging the foundation of the system. Amaziah would argue that the *cultus,* the state religion of Israel and Judah, was not man's invention but Yahweh's. Yet Amaziah's religion was man's invention. He had only the horizontal dimension—the dimension of traditional religion. That is why Amaziah could not understand the vertical dimension of Amos. As a result he ascribes selfish motives to him. There is no place in his system for a prophet.

How often the church is accused of unpatriotic disloyalty to national civil religion. When the church tries to speak a prophetic word to a self-satisfied, religiously dull-minded and complacent people, it is condemned, like Amos. But the power of God shatters the system and encounters the man. We cannot live without the system (the church), but we must not lose the vertical dimension taught by the prophets. The system resists the knowledge of God.

This is why it is erroneous to conceive of the prophets as giving forth an irrational attack on the cultus, which can be psychologically explained. It is also erroneous to think of the prophets as social reformers who stressed ethics rather than faith. Childs writes,

> The book of Amos in its canonical shape functions for the contemporary church and synagogue, not to provide a model on how the modern clergyman is to become a prophet like Amos for his day—the prophetic "office" is time-bound in God's economy—but rather the book serves as a faithful witness to the God of Israel whose will we now understand more *clearly through the medium of Scripture.* This living God calls his people into obedient worship which is tested by the standard of God's justice and righteousness.[12]

When we consider faith and prophetic teaching, we have to look at the career of Isaiah of Jerusalem. Quite unlike Amos, Isaiah is on the king's side. He is supportive of the establishment. He is historically positive: "O house of David" (7:13). The only challenge he throws at King Ahaz of Judah is the demand that the king place his trust squarely on Yahweh his God: "If you do not stand firm in faith, you shall not stand at all" (7:9). Moffatt rendered the phrase with his native Scottish tongue, "If you have not faith, you shall not have staith." National stability can be bought only from God who reigns as sovereign Lord of history. A national stance of neutrality, trusting God to act decisively in human events, may often show greater faith and obedience than frenetic eagerness to take sides and rush headlong prematurely into battle.

The prophets are champions of *truth vs. vested authority*. They were not always antiestablishment. Indeed, 2 Kings 3 shows the prophet Elisha, the immediate successor to Elijah in the ninth century B.C.E., in a decisively pro-establishment role. Under the influence of the music of a minstrel, this ecstatic prophet, a throwback to an earlier era, this wonder-working thaumaturgist, is seized by the power of Yahweh. He predicts that Israel's king Jehoram, along with Judah's king Jehoshaphat and the king of Edom, will lead their armies to surprise and rout King Mesha of Moab with his men across the Jordan. It is the will of Yahweh to destroy Mesha (Moab) and give victory to Israel, Judah, and Edom. The story ends with the sacrifice of Mesha's son as a desperate and despairing "burnt offering on the wall" (v. 27).

R. E. Clements comments:

> Undoubtedly, therefore, the prophets cannot be adequately characterized as 'opposition prophets' as though opposition to existing institutions was the basis of their calling. This is not to deny, however, that they were forced into a very sharp opposition to the political and religious leadership of their day.[13]

Did ancient Israel produce any female prophets? Absolutely. Sarah, Miriam, Deborah, Hannah, Abigail, Huldah, Esther—and one false prophet, Noadiah (Nehemiah 6:14); all these are prophets, at least in Jewish tradition. The "Song of Deborah" (Judges 5), emanating from the twelfth century B.C.E., tells the exciting tale of a female prophet who literally rose to the occasion in a time of tribal crisis. It takes place two centuries before the establishment of Israel's monarchy under Saul and David, and the twelve tribes of Israel are digging into their land allocations trying for permanency. The richest part of Canaan was the great Plain of Jezreel (Esdraelon in the New Testament) whose fertile earth supports a lush agriculture. The Hebrew tribes needed that breadbasket, but the indigenous Canaanites were not about to give it up without a fight. Barak, leader of one of the tribes, saw the crisis but was too weak to know what to do. Then the "Joan of Arc" of the Old Testament, the prophet Deborah, confronted Barak and the people of the tribe, going so far as to issue a bold call to the eleven other tribes to send reinforcements and form a coalition of tribal armies.

Judges 4 provides a later prose account of the song, filling in details the poem only suggests in masterly broad strokes. In chapter 4, Deborah summons Barak, tribal chieftain, and says in a commanding (rather prophetic) tone, "The LORD, the God of Israel, commands you, 'Go, take position at Mount Tabor, bringing ten thousand...and I will draw out Sisera, the general of Jabin's [Canaanite] army, to meet you by the Wadi Kishon with his chariots and his troops; and I will give him into your hand.'" Barak said to her, "If you will go with me, I will go; but if you will not go with me, I will not go" [the weak leader groveling before the strong prophetess]. And she said, "I will surely go with you; nevertheless, the road on which you are going will not lead to your glory, for the LORD will sell Sisera into the hand of a woman'" (vv. 6–9). The triumph of Barak's army over the Jabinites was decisive, and the General Sisera was deceived and killed by the woman Jael, "wife of Heber the Kenite," by brave cunning and sheer courage. The ending of Judges 5 is one of the great ironies of the Bible, and the whole poem (song) is an ancient literary masterpiece, the oldest long poem in Scripture.

The church must not forget that the role of prophetic challenger is ungrudgingly ascribed to women as well as to men in the Bible, without prejudice. William E. Phipps's book, *Assertive Biblical Women,* marshals the evidence.[14]

Does the role of prophet entail paying a price? The Old Testament seems to argue for a *martyr's* role for the prophet. "The history of the Israelite prophets is a history of martyrdom, the outstanding example being Jeremiah," writes Lindblom.[15] "The history of prophecy is one of bitter disappointment; the prophet Hosea sums up the prophetic impact upon society in succinct fashion: 'the prophet is a fool, the man of the spirit is mad, because of your great iniquity and great hatred'" (Hosea 9:7c d). So did Crenshaw: "At no time did the prophets meet with success, save in fiction (Jonah) [or in matters of the cult (Haggai and Zechariah)]."[16] Poor Jeremiah in the seventh-century B.C.E. suffered so keenly that he complained apparently bitterly and incessantly—so poignantly that the whole poem of Lamentations was traditionally ascribed to his authorship. Jeremiah was considered quirky; his own kinsmen hatched a murder plot against him; he was imprisoned, beaten, placed in a dungeon, thrown in the stocks, and forced to accompany murderous insurrectionists to Egypt.

He found Yahweh a "deceitful brook" who promised to safeguard him as a fortified tower against his enemies but abandoned and betrayed him.

Jeremiah gives a clear picture of what the dominant elements in Judean society expected of their prophets: They should be upholders of the status quo (compare 26:7–9).

> Jeremiah's activity was perceived to be detrimental to the national welfare, and so he was imprisoned. In the end he could no longer proclaim his words publicly lest he be killed (38:24–28). He took himself out of action: a prophet who does not operate publicly is no threat because he is no prophet.[17]

The very apex of prophetic suffering, possibly modeled on the life of Jeremiah, is Isaiah's beloved poems of the Suffering Servant (Isaiah 42:1–7, 49:1–6, 50:4–9, 52:13, 53:12). Why all this suffering? We observe that the prophets who did *not* suffer were the false prophets, "prophets who teach lies" (Isaiah 9:15). Micah in the eighth century describes "the prophets who lead my people astray, who cry 'Peace' when they have something to eat, but declare war against those who put nothing into their mouths" (3:5). Crenshaw finds the reason for prophetic suffering in the absolute fact that it was impossible for the prophets—as for the church today—to find convincing authentication for their claim to have received their message directly from the Council of God.

> A closer look at the response to the prophets by those to whom the "authoritative" words were spoken proves how devoid of authority the prophetic message was, despite the claim that its origin was divine...Without exception the prophet was scorned and vilified, his words finding receptive minds only in a few "disciples" who preserved them until the course of history vindicated a message of doom. Where the prophets addressed themselves to the question of **success** the judgment is always the same, namely **utter failure** (thus Isaiah, Jeremiah, Ezekiel, [and Amos]).[18]

The prophet Ezekiel was perceived as walking "among a people whose words made him appear to be dwelling amid briers and thorns and sitting upon scorpions" (2:6). In our day the rise of the mega churches (over 2,000 active members) has given new meaning to ecclesiastical "success." The church at large must never lose sight of the suffering of biblical prophets. The struggle to vindicate their divine call and to authenticate their authority and the truth of their message plagued the prophets and will plague the church forever. Prophetic conflicts among "true" and "false" prophets were the inevitable outcome of this struggle for authentication, for "certification" as spokesmen for God. Clearly a prophet's claim to be speaking for God did not go unchallenged. Even when the word spoken was completely favorable, as in Second Isaiah's majestic promises, disputations about the prophets erupted. "The presence of disputes in messages of weal and woe suggests that the prophets were aware that their words did not automatically carry authority, but *had to be legitimated by persuasive argument*."[19]

How is the Christian church to authenticate the gospel? How is the church to convince hearers today that its perception of the will of God in the crises of contemporary affairs is correct? Must the church always be able to legitimate its positions "by persuasive argument"? That the church must always try to do so mandates its time-honored leadership in education. The minds of laypersons must be prepared for the Church's message; ignorance is ever the enemy of the gospel of Christ.

Does this generation seek for a "sign"? The only sign Jesus offered that generation was the sign of Jonah. What sign was that? When we turn to the story of that most remarkable prophet, contained in four short chapters of the book by his name, we are confronted by the very opposite of the prophets we have considered thus far. Here is the Bible's only "successful" prophet. Everything in the story is contrary to prophetic expectation. Jonah is the reluctant prophet, more effectively reluctant than Moses, whose fourfold objections in Exodus 3 are arresting: not knowing what to say to the Pharaoh, not knowing God's proper name, not being able to convince the Hebrew people he has been sent by God, and being a poor public speaker. And Jonah is more effectively reluctant than Jeremiah, who protested he was "only a youth." Jonah jumped into a ship headed in the opposite direction from the destination God had set for him (Nineveh) and fell asleep while the pagan sailors were fervently praying to their various gods for relief from a storm at sea. When he finally arrived at Nineveh after being thrown overboard, swallowed up then vomited out by a "great fish," he most reluctantly announced his missionary sermon: "Forty days more, and Nineveh shall be overthrown" (3:4)! Never has such a doleful bit of evangelism resulted in such massive conversion: "And the people of Nineveh believed God; they proclaimed a fast, and everyone, great and small, put on sackcloth" (3:5). When news of this reached the king, he ordered wholesale repentance—including the livestock—and proclaimed a general fast of both food and water and a genuine turning away from evildoing on the part of everyone in Nineveh! A more successful piece of productive and effective preaching has never occurred. Jonah had only entered the city one-third of the way (one day's journey into a city "three days' walk across"). The message of the book of Jonah is contained in chapter 4. And that message has important relevance for our contemporary Christian church. In all his success at effecting Nineveh's conversion and repentance, Jonah's emphasis lay in his articulation of doom on Israel's traditional enemy from the eighth century. (The book of Jonah dates from the mid-fourth century B.C.E.) Absent from Jonah is any expression of concern for the "godless" of the world whom God created and for whom Christ later died. Jonah is petulant and crabby; he made himself a little gazebo on the cliff overlooking Nineveh, the better to witness Nineveh's destruction. Overnight a bush pops up to provide a bit of shade from the afternoon sun; next night a big "worm" (caterpillar?) gobbles up the bush and away with the shade. Jonah is furious—with whom? Not Nineveh, not the bush, not the worm, not the hot sun; Jonah is angry with God, yes, "angry enough to die" (4:8).

Do we have here an image of the church? See with what sensitivity the exegete B. Davie Napier interprets the story in poetry:

> My name is Johnny Jonah. I am one
> who never was but always am—always
> in search of Tarshish; always brought again
> to Nineveh; and never satisfied.
> If Yahweh burns in anger at the ways
> of men in anybody's Nineveh,
> he cools it when he sees a sign of hope.
> And I, who have proclaimed his wrath, am left
> Holding the bag. No wonder that I burn!...
> That really isn't how it is at all.
> We Johnny Jonah's aren't disposed to sing
> when we are caught by Yahweh in a fish
> somewhere between Tarshish and Nineveh.
> No one rejoices when he finds himself
> restrained from breaking loose, brought back again
> to face some kind of crucifixion.
> Look at Jesus' anguish in Gethsemane.[20]

The story of Jonah brings us to Jesus of Nazareth. However much people differ in their christologies, all agree that whatever else Jesus was, Jesus was a teacher. In the New Testament the role of prophet was transformed into that of teacher, announcer of the word and will of God for one's generation. Did Jesus' teaching enjoy the success of that of Jonah? That question is answered by the event of the crucifixion.

The last books of the Old Testament reveal a decline in prophecy, a gradual cessation of the prophetic movement. We have seen that prophetic claims made in the name of God were not borne out in historical experience, and this resulted in the clash between true and false prophets. It is this clash that destroyed the movement.[21]

> From Zechariah it can be assumed that prophecy had become so distasteful to society that it no longer is reckoned in the divine economy of salvation; it is even said that the prophet is to be put to death by his parents, and that every prophet will be ashamed of his vision and will seek to hide his identity by refusing to wear the distinctive garb of the people and by explaining his flesh marks, probably acquired in ecstatic prophecy, as the result of a brawl.[22]

By Ezekiel's time (sixth century B.C.E.) the prophet had become a successful entertainer, "like one who sings with a beautiful voice and plays well on an instrument," but they hear what he says and refuse to do it.

Has the church's gospel degenerated into "entertainment" instead of confrontation? Is the frenetic effort in contemporary American Protestantism to lure people in "so we can hook 'em" a reduction of the church's legitimate prophetic role as challenger of authority (and of society at large) into an alternative entertainment medium aimed at stroking our egocentric, consumer-oriented culture?

The very existence of the Christian church testifies to the truth and reality of the resurrection of the Crucified One, however critically even church members differ in their interpretations of that event. For the church is the Body of Christ at work in the world to preach repentance and palpably change both individuals and society for the betterment of humanity as a whole.

Jesus gave us the sign of Jonah. Are we, like Jonah, petulant, petty, judgmental, indignant not with ourselves but with God, impatient with the slow pace of God's kingdom, always coming but not yet quite here? Dean Leander E. Keck, in his memorable Lyman Beecher Lectures at Yale University for 1992, addressed the formidable topic of renewing the mainline churches for the twenty-first century. His keynote for these lectures was a quotation from the Beecher Lecturer for 1939, Charles Clayton Morrison: "Christianity must repent, but it must not whimper." Keck entitled his treatment *The Church Confident*, and he calls not for improvement but for renewal "that reforms the churches' worship, theology, ethos, and communication. Changes in these four, taken together, can restore *the church confident*—a less abrasive image today than the earlier "church militant."[23] He eschews the idea of triumphalism, but he urges a renewal of that confidence in truth that characterizes the biblical prophets: "Now a new era is dawning. If in this yet ill-defined era the churches are renewed within because they recover their confidence in the gospel, they will be able to offer the twenty-first century a vital witness to the truth about God—and about ourselves."[24]

The prophet speaks God's word regardless of consequences. It is the business of the church to find the prophetic word for today at any given moment. If that divine word is destructive of the status quo, then it is squarely in the biblical prophetic pattern. If proclaiming the prophetic word is painful to the church, costing it members, prestige, worldly "success," and even temporal security, it may simply be putting obedience to the command of Christ ahead of mundane and selfish concerns.

SECTION I
The Prophetic Call to Restore and Celebrate Community

2

The Failure of Community

Sharon G. Thornton

When I was nine years old, my next-door neighbor and I decided we would form a club. We spent hours constructing a clubhouse from a discarded box that once held someone's new washing machine. We initiated new members by placing a large *X* on their foreheads made with the lipstick we "borrowed" from my sister's dresser drawer. We devised a secret password, known only to us, that would allow others access to our exclusive little domain. We were a "girls only" club, the envy of the fourth-grade class. Our fame was short-lived, however. One day two big boys, sixth graders, found our cardboard hideout and kicked in one side, making a huge hole. Soon the rains came and finished the job, leaving only an ugly heap of soggy brown pulp. That was the end of our "club." Our dreams were destroyed; our "community" had failed! Before long our little band of members parted company to find other adventures, leaving my next-door neighbor and me to grumble about what might have been and to cook up new schemes for another day.

The longing for community appears to be programmed into our genetic code. Or as Simone Weil has said, "To be rooted, is perhaps the most important and least recognized need of the human soul." [1] As children we form play groups, all kinds of "clubs," neighborhood pals, best friends. As graduate students many of us experienced "community-building" activities on our various campuses to address the needs of those of us who were feeling homesick, lonely, and isolated. In every church I have participated in, a sense of "community" has been a high priority, especially when tensions between members became accentuated. In the seminary where I teach, the longing for community is strong, particularly at this time when we are struggling to respect our diversity and engage each other across differences. I cannot remember a time when I have not heard people expressing a desire for community, often precisely when a particular community is experiencing its life as fragile, weak, or absent. Yet once we attempt a living facsimile, its failure seems to quickly follow. Why do we not seem to "get it right"?

The lure of community with its attending difficulties and inevitable demise always seems to haunt us. Yet, if communities come and go, almost like the seasons, why is the failure of community such an urgent need and pressing challenge at this particular time in our common life? Moreover, what is this "community" that draws our imaginations and prompts our creative undertaking—and then causes us such grief when we feel its loss?

Fractured from the Beginning

Somewhere in the collective imagination of many North American people is a version of our national identity that we suppose is reflected in our neighborhood communities and places of worship. It is one that portrays a way of life where people are happily living together in a spirit of cooperation and goodwill. It arises out of the dream voiced in our Declaration of Independence, penned into our Constitution, and amplified by the Bill of Rights. Our founders who composed the words believed our public life could reflect the ideals represented in these documents. Their vision inspired the words inscribed on our coins: *e pluribus unum* (Out of many we are one). From the beginning the dream of one nation conflated with religious imagery depicted America as the new "Promised Land," and by and large our religious institutions endorsed this Manifest Destiny.[2] But we are not "one" people today. And we were never a truly united people when these words were first engraved on our currency. Our communities have never been equal, free, and whole in the United States. Instead, they have been fractured from the beginning and remain so today.

The truth is, we built the foundations of our nation on the ruins of prior existing, legitimate communities here in North America—ruins that we created. We destroyed the communities of those we brought for cheap labor, particularly from Africa, in order to build a powerful empire. In a speech delivered at the University of California in 1997, President Clinton reminded the audience:

> We were born with a declaration of independence which asserted that we all were created equal and a constitution that enshrined slavery. We fought a bloody civil war to abolish slavery, but we remained unequal by law for another century. We advanced across the continent in the name of freedom, yet in doing so we pushed Native Americans off their land. We welcome immigrants, but each new wave has felt the sting of discrimination.[3]

We were fractured from the beginning. We are broken now. The implication of this is that fractured communities are not something we can simply restore. The longing for community we experience today cannot be assuaged by evoking something from the past—because it never existed in the first place. As Benjamin Mays has said, "a nation cannot restore what it has not established."[4]

The failure of community in the United States today is rooted in our founding genocide and fueled by our ongoing abusive structures of race, class, gender, and other forms of exclusionary politics in spite of our lofty public rhetoric about what this nation stands for. There is no way to soften this reality. It is a trajectory for failure supported by what Sydney Ahlstrom has called "rampant economic anarchic individualism,"[5] an unrestricted expression of social organization that has led to extreme and unjust forms of abusive market capitalism. Our imaginations are formed by this brand of market capitalism that militates against the spirit of cooperation necessary for sustainable communities, promoting instead competition, consumption, and the entrepreneurial spirit toward exclusionary private gain.

Robert Jay Lifton has explored the implications of our violent history for people who live with it and try to make some moral sense out of their lives. He says that it is very difficult for American citizens, who think of themselves as good and decent people and who value what their country stands for in terms of democracy and human rights, to also recognize their country's violent history and actions. In other words, it is difficult for many Americans to answer the question "How can I be a good person and be a part of a people who have perpetrated such harm on others?" In order to deal with the deep contradiction in this question, Lifton suggests that we as a nation have engaged in what he calls "psychic numbing." We rationalize, forget, ignore, "numb" ourselves to the realities we inherit, benefit from, feel little control over, cannot justify, and which we do not want to admit we participate in. Because we numb ourselves to these realities, we distort our history and position ourselves to justify all kinds of other atrocities. Lifton believes, and he is convincing, that this historical numbing on many of our parts is what furthers our willingness to justify slavery, our reluctance to see the Holocaust of the Jews, our ambivalent responses to our dropping the atomic bombs on Hiroshima and Nagasaki, even our drift into Vietnam as well as many of our continuing military engagements.[6] Psychic numbing, then, not only denies history but also reinforces our willingness to resist fundamental changes in the way we understand our lives, our communities, and our places in them.

The old truism, that those who refuse to learn from history are the ones doomed to repeat their follies, applies to our situation today. Instead of learning from our mistakes, we often deny them and distance ourselves from their orbit of harm. Then when we do respond to the suffering of people, particularly sufferings in which we are implicated, we falsely believe our feelings of remorse and stabs of compassion absolve us of further responsible action or any deep changes in our living arrangements. Strangely, at this time in our national life, to question root causes of failed community is viewed as unpatriotic. Yet, as Ronald Herring, Professor of International Relations at Cornell University, warns, "If we fail to understand causes [of our current social and political situation], we will as a nation exacerbate and replicate the threatening conditions that now affect us."[7]

Our ongoing denial (psychic numbing) and unwillingness to deal with our moral and social contradictions as a nation is keeping us in a politically and environmentally toxic environment that is killing us. Some of us die instantly; the rest of us die inch by inch through the kinds of apathy and hopelessness that become somaticized in the body politic as well as individual bodies in depression; rage; cancers of all sorts; and malnutrition of body, mind, and spirit. This is failure of community. But instead of recognizing it as such, we employ military and violent maneuvers to conceal our failure, trying to convince ourselves that through power and force we will somehow prevail. Or we turn inward and falsely believe we can become whole and good through individual efforts and spiritual gymnastics—but there is no such thing as individual health, no personal morality, apart from our communal integrity and well-being. And instead of health, we will bequeath fear to the following generations.

Our media is playing a critical role in legitimating the use of violence and force to address complex issues facing our communities. It is doing so, in part, by manipulating people's fears toward conforming to the dominant national rhetoric calling for armed conflict to oppose terrorism and, at the time of this writing, the deposing of Saddam Hussein's government in Iraq. The media has, in fact, been restricting its coverage to proceedings and opinions that reinforce this point of view, perpetuating a distorted reading of world events and options to the American people. A professor visiting from Australia remarked that he was profoundly surprised by the limited access to world journalism in the United States. His comment confirms what Ziauddin Sardar and Merryl Wyn Davies wrote: "The American media...[w]orks to keep American people closed to experience and ideas from the rest of the world and thereby increases the insularity, self-absorption and ignorance that is the overriding problem the rest of the world has with America."[8] Too often our longing for community has only meant securing our own direct experience of our circumscribed world.

By limiting what we are told, and by whom we can be informed, we are cultivating a climate conducive for conformist thinking. This has all kinds of repercussions, not the least of which is making us vulnerable to authoritarian ways of relating with each other. Authoritarianism and conformist thinking were two interrelated concerns coming out of World War II that we sought to resist by all means. As these destructive forces infiltrate our national ethos, we are beginning to live what we deplore and we move farther and farther away from our hearts, longing for vibrant and meaningful communities.

Community has always failed when it produces and perpetuates practices of destruction, distortion, and exclusion. The schoolyard clique and the neighborhood "clubhouse" are simply smaller and less sophisticated versions of this wider entrenched phenomenon. Furthermore, when schoolchildren engage in exclusionary games, their play is not simply the product of an immature imagination. Exclusionary play is learned behavior that reflects the ethos of the wider society in which children are nurtured. If we are honest about it, we will recognize the failure of our exclusionary politics and that we have yet to establish a community, whether in a local setting, a national setting, or a global setting, that reflects the mutual and inclusive participation of all people over time. In many ways we do long for something that we have yet to conceive.

Recognizing Our Failure

Failure of a community points to the failure of an ideal, in this case the "American dream," which was a "broken dream" from its beginning—in fact a nightmare for the Native Americans and many non-Europeans who have come here since. Without recognizing this initial brokenness, the "ideal," lacking corroboration in history, becomes an idol that is untouchable—because it does not exist and never did. This is the recipe for idolatry where the ideal becomes raised to what is valued and revered as something of ultimate importance in and of itself. Whether it is the ultimate importance of a small group of schoolchildren or small groups of powerful people in a nation, or whether it is the ultimate importance of a particular people, community, or nation as a whole (manifest destiny), "ultimacy" points to the formation of the idolatrous imagination that mitigates against mutuality and inclusion or any recognition of authority outside its own sphere of reference. An ideal community that becomes an idol will be *failed* because the idolatry it generates cannot endure.

If we consider our present ways of living together, is there any hope for a future where people are related by bonds that are forged through trust and mutual respect? Do we simply name our failed community and resign ourselves to a perpetual state of alienation? Although there are no guarantees that our future will be any different from what we experience now, we must not let our failed attempts at community be our last word. We live with a myth that failure is always with us; there have always been wars and rumors of wars. But we also have access to a tradition that calls us to turn in our swords for pruning shears and to hope against hope. The kind of hope we are called to live, however, has never been associated with what we have come to know as "optimism." Instead, genuine hope has always insisted on recognizing the true reality of our circumstances and confessing our failures. Hope always begins in failure and arises out of the realization that an alternate way of living must be proclaimed. Archbishop Desmond Tutu staked his life on this, believing that telling the truth about our lives can move people toward reconciliation and new life.

Recognizing and confessing our failure of community can offer a new, however painful, perspective from which to view our history and our lives. Or it may not. Failure can propel people into isolation, cynicism, and further destructive practices. Whereas confessing can be revealing, it does not necessarily guarantee new and redemptive possibilities. While this may seem pessimistic, it need not be. In fact, the null point of failure can become precisely that place from which something entirely new can emerge. It can become the birthplace of a new imagination.

The null point of failure offers a place from which we might allow the reforming of our lives through critical reevaluations of our history and the theories and theologies we have relied on to interpret it. It could be a time for "decolonizing" our minds, to use a phrase borrowed from postcolonial scholars, only the minds to be decolonized in this instance are those that perpetuate modern Western certitude and domination and, predominantly, white privilege. It invites us to relinquish the worldviews that have become lodged in our theories, theologies, and liturgical practices that foster exclusionary visions and models of persons and communities.

Failure, from this angle of vision, can provide an opening for a radical faith where people and communities stand poised to become transformed into something they have never known or experienced before. It will involve a kind of deepening of our disintegration until we become free, open to a future beyond our control. But the courage and risk involved in this is enormous. It means relinquishing the familiar for something completely unknown. It means being willing to depend on others who know the underside of history, especially those we have not previously known and trusted before. This situation we face at the crossroads of history in our common life has something to do with the condition of disruption and dislocation where failed community imposes its own kind of exile.

The Experience of Exile

In my kitchen is a framed picture of a chicken, with obviously wet feathers, standing next to an egg broken open into two jagged pieces. The title of the etching is "You Can't Go Home Again." Like this chick, we find ourselves in a similar situation outside our familiar and secure surroundings, longing for something we cannot retrieve. Our longing for community is our longing for "home," and we are finding ourselves homesick without end. Separated from everything we have known and taken for granted, unable to regain our bearings, we are faced with a situation that is irreversible, and so we find ourselves living a kind of exile.

Walter Brueggemann has written that exile is indeed an appropriate metaphor to express the serious rip that is torn through our communal fabric. In fact, he compares our time to that of great crisis in 587 B.C.E., when the temple of the Hebrews was destroyed. He states, "Our present deep social dislocation is a parallel to that of Israel's ancient exile in depth, intensity, massiveness, and urgency." [9] Now, like then, our public life is in jeopardy as our public institutions falter and we face the end of a sustaining social fabric. He goes on to say that we are now in the situation where we must recognize that "Even the life guaranteed by God is tenuous and can end." [10]

This is no time, then, for any gestures that suggest we might be able to get out of this mess anytime soon, especially not by our own efforts. We do not live in exile as though the viability of our previous and carefully hewn opinions or our tentatively held solutions are simply being tested. This would misread the extreme environment we now inhabit, trivializing its radical disjuncture. Exile does not invite the rush toward quick solutions and answers. That would simply replicate the dynamics of coercive power and militaristic force and take us to a place no different from where we are now. Like the exiles of old we must come to face an alternative community, "deeply placed at risk, in which God of Israel is a pivotal player." [11]

Edward Said has described exile as an alternative to the mass institutions that dominate modern life. However, it is not something we can choose. We are either born into it, or it happens to us. [12] So, while exile is a place of excruciating failure, or according to Said, "the perilous territory of not-belonging," [13] it is also a place of possibility precisely because we do *not* decide to be there.

Brueggemann warns us that the temptations of exile include denial and despair. We will be tempted to deny the experience. If we do admit how dangerous it is, we will be tempted to despair that there is anything we can do, now that we are in such a situation, to alter it. [14] Denial and despair can combine to foster a spirituality of cynicism that forms around us like a cement prison wall through which no light can penetrate. Cynicism cannot generate hope. So, what is the alternative in such grave times? As Brueggemann says, we need "access to the crisis that can go deep into the crisis and so avoid denial and imagine past the crisis, and so avoid despair." [15] And here is the point of connection to this volume of essays, which focuses on recovering the prophetic voice of the church. Access is given through the prophetic tradition that remembers its ancient miracles and grants the courage to speak with honesty, sadness, rage, and anger over the losses that are real: "[S]peeches of complaint and lamentation that dare to say out loud how overwhelming is the loss, how great the anxiety, how deep the consequent fear." [16]

The prophet emerges in exile. The prophet arrives when the people are stripped of their self-confidence and previously construed ways of living. Into their bankruptcy the prophet announces a radical new possibility, giving expression to the alternative reading that another world is possible. While the prophet's words may appear as "over and against," they arise from the workings of alternity already hidden in the rhetoric of despair and the workings of destruction. Through the prophet's speech the old imagination that believes we have only the world in which we are living is weaned away from the powers that have kept it captive too long. Exile can give us a new perspective on who we are, and a new self-awareness of whom we might yet become.

The new self we may encounter in exile will, by necessity, be radically different from the one we knew before exile. No longer will the autonomous individual be able to retreat into a private domain or form exclusionary clubs secluded from the terrors and suffering of the world. In exile, the community can no longer be viewed as a backdrop against which the private individual lives out the drama of life. The Biblical response to exile speaks against this false notion of community and insists instead on the cultivation and maintenance of a public economy of compassion and justice as the way beyond despair.[17] "[M]otivated by a memory of earlier times of one's own disadvantage that continues to propel us with commanding authority," exile is a time for communities to regroup and reorder their public policies for the sake of all of the members of society.[18] By engendering such new awareness, Said observes that exile carries within it "a touch of solitude and spirituality."[19] However, exile's solitude will be a solitude without the guarantee of peace, and its spirituality will be marked by insecurity, although a holy insecurity, that will indicate a new way "home."

Intimations of Return

The signs and marks of an exodus from exile toward our true home will take us on a "journey in reverse." Instead of moving on and building on what has been, we will need to return to "ground zero," the place where fracture and failure originate, and see it as though for the first time. In a way this beginning will be a place we have never been before because we have never allowed ourselves the full impact of our origins. However, this journey in reverse will not satisfy our nostalgia for the community we previously imagined and now hope to retrieve. Instead, it will lead us somewhere else, toward a new community we can never accomplish completely and only approximate partially. Elie Wiesel speaks of our hope for a new home as a yearning for the future, a longing for the "humanity in human beings that moves them away from the need to conquer, to dominate, and above all to humiliate others."[20] This is a future that is not yet; as such it will require of us new ways of living that are tentative and provisional, open to the unexpected, where we take seriously the place of others as well as ourselves.

The contours of our new home will need to be forged through forgiveness and shaped by promises we keep. We need the power of forgiveness to free us for a future not dominated by the past. We need to make promises so we can receive the promise of a future that does not replicate the past. Forgiving and promising are gifts of an "exilic consciousness" that reveals to us our lives as far more interconnected and interdependent than we once thought they were. So, if we manage to avoid the temptations of denial and despair in exile that threaten to draw us into a debilitating self-absorption, we might discover a new self-understanding grounded in forgiving and promising activities that helps prepare us for the kind of community building that will be required of us all.

The world, our communities, and even our families are shaped by spheres of knowledge and influence far beyond our control. The complexity of our lives requires a new kind of relational imagination that acknowledges that we have no future without each other. Our future will involve cultivating a mutuality based on radical respect, particularly for those whom we perceive as different from who we are. The kind of radical respect whose seeds are sewn in exile is more than the Rogerian notion of unconditional positive regard. Rather, exilic respect is proactive, involving our willingness to make commitments to the deep humanness of others in their complete integrity. In other words, radical respect prompts us to act self consciously toward realizing Wiesel's humanity that moves away from the need to conquer, to dominate, and to humiliate others, since exilic respect for all of life reveals that in our differences is our inescapable relatedness. What we are calling radical respect, theologian Dorothee Soelle describes as a kind of critical attentiveness that prepares us to "become empty and ready to perceive what another person is expressing" entirely independent of my evaluations. [21]

Radical respect born in exile prepares us to become surprised. We become open to ideas and behaviors that shake our previously held convictions about community and the way that the world is. This is painful. It throws us off center, making us vulnerable again and again to displacement. With Wiesel we might ask, "Is history, then, nothing but a journey from exile to exile?" [22] Yet, it is the shattering of assumptions that can open us and change us. The way into a different future, of which we may not be the chief architects, is to allow the play of many voices and imaginations in the struggle for new communities free from the stranglehold of greed, fear, and humiliation. Radical respect involves our willingness to be changed and formed by others. [23]

The journey in reverse, then, will require much from us. It will involve the formation of a new consciousness that expresses itself in radical respect. It will mean cultivating an attentiveness to others that will open us to new forms of knowledge. It will call us to practices of relinquishment that require our unlearning familiar patterns of interactions and letting go of cherished ideas about community. For those of us whose lives have been supported by privilege, Soelle reminds us that we need to unlearn our dependency on consumerism and militarism, violence, and the ways we plunder our Earth. We need to relinquish coercive forms of power, spiritual apathy, and postures of cynicism and defeat. [24] Relinquishment will involve us in patterns of *joining* and *following,* and this will make those of us who are used to offering the directions and taking the lead feel uncomfortable and disoriented. If denial and despair mark the temptations of exile, our resistance to and ambivalence about the fundamental changes required of us dot the terrain of return. Said cautions, "Homecoming is an enactment expressed through defiance and loss."[25] Will we tolerate the kind of ambiguity that accompanies us out of exile? Can we embrace what some have called the life of "liminality," where uncertainty resides and reassurances are few? For the journey in reverse is filled with insecurity because it is a way of not knowing.

Yet, the way of not knowing is precisely the route we must take. It gathers up the exilic imagination marked by the cross-currents of courage and modesty, perseverance, and tentative beginnings, a keen resistance to what we know is destructive and a commitment to nonviolence. Not knowing prepares us for the way of holy insecurity, the way of truth and reconciliation, the way of not "knowing" but *trusting*. The way of not knowing is like the *via negativa* of classical spirituality. It is the spirituality that allows us to live with a kind of holy insecurity so we might enter into the crises of our day without despair. Here is where we learn to trust a hand that guides our lives in a direction we can but dimly see, knowing again that the God of Israel is indeed a pivotal player. This spirituality is totally opposite to nostalgic longings for what has never been; however, it is the faith posture of holy insecurity necessary for "journey in reverse."

During the time of holy insecurity, we let the power of our faith story take hold of us to form a new angle of vision marked by humility—provisional offerings always open to be changed by those who are suffering. The time of holy insecurity is where we become increasingly relational, self-critical, and open to see the pain of the world. We learn that there is a deep connection between the injustice that we of the so-called first world perpetrate on the rest of the world and our own psychological and spiritual misery. On the long trek toward our unknown future, we feel in our bodies the material suffering of the two-thirds world and our unease in the first as one piece. We met in exile. We join together in return, where our intimations of community begin to foster global citizens.

Edward Said wrote: "What is true of all exile is not that home and love of home are lost, but that loss is inherent in the very existence of both."[26] This is what we are saying about community. Loss is inherent in the very existence of community and our longing for it. And the particular expression of loss through the fundamental broken nature of community is the only reality we know. What do we do with brokenness? How do we engage the broken reality of our community life without abandoning it or trivializing it? In a way, what we are suggesting about failed community through our inquiry into exile is similar to the conclusion Dorothee Soelle reaches in her response to the problem of suffering. In her now classic little book *Suffering,* she begins with the "givenness" of suffering. In other words, we do not know or experience a world without suffering. Given this, we have only two responses we can make: We can work to eliminate the causes of suffering where we can, and where suffering cannot be eliminated, we must discover how suffering can make us more human. This means we must take suffering seriously and commit ourselves to what we are willing to *suffer for* so that suffering might be transformed. In no way does she condone masochistic tendencies or its twin self-pity. Rather, she condemns all forms of denial and rationalization of suffering that lead to apathy and indifference. Particularly, we are not to abandon those who are suffering. [27] What this line of thought suggests to us, since we do not know or experience a community that is without failure, is this: How will we work to eliminate the causes of failure in our community life, and where we cannot eliminate the failure, how might failure make us more human? In other words, since brokenness is a given, what are we willing to be broken for that we might be transformed? Where do we practice this nascent spiritual awareness we begin to discern in our journey in reverse? For the task before us is a holy one indeed.

Failure is no stranger to those of us who identify with the Christian tradition. The liturgical calendar marks our day of failure as Good Friday. I always wondered how that Friday ever became named "good." But it has been named just that—"good." So we ask ourselves how can failure become good? What is the gift of brokenness or failure? These are the musings of those on the journey in reverse; they are the haunting questions of a spirituality based on an insecurity that prompts a new religious imagination that Brueggemann calls the "sacramental imagination." [28]

Sacramental Renewal

Human brokenness and the failure of community have been powerful themes in the biblical tradition. The profound brokenness of the one named Jesus and failure of Jesus' dream on a cross outside Jerusalem speak particularly to Christians. Yet strangely the themes and experiences of failure have also been closely associated with notions of hope and healing. There is something about the significance of utter failure or brokenness that makes us so completely vulnerable that the barriers between us and the rest of the world begin to crumble. We recognize, name, and grieve the failures that we live. We stretch ourselves out, prostrate, before the vast broken terrain that extends across neighborhoods, cultures, and histories of abuse. We recognize the suffering of injustice and broken dreams and enter the landscape of abuse. We recognize the suffering of injustice and broken dreams and enter the landscape of grief. Although we know this can lead to despair, we also know it need not. Where barriers are lowered and new access to each other and ourselves becomes possible, here, too, is the possibility for healing. This juncture is the prophetic moment whose origins begin in sacrament. Sacrament is the alternative to despair. [29]

The liturgy of the Lord's supper involves us in a profound countermeaning to our despairing inclinations. In this event we recall, "This is my body broken for you," suggesting to us that all human failure and brokenness can be brought to this particular broken body in order to be healed. The breaking of the bread, in fact, becomes an invitation to the "journey in reverse," where the holy space is opened for our healing. As such, the public nature of sacrament becomes the focus of our eating and drinking. It ritualizes the prophetic moment, allowing us to grieve our failed community, to recognize we cannot get out of this by ourselves, and to remember our traditions of restored communities in order to kindle afresh our desires for an alternative future.

The liturgy of the holy meal prepares us to meet each other anew because we are met by the astonishing God who surprises us by coming to dwell among us—"the God of Israel is a pivotal player." The sacrament offers us the possibility of recognizing one another in the embrace of this holy God, as those who are willing to see our lives through to an alternative future. [30] When we tell the truth about our lives, and our failures find a true hearing in the presence of others, holiness and brokenness do come together in sacramental expression. As the community of faith journeys in reverse through sacramental renewal, we dare to become "The outward and visible sign of an inward and spiritual grace." [31] In this way we "prepare a place that is a suitable habitat for God's presence." [32]

Conclusion

The prophetic moment we inhabit calls us to practice our faith in a post–Good Friday world as an alternative to despair. This is not the Easter faith we have come to celebrate that speaks of certain victory. No, we are much less confident these days and closer to those who waited "the day after" that horrible Friday without signs, except for their own fear and tears of anguish to guide them. "Holy Saturday" is the name the tradition gives it. And the day after is the day in which we find ourselves. It is the time of our journey in reverse filled with memories of failure and remorse. It is precisely across this seemingly frozen time between yesterday and tomorrow that we are to travel even without evidence that this is a holy time. This long Saturday is a barrier that prevents both our knowing and our onward rush to victory and joy. It is the boundary point that serves both to conjoin and to separate the Friday cross and the Sunday garden, preventing absolute despair and cheap triumphalism, both the nonoccurrence and the premature arrival of a resurrection sequel to the crucifixion.

At this precarious hour of exile and our longing for return, we are not to sacrifice our genuine human need for community for the chimera of national security based on our own weapons of mass destruction or our fear of others'. Instead, it is through participation in the patience of even God's holy insecurity that we break bread and learn the gifts of the spirit that can restore our communities and us to each other. After all, participation is the whole point of incarnation. Between yesterday and tomorrow is where intimations of holiness and broken people come together toward an alternative future that is truly a homecoming for all. We are to wait with the broken Christ of Holy Saturday, who is still the one who embraces our broken world, promising a future instead of a bombed out wilderness. This means, as Frederick Buechner reminds us, "To be really home is to be really at peace, and our lives are so intrinsically interwoven that there can be no peace [and I would add justice] for any of us until there is real peace [and justice] for all of us."[33] Authentic community requires both.

3

Building Authentic Faith Communities

Ismael Garcia

Most of us living in North America express ambiguous feelings about the role of community in our lives. This is due in part to our having few experiences of living within formative communities. Lacking this experience, we do not fully understand why we ought to give priority to the development of those virtues necessary to sustain communal life. Still, we assume that community is something good, fitting our nature as social creatures who have, as one of our basic needs, the need to belong and enjoy membership and recognition. Thus, we long for community while remaining uncertain as to whether or not it is an intrinsic part of a good life. We are suspicious as to whether or not the commitments community life entails will significantly diminish our personal freedoms and personal life plans. [1]

Our diminished experience of community is in part the result of the development of the global market economy. The fast and radically changing nature of transnational capitalism is making the creation of stable communities, within all spheres of life, harder to sustain. For example, while our parents stayed twenty-five years at their jobs and were known by and knew everyone in the workplace, our children and friends are changing jobs every three years and complain about being anonymous cogs at their workplaces. The dynamic nature of the market motivates us to live in a state of constant readiness, always willing to "pick up our tents" and follow the jobs through which we can fulfill our calling. Families find it harder to live close enough so as to exercise a formative influence on each other. Long gone are the days in which our grandparents served as our mentors and nurtured our religious and moral formation. Our children rarely or never get to see their relatives. We have even conceived of commuter marriages as a way for each partner to fulfill his or her vocation.

We are increasingly becoming a society in which traditional personal connections are giving way to more impersonal ones. Less and less do we serve the needs of others based on an understanding of the obligations due to family, neighbors, and friends. Most services and needs are met through a market view of obligation; the personal links give way to the more effective and efficient link of money exchanges among strangers.

Churches have not been spared from these dynamics. They, too, find themselves living in a state of constant flux, saying goodbye to their members, welcoming newcomers, and hiring new pastors at a rate never seen before. In an almost literal sense churches themselves have become "gatherings of strangers," functioning more and more like communities of migrants. These dynamics contribute to their losing their capacity for offering alternative visions, values, and ways of life to the ones advocated and subsidized by the state. They are more and more confined to the "mission" of providing palliative responses to the anonymity, loneliness, and multiple fears and insecurities experienced by their constituencies.

The changing nature of the global market has not only reduced significantly our experience of community but also conditioned us to think and behave in terms of "looking out for number one." Career options, at best secondarily informed by a sense of service to others and the community, are frequently chosen on the basis of personal self-advancement, measured primarily on the basis of economic gain and capacity to consume. Not that we have become more selfish; there are many examples of generous altruism both at the personal and social level. Still it seems undeniable that we have become habituated, within all spheres of life, to seek our own good without seriously taking into account how our actions, goals, and long-term plans affect others and our society as a whole.

Our present challenge is to discern whether or not we are capable of conceiving and acting in ways that forward community within this more dynamic and plural global context. What we must do is to come to terms with both the obstacles and new possibilities for community brought to us by the dominance of the global market economy. The same global market forces that have led to the undermining of our "traditional" sense of community have also created conditions for "new" forms of community to emerge. The global market presented us with the opportunity of creating a truly inclusive multicultural society. The notion of the global village is no longer an imaginary and external reality for us. Our national identity has always been that of being a gathering of peoples with strong national and cultural identities, requiring the development of the virtues of living together while finding ways to preserve and honor diversity and differences. Our destiny points in the direction of our becoming a multicultural society and a culturally and racially mestizo, or hybrid, people.

For us, a sustainable community can no longer be based on a conception of cultural uniformity.[2] More and more voices resist merely being fitted into the dominant culture. Our challenge today is to find ways for these culturally diverse groups to become active participants in the journey of redefining what it means to be a North American. The new vision of America must be that of a national community that allows different groups to flourish in their difference, to share power justly within all spheres of life, and to grant recognition and respect for each other.

Where Are We?

Let us examine the character of three spheres that obviously affect our capacity to contribute to the creation of a sustainable community: the economic sphere, the political sphere, and the cultural sphere. My aim is to uplift some of the key dilemmas we presently confront within each sphere.[3]

The Economic Sphere

No one feels economically secure today. The economy is unstable and unpredictable. Periods of rapid growth are followed by equally rapid periods of decline, and uneven economic growth leads to significant social inequality. Even during the best of economic times, many citizens are marginalized, unable to participate in the economy to their benefit. We confront the reality of a permanent and ever growing economic underclass.

Racial and ethnic minorities experience economic hardships more acutely. Even those who might hold two jobs cannot secure a living wage. We might be the wealthiest and most productive nation in the world, but we seem to lack the will to overcome the poverty that adversely affects a significant number of our fellow citizens.

Economic fear and insecurity are also manifest in our national consciousness. We have not yet come to terms with the fact that we can no longer dictate to other nations how they are to conduct their economic affairs. We resent our dependence on other nations.

The Political Sphere

Politically, we are experiencing a chronic lack of vision and purpose. Political apathy and lethargy on the part of citizens and reactionary responses to key social problems on the part of professional politicians perpetuate cynicism and hopelessness among the general citizenry. Political power and influence continue to move away from the hands of citizens into the control of professional politicians. Public concerns are given secondary consideration to the desires of private interest groups. Citizens' apathy encourages public leaders to give themselves permission to be minimally accountable to those they are supposed to serve, and political cynicism feeds the conviction that, no matter how politically involved we become, few things will actually change. Apathy and cynicism kill our will and adversely affect our capacity to organize and struggle, depriving us of the possibility of a better and more humane future. [4]

Citizens have become chronically suspicious and show their disregard for government solutions to the problems they confront. Although it is true that the tyranny of the political sphere can be worse than the tyranny of the economic sphere, it is still important to recognize that there are issues that only the government has the resources and expertise to address. Political solutions, however, do not have to be limited to those provided by the state. Authentic politics engages citizens in conversations about the common good. When citizens fail to express their values through the political process, the door is left open for market values to rule our common lives. The boundaries between private needs and wants and public goods are blurred and transgressed. This is precisely what has happened. We have been led to rely on the economic sphere to solve problems that affect our common life.

The dominance of the economic sphere within the public sphere is seen in the process of privatization. Privatization has become the new mantra to solve issues dealing with the education of our children, the health and retirement needs of the elderly, and even the poverty that affects the life possibilities of many of our fellow citizens. In this process we have allowed the economic sphere to determine for us solutions guided by the concerns of effectiveness and quick fixes. We have lost the political sense that goodness is to be achieved intentionally and slowly and that it requires constant public encounters, dialogue, vigilance, patience, and nurturing to sustain itself.

The violation of the boundaries between the economic and the political spheres and the dominance of market values within the political sphere have significantly redefined the nature and content of the good life. The market vision of the good life, both personal and social, is defined mostly in terms of instant gratification, conspicuous consumption, convenience, and the never-ending quest for bodily pleasures, in particular sexual stimulation. Politics under the dominance of the market is not about acting and expressing our uniqueness but about acting and being for the sake of having and consuming.

The Cultural Sphere

Today we long for meaning, self-worth, recognition, and respect as we seek to affirm and fulfill our distinct cultural identities. Our culture has also been greatly affected by the distortions that manifest themselves within the economic and the political spheres. The pleasure-seeking and possessive individualistic lifestyle promoted by the economic sphere together with the cynicism and lack of vision that defines the political sphere have led to a state of cultural decay and spiritual impoverishment that creates attitudes of self-loathing and a lack of meaning. This cultural chaos is one of the most serious problems, if not the most serious one, we presently confront. It is no wonder that the language of spirituality and spiritual nurture has become so prevalent in our culture with both religious and even nonreligious communities.

The new coalition between market values and the media, informed and guided by the psychological sciences, that dominates our present cultural moment has led to a new conception of the good life: the narcissistic lifestyle. The characters of the ever-popular soap operas best depict this lifestyle. Most soap opera characters live chaotic lives: Failed businesses and personal relationships, dysfunctional families, and betrayal of friendships are the norm. In spite of all this, these characters project themselves as happy because they possess the inner strength of feeling and seeing themselves, and of presenting themselves to others, in a positive light. The good life depends not on the performance of duties or the achievement of goals. Rather, it depends solely on our capacity to subjectively manipulate ourselves in order to feel good about ourselves and project ourselves as self-confident and attractive human beings.

The culture nurtured by the alliance of the global market with the mass media presents to us one consistent message regarding the content of the good life—develop the capacity to control how you feel about yourself and how you project yourself to others. On this basis, seek the exotic self-affirming life by expanding and intensifying pleasure; enhancing your consumption, comfort, and convenience; and engaging in never-ending sexual stimulation and other hedonistic indulgences.

Culturally, we are at a state in which too many of us, in particular socially marginal groups, feel directionless and lacking in meaning. It is a life lived in a vacuum of hope. In this social context the greatest need is the need to be loved, not just loved by others, but more fundamentally to be able to engage in proper forms of self-love. Increasingly, the culture shows signs of self-loathing and a sense of worthlessness. Racial and ethnic groups who are depicted in negative terms through multiple stereotypes, and whose cultures and ways of life are depicted by the dominant culture as inferior or worthless, are particularly prone to self-loathing and lack of self-love. Cultural meaninglessness and lovelessness toward self and others sustain other forms of destructive behavior, including violence toward life and property.

We know that proper self-love is intrinsically related to our capacity to love others and that both of these are indispensable if we are to create sustainable communities. People who have no sense of being loved and who are dominated by despair can harbor self-destructive dispositions toward themselves, the world, and others. The violence that is taking place within our schools reveals the meaningless, hopeless, and loveless feelings of many of our young citizens. Equally scandalous are the high rate of suicide among our youth and the way their sense of being unattached nurtures a cold-hearted and mean-spirited outlook toward others.

Where Do We Go from Here?

It is always harder to offer concrete solutions to our dilemmas than it is to describe them. However, the description in itself already presupposes elements of possible solutions. First of all, clear boundaries must be established between the economic, political, and cultural spheres to enhance the quality of justice within the community. Each of these spheres must enjoy relative autonomy, and the problems that emerge within each of them must be treated on their own terms.

We mentioned that market forces by their very nature breed inequalities. As long as these inequalities relate to the activities of purchasing goods and services that express our preferences, they are not dangerous. It is important, however, to keep economic inequalities within limits so that they do not become an obstacle to citizens recognizing each other as equals and treating each other with respect. All citizens must participate in both the process of production and the process of consumption. Living wages must become socially normative. People who perform socially-needed work ought to have what they need to live with dignity. If the private sector cannot compensate workers properly, we must find alternative ways to improve worker income. This is imperative for us because, in our social context, not being able to consume makes us invisible and insignificant. It is necessary to establish ways to delimit the forces of the global market so as to curtail its dominance over the political sphere. The present political debate over campaign finance reform is one indication, although a timid one, of our awareness of the distortion money brings when it moves outside its proper sphere.

Politics must remain the sphere where citizens come to meet and dialogue with each other as equals and recognize and treat each other with respect. The political sphere provides the space where citizens gather to discuss matters pertaining to the common good and the quality of life they share. Through political encounters and interactions they teach and learn from each other about their particularities and how to negotiate a life together.

Political power must be widely distributed to avoid some groups dominating others. A just and sustainable community understands and organizes power not as a zero sum game but as a process in which the more widely power is shared, the more power is generated, and the more possibilities for a fuller life are created. Such is the nature of political justice. [5]

We need to recover some of the best traits of our political traditions to overcome all the obstacles against the full realization of democracy, freedom, equality, and mutual accountability. Given our understanding of political life, politics must be democratic, promote democratic virtues, and sustain democratic institutions. Thus, not only the government and the state ought to embody a democratic spirit, but also businesses and other economic institutions ought to promote the participation of laborers in the decision-making processes through which they regulate their common life. The same is true for cultural institutions.

A central political agenda for us today is to move intentionally toward the creation of a genuine multicultural democracy. This is a society that nurtures differences while at the same time being committed to the defense of basic human rights. The creation of such a society necessitates a political leadership which instills hope and educates the people in the skills of perseverance, endurance, discipline, self-sacrifice, love of self, and love of others.

Sustainable communities depend on the existence of strong local institutions and voluntary associations that address the issues of spiritual emptiness and social and personal disconnection that affect so many of us. These institutions can empower us to meet the cultural challenges of overcoming self-loathing, the lack of meaning, and the diminution of hope that have become culturally dominant. We need more voluntary associations whose nature and commitment encourage something other than the pursuit of self-serving goals. They must empower members to develop strategies for genuine solidarity with those deeply committed to the creation of a more inclusive community. They are to contribute to the eradication of dehumanizing poverty, racism, cultural imperialism, sexism, and homophobic attitudes. They are to be communities of hope and meaning, associations that make us aware that a better life, though requiring long-term commitment and sacrifice, is still possible.

These voluntary associations contribute to the democratization of our political life by providing alternative visions of the good life and a critical public spirit among citizens. They make us aware of and give us occasions to practice the virtues of service, sacrifice, love, and care for self and others. Such institutions and voluntary associations make us aware that personal meaning and hope ultimately come from committing ourselves to causes that can push us beyond narrow self-interest. They reveal to us the old religious wisdom that the good life is one that necessarily includes service to others, that is, the generous sharing and giving of one's time and resources.

In matters pertaining to the reestablishment of hope and meaning, the church has traditionally played a central role. This might be the primary reason why nonreligious people enroll their children in religious schools; they do so because they believe their children will derive a structure of discipline and a vision of life, including commitment to decency, moral goodness, beauty, and excellence. Religious communities understand quite well that the conversion we need today within our neighborhoods, cities, and nations entails a spiritual change, a change of our personal and collective souls, enabling people to believe once again that there is meaning sustaining their struggles and hope for the future. Thus the church can help us resist the threats of individualism, hedonism, and radical subjectivism that dominate the present cultural scene. The church does not have a monopoly over the language and commitment to empathy, compassion, and conversion, but this language is at the core of its identity as a church. To fulfill its mission, the church must recover its identity as a community that provides an alternative vision of the good life, affirming service to the needy and love of strangers.

In order to accomplish this, the church needs to provide many occasions for people to engage in proper self-love, self-worth, and self-affirmation. While it knows that self-sacrifice is one element in the process of creating and sustaining community, it also recognizes that healthy communities endure on the basis of mutuality. It is part of the wisdom of the church that self-love is necessary to motivate us to love others. It also makes us aware that in the struggle to serve the poor, we can find a justification for self-love. In this sense we can claim that a love ethic, and an ethics of care, is at the center of the church's political commitment to convert the souls of people.

It is imperative for churches not just to encourage their members to remain politically active but to give some direction to the politics that fit what it means to be a Christian. This ought to be a politics that seeks inclusion, respect for differences, empowerment of the weak, and a commitment to resist our present cultural decay and encourage a democratic lifestyle. The church has to denounce the political cynicism that plagues our culture and call us to remain politically involved. Christians have always understood that hope emerges precisely within the midst of moral crisis, not in its absence. They have also understood that the good life and the creation of a good society are neither achieved easily nor without significant cost. Rather, both require the development of those character traits that enable us to keep in struggle within different realms. Although our victories and achievements, both large and small, fuel our hopes and sustain our commitments to the struggle for a better life, it is part of the prophetic function of the church to remind us that ultimately it is the struggle itself, the journey toward the creation of a life committed to decency, beauty, goodness, and truth, that bestows meaning and purpose to our lives.

In our present social context, the possibilities of building sustainable communities must move in the direction of creating a multicultural and inclusive society committed to the eradication of poverty, powerlessness, and cultural imperialism. This new vision of the good life argues for a new social covenant in which all parties can preserve their unique cultural identity. Unity comes from the establishment of just cultural, economic, and political arrangements. For this reason the good society gives priority to the creation of public spaces and democratic structures that allow different social groups to encounter each other and negotiate bounds of unity based on mutual recognition and respect.

A Christian Vision of Community

It is no longer possible to claim that Christians have the solutions to all problems, much less that they can solve them alone. However, those of us who belong to faith communities and who also aspire to be responsible citizens ought not to surrender our distinct religious and theological voices and contributions in these matters. Although we cannot afford to be arrogant and assume that we can dictate what ought to be done, we are called to participate, respectfully listening as much as suggesting and advocating, in all conversations dealing with the quality of our common life.

A central motif of the Christian vision of community, the roots of which lie within the biblical tradition, is that of the covenant community.[6] The covenant and the practice of the Sabbath that is intrinsic to it provide us with moral insights relevant for the creation of sustainable communities. The covenant points to an agreement, initiated by God, between God and God's people. Thanks to God's creative action, the people become a community. Thus, community is a gift granted by God for the sake of human flourishing; it has priority because it is essential to the possibility of becoming fully human. We were not created nor should we aspire to be self-sufficient and isolated from each other. We are created as relational and dialogical creatures whose identities are shaped in the company and with the assistance of others. The proper response of the people to God's gracious gift is to create relationships and social structures of mutual obligation and care.

God's covenant, and the covenants humans give themselves by modeling God's initial gift, are not understood as law but as means of grace. Covenants do entail regulations and specify the rights and obligations that are part of our multiple relationships. Still, our agreements are not legalistic. Rather, the regulations are quite fluid and flexible; they remain open to change, to renegotiation and accommodation in light of new events and experiences that are born out of the dynamics of the relationships themselves. The openness of covenant regulations is what gives our personal and social relationships greater stability and lasting power. Covenants are open and flexible because life is essentially unpredictable, full of surprises and unexpected outcomes and developments that need creative yet fitting responses to maintain relationships. Within this context, forgiveness and promise keeping are two indispensable poles of all covenant relationships. The former enables us to begin again, and the latter enables us to create islands of stability within a future that is open and unpredictable.

The notion of the covenant reveals to us some of the basic conditions that are required to sustain human community. Order, regularity, and dependability are among the factors that contribute to the creation and preservation of sustainable communities. Humans are dependent and interdependent creatures. This becomes self-evident from the moment we are born because, contrary to many other animals, we depend on a lot of nurturing from parents and others before we become relatively self-sufficient and interdependent. Our dependence reemerges as we grow old and depend on the graces of others to end our last days with dignity. Our dependence and interdependence highlight our need to be in relationships of mutuality and care and to create structures that support us in these efforts. A covenant point of view keeps us mindful of how our actions affect the life possibilities of others.

A covenant point of view also makes us aware that the good life is not always the happy life. Tragedy intrudes our lives, and no one is spared the possibility of pain, suffering, or even premature death. Still, covenant people are to develop the skills and virtues necessary to respond to these negative dimensions of life with courage and hope. This hope is nurtured precisely because they have available to them the resources and support of the community as well as the courage to remain in the struggle for a better life. This struggle is what bestows meaning on our lives, even when we are not always successful and fall short of our ideals. Covenant motifs make it clear that love of God and love of others are not just interpersonal but take place through God's orders of creation: the family, state, workplace, school, and church. Thus, love is as much political and social as it is personal.

The covenant notion of community stresses the centrality of people's generosity in sharing their gifts, talents, and resources with, and making them available to, others. Since life, including life in community, is itself a gift, it ought not to be ruled by the principle of self-ownership but by the inclination and motivation to share with others. The covenant notion of community keeps us mindful that many of our achievements and successes are due in part to the gifts we have received directly or indirectly from others and the resources provided by the community. Thus, we are called to respond appropriately by generously giving and sharing of who we are and what we have. The use of our skills and talents should include the consideration of how we serve the well-being of the whole.

Economically speaking, a covenant point of view calls us to establish a process of production and consumption that allows all members of the community to participate and benefit from the fruits of the system of social cooperation. In principle, no one ought to be left out. All must be provided with what they need to develop their skills and talents so they can share in the process of social production. Even the poor are to benefit from and to contribute a measure of what they have.

While the covenant notion of community promotes economic creativity and productivity, it also recognizes that the purpose of life is not limited to the never-ending process of production and consumption. If we need to have goods and services in order to be and fulfill ourselves, it is important that we do not exhaust our life energy in the never-ending process of producing and consuming. Thus, the covenant community structures the time of Sabbath. The first requirement of Sabbath is that no one is left out of the productive process and that the community sees to it that all are integrated into the work process. As well as emphasizing the importance of being freed from work, Sabbath also calls for stewardship—disciplined and limited consumption that will allow the community to reinvest in and improve the life conditions of future generations.

Sabbath regulations ought to affect how the community organizes itself as a whole. Rest is due not just to all humans, whatever their status, but also to the land and to the beasts. One ought not to forget that the land and the beasts are also gifts over which we are not able to make the false claim of absolute ownership. Both have an integrity of their own that ought to limit our use of them and the way we benefit from them. We are as accountable for the well-being of the land and beasts as we are accountable to each other's well-being.

Sabbath places limits not just on production and acquisition but also on debts. Sabbath allows for new beginnings; in particular the least advantaged are given a new chance to achieve their self-realization and reintegrate themselves into the community as productive members. Debts are to be canceled, and the enslaved are to be made free. To empower them to use their newly gained freedom, those freed from forms of enslavement are to be provided with enough goods to make a living. These are ways in which the covenant community can become more inclusive and attempt to eradicate relationships of domination and exploitation. In short, the Sabbath of rest, debt cancellation, and emancipation moves against the temptation of viewing life as primarily a matter of ownership, hard work, good management, and deserved success.

The covenant community even recognizes the needs and the legitimate claims of the stranger—the alien. Love of neighbor includes those who have no land or power and who are not full members of the community. The poor and the marginal as well as the stranger and alien cannot be left out. They are to be cared for and share in the fruits of the covenant community. The justice that fits the community includes nonmembers.

What Kind of Prophetic Community Should the Church Be?

How should churches exercise their prophetic role and contribute to the creation of a multicultural society? There are at least three ways in which the covenantal faith community has understood its prophetic ethos.[7]

The Prophet as an Outsider

The outsider prophetic community intentionally assumes a moral distance from the established cultural, political, and economic reality in which it lives. As separate from the culture, it assumes an objective stance from which it engages in radical social critique. It distrusts the wisdom of the world, neither appealing to nor relying on the knowledge, technological know-how, or moral wisdom offered by the culture in which it dwells. It sees the culture as decadent and questions not only its present spiritual and moral health but also the possibility of its renewal. Its critique is dominated by the moral indignation it feels against society's complacency, injustice, and the lack of love within the community.

From this perspective nothing less than a radical transformation of our sociocultural context will do if we are to create conditions for the establishment of sustainable communities that are both peaceful and loving. Since the powers and principalities of the world will not change, given the radical nature of sin, the prophetic community looks internally and calls its members to be different from the ways of culture, the market, and politics and to witness and commit their lives to the love and justice of God. In a world ruled by violence and self-interest, faith communities find their reason for being precisely in the call to establish themselves as peaceful, loving communities grounded on mutual care. This is the only fitting response to God's calling of humanity to once more follow God's way of justice and love.

The church becomes the alternative community that lives out the costly life of loving service that God expects from God's people. It constitutes itself as an alternative social–cultural and political context in which God's liberating purpose is to be realized. Thus, prophetic denunciation starts at home. The church itself lives in a continuous process of prophetic moral regeneration and, on this basis, models to the world a different way of living and relating. It summons its members to resist compromises with the fallen world and decayed culture and to live in light of ultimate values.

Churches provide the vision, motivation, and support necessary for their members to sustain the discipline and sacrifice necessary to become a faithful community. The church must be faithful to its vision and mission even though it knows that the world will not change in any morally significant way. The church's main responsibility is to be truthful and faithful to God's call, not to take responsibility for transforming the world. Faithfulness to God's way takes priority over effectiveness in transforming the world. While the outsider prophetic community is humanly pessimistic, it remains theologically optimistic. The improvement of the human condition is less in human hands than it is dependent on the creative agency of God.

Still, members of the outsider prophetic church see themselves as having a worldly vocation. They are to become professional naggers who attempt to shame others for doing what they know is wrong and not doing what they know is right. They confront, but never coerce, others into accepting the new way of life that God, through Jesus, has given to the community. It seeks to instill in all its members the importance of being active participants in the life of the community and of assuring that the resources and talents of the believing community are widely and generously shared. It also understands that the life of faith is a life of disciplined commitment and one of willing sacrifice for the well-being of the whole. The creation of a community of peace, truth, and beauty that was initiated by Jesus is both its hope and that which sustains its struggle.

The outside prophet thus calls the church to embody within its own life a multicultural and inclusive way of life. It creates spaces and occasions for people to live in light of their cultural distinctiveness and still be recognized, respected, and accepted by all as equal members of the faith community. It acknowledges that different interpretations of the Jesus story are necessary and indispensable to discern more fully God's purpose. This fits its commitment to uphold different theological perspectives as necessary for a more accurate understanding of theological truth. With the same passion that it resists listening to the wisdom of culture, it commits itself to dialogue with all those different groups who profess to be members of the Christian community.

The Prophet as an Insider

Insider prophets encourage the community of faith not to withdraw but rather to relate to, to learn from, and to influence the social world of which they are a part. They uplift the positive moral impact the faith community has had on many of our basic social institutions and on the values that shape our culture. The practices of forgiveness, love, justice, service to the poor, fidelity in relationships, self-sacrifice, self-discipline, delayed gratification, respect for life, and human dignity, just to name a few, are seen as part of the long historical legacy Christianity has contributed to our secular cultural heritage. These values are to be jealously guarded because they have been shown to work in creating sustainable communities.

Insider prophets value the role of being the priestly preserver of culture. They are defenders and function as gatekeepers of those traditional institutions and social values they understand as being related to God's ordering of historical activity. Thus the church has a stake in the preservation of culture as an act of theological faithfulness. Insider prophets tend to take a defensive attitude toward social change. Embedded social evils are on the whole preferable to the evils of social instability and chaos brought about by radical change. Social change places at risk the costly gains humanity has already achieved. Change is welcomed, but it must be gradual, orderly achieved, and brought about within established procedures so as to protect the hard-won achievements.

Culture is good precisely because it embodies the gradual realization of God's moral and redemptive purposes for humanity. Every step toward justice and inclusiveness is a manifestation of the presence and impact of God's spirit on human history. History's goodness is not only past and present but also future. This is the foundation for humanity to remain hopeful, particularly when things do not seem to go in a constructive direction.

Humanity not only has a stake in what happens within history; it is also called to be an active agent of historical developments. The kingdom of God is not just God's creation—we have been called to participate in its realization. We contribute to the kingdom by nurturing and preserving those institutions and procedures that fit God's orders of creation. Our historical commitment is expressed primarily through the preservation and improvement of the existing order. This conservative and tradition-based perspective does not argue for the existence of absolute values and ideals. On the contrary, it harbors a strong social realism that enables it to understand that within history it is never a matter of all or nothing, but a matter of more or less justice and peace.

Insider prophets see the creation of a new multicultural community as something positive, as long as the inclusion of new members and the diversification of the community take place gradually and through channels that allow it to preserve the values through which the community has been able to establish its identity and organize its life. It is important to society and to the church that the stability and unity we presently enjoy not be lost as we intentionally move in the direction of a more differentiated and diversified community. The multicultural community, contrary to the views of the outsider prophet, is to be created not only within the church but also with society at large.

The Prophet as Insider/Outsider

The insider/outsider prophetic church attempts to keep the strengths and avoid the weaknesses of both the prophetic insider and the prophetic outsider church. It promotes the active participation of Christians within all spheres of life. The creation of a multicultural society is primarily a political task as well as a task internal to the life of the church. It encourages the faithful to be active partners in the public dialogue through which the process of public opinion is shaped. It grounds its thoughts and actions within the Christian tradition but still listens to the technological, scientific, political, and moral expertise of others. It claims that if worldly wisdom is true, it is an intrinsic part of God's disclosure of God's purpose. The world can teach and correct the church, and most of the time it also leads the way for progressive reforms or radical transformations. Insider/outsider prophets are also open to the possibility of establishing coalitions with all people of goodwill who are committed to the creation of a more inclusive and humane society.

Insider/outsider prophets look at society from the perspectives of those who have been wronged: the poor, the powerless, the socially marginalized, and the culturally discriminated against. In solidarity with these groups, they join the multiple struggles through which those victimized by society struggle for their empowerment and inclusion within a new social order. Insider/outsider prophets do not treat those who have been victimized as victims. They treat them as moral agents who can participate in, and have moral responsibility for, their own emancipation. However, they neither condemn nor support the status quo as a matter of principle. Insider/outsider prophets assume a pragmatic attitude as they engage with others in addressing particular human problems and challenges. Their claims about the primary purposes of human existence and history, what the qualities of life ought to be, and what values are in accord with God's activity and purpose are not given with absolute certitude; rather, these are seen as historically relative and conditioned. Their intention is to respond creatively to new events and circumstances rather than with indignation or in a defensive manner. They see possibilities for social and moral growth without denying the potential dangers, due to our sinfulness, of our new achievements and the costs involved in bringing them about.

Insider/outsider prophets understand God not as a disengaged observer, nor primarily in terms of judgment, nor as the changeless basis of the law and the established order. Rather, God is an active historical presence—the power within history that brings new possibility and makes possible human creative responses.

God guides history and gives the future an ordered pattern but not a given outcome. The mighty deeds of God demand a fitting human response. We are called to be involved, as God is involved, in the temporal and historical existence of the human community, bringing it toward a more universal and loving communion. This is at the core of the claim that we are created in the image of God. In one sense we humans are cocreators with God of the future that will give shape to our lives. Our responses can truly redirect the course of social and human events. The future remains open to either greater destruction or to more goodness—thus, the importance of being careful in our commitments and the processes through which we discern God's intention for humanity.

While avoiding radical critiques of the status quo and not willing merely to be custodians of the system in place, insider/outsider prophets remain committed to change social conditions, to convert the soul, and to give people a new vision and the motivation to pursue it. They call all people of goodwill to be creative agents of transformation. They want people to have the political hope, trust, and love to extend and intensify love and justice. This forward–looking vision and disposition frees us from the hate, despair, and distrust that feed political cynicism.

The insider/outsider prophetic vision understands that within history, sin stubbornly abounds. There is no way humans can free themselves from it and its consequences. Still, there is room for creative betterment of the human condition. Oppression should and can give way to greater freedom, the ways of war to lasting peace, the concentration of wealth and power to distributive justice, cultural discrimination to respect and recognition, and paralyzing cynicism to active and creative historical participation in the determination of our shared lives.

The insider/outsider church is an involved community. The church is one of the few communities left that provides a place and occasion for moral discourse to take place among people of many cultures and generations. It is an important institution that can make significant contributions to clarify the ends and means of human action. It has been called by God to live and work together with others, sharing common dreams and engaging in a plurality of struggles toward the creation of a better life for all of God's children. It calls its members to be actively engaged in moral deliberation within and outside the church.

At this stage of our history, this is the kind of church that can best contribute to the creation of a multicultural community, both modeling and allowing itself to be taught how our nation and church can be redefined in ways that embrace all their members. The insider/outsider prophetic voice is the one best suited to call all people to express who they are and what they value so that they can find the common ground to negotiate a life together that is life affirming for all.

4

A Prophetic Vision of Building Worldwide Community

Ann Bragdon

What Do People Need to Hear?

Most profoundly, we need to hear that "another world is possible!" Indeed, this is the function of prophecy. The prophets of old spoke to human communities in times of turbulence and uncertainty and heralded a direction out of troubled and difficult circumstances. Clear in their proclamations was a critique of the motivations and actions of whole societies, their leaders, and political and economic institutions.

American leaders have spoken, acted, and disclosed their intentions—their vision. They tell us that we must pursue the path of war, violence, and intimidation against all the world should the world impede our interests. It is not enough to be neutral; "one is either with us or against us" to the almost-elected president. It is clear that these policies and actions seize for us a future that is hardly Christian and cannot be sustainable. War steals the resources of the future and inflicts wounds that are not easily healed.

In contrast to the United States' battle against all for all time was the meeting of a large number of people described as the "civil society" of our worldwide community, full of energy and intent on solving the problems and issues of our globalized world. Some 50,000 delegates from 123 countries met in Pôrto Alegre, Brazil, at the World Social Forum in January–February 2002.[1] They participated in 27 conferences, 96 seminars, and 652 workshops. The forum represented what Jeremy Bredher and Tim Costello referred to as "globalization from below."[2] Globalization from below refers to the process and organization of *people* reaching out to *other people* around the world in an effort to counter and resist the destructive forces of "globalization from above"—the financial, technological, economic, and political end of globalization controlled by big money, institutions, and power and its consequences.

That same week in January 2002, a group representing global elites and their political and economic institutions, interests, and practices met at the 32d World Economic Forum. (Rather than convening at Davos, a Swiss ski resort, as usual, the group convened at the Waldorf Astoria Hotel in New York.) Even this usually confident, self-assured group was forced to hear troubling criticisms: One U.S. economist reported that the policies of the rich nations cause 25,000 deaths from starvation every day.[3] At opposite ends of the hemisphere, two conferences with different constituencies and processes—two quite different agendas and concerns—expressed some basic divisions in the global community. Young adult women from Colombia, attending the meetings in Pôrto Alegre in response and resistance to the destruction and war gripping their country and lives, raised a banner stating their vision and hope for "another world." The words were simple: "A home, a country, a planet free of fear, wars, and violence."

Who could not understand their wish for relief from the duress of ongoing war in Columbia? Let us lift up their hope and evaluate the possibilities as we consider the hope of so many around the globe and the task of building worldwide community and "A home, a country, a planet free of fear, wars, and violence."

Wholeness and an American September

The Semitic terms *shalom* (Hebrew) and *salaam* (Arabic) have the same three-consonant root—s/l/m. The translation and etiology of these words refer us to a vision of wholeness derived through a "right relationship" with God. When you give the salutation "salaam" or "shalom," you are wishing another to live in peace and harmony according to a theological notion of wholeness.[4]

Are the salutations "shalom," "salaam," and "peace be with you" outdated and irrelevant in the contemporary era? What is wholeness in the contemporary world? Looking at events of 2001 and afterward, one might doubt that wholeness can be found. Perhaps, in despair, we might conclude that our world is "fractured" beyond repair!

Indeed, on September 11, 2001, domestic airliners, filled with unsuspecting travelers and their *misguided* hijackers, became missiles of destruction as they crashed into the Twin Towers of the World Trade Center in New York City and the Pentagon in Washington, D.C. Time stood still for those of us waiting and watching events reported on television and radio. Destruction of landmark buildings and human deaths numbering around 2,800 individuals were only part of the final toll.

The horrific events of September 11, 2001, got our attention. The powerful and violent assault on our living space, population, and "business as usual" routines was a dramatic strike of anger, if not rage, directed at our society. How could this happen to us? Who would do this? *Why* would anyone do this? Many questions about September 11 will never be answered and will leave us to speculate.

Our nation, and indeed the world, was irreversibly propelled into a new era on that fateful day of that September. More than the questions, the horror of destruction and death—the trauma of "9/11"—was the heightened sense of uncertainty about how the world operates. Americans, until recently, may not have understood the terror of sudden and overwhelming destruction and violence and the trauma it evokes. Into our consciousness came a deep sense of foreboding, insecurity, and *fear*. These profound and unsettling emotions had never been so present for vast numbers of ordinary Americans before. Every single person was traumatized by the events of the attack of 9/11 (and the continued media replays and coverage of the events). *Fear* and now the presence of *war* permeate our mental landscape—our daily lives and routines in the institutions of our society. Our lives and world will never be or look the same to us.

The government of the United States moved to "go it alone." The George W. Bush administration proclaimed that the United States would be in a permanent state of *war*. This is their response and unimaginative *vision of the future*. Of a host of possibilities, including working to strengthen the system of international law and its process across the globe, they articulated a policy of permanent war: simple, brutal, destructive, unnuanced, and unilateral. The policy of the world's one superpower would be *war*. The war policy was opportunistic, as their later initiatives and actions would demonstrate.[5] With the world's only superpower proclaiming its intentions to launch unlimited military assaults, other governments unleashed their forces against civilian populations without care for accusations of human rights violations. Worldwide, violence escalated, and the "slaughter of innocents" continues, for example, in Chechnya, Palestine and Israel, Southeast Asia, Iraq, and Afghanistan.

The prospect of permanent war is neither a comforting nor a Christian vision. "Perpetual War for Permanent Peace" has the numbing logic of

"1984 Speak." Elected officials who dared to question the mantra of "patriotism equals lock-step agreement" with our government's militaristic response and *shortsighted* vision for the future are few. How refreshing when the courageous speak, as did one lonely U.S. Congressman. Rep. Dennis Kucinich reflected on the prospect of war without end:

> Let us pray for our children. Our children deserve a world without end. Not a war without end. Our children deserve a world free of the terror of hunger, free of the terror of poor health care, free of the terror of homelessness, free of the terror of ignorance, free of the terror of hopelessness, free of the terror of policies which are committed to a world view which is not appropriate for the survival of a free people, not appropriate for the survival of democratic values, not appropriate for the survival of our nation, and not appropriate for the survival of the world.
>
> Let us pray that we have the courage and the will as a people and as a nation to shore ourselves up, to reclaim from the ruins of September the Eleventh our democratic traditions. Let us declare our love for democracy. Let us declare our intent for peace. Let us work to make nonviolence an organizing principle in our own society. Let us recommit ourselves to the slow and painstaking work of statecraft, which sees peace, not war, as being inevitable. Let us work for a world where someday war becomes archaic.[6]

Making Connections in the "New World Order"

"The New World Order" was a term used by the U.S. government at the time of the Gulf crisis in 1990. It describes "the end of an international order determined by the struggle for hegemony between the United States and the USSR; and the initiation of a U.S. foreign policy doctrine based on U.S. hegemony in the international order."[7] The implications of a unipolar world are reflected in the unilateral positions taken by the United States and its arrogance and independence in the international arena. A host of books with telling titles reflects current focus and analysis of the large global economic and political system: *Empire* (Michael Hardt); *Silent Takeover: Globalization and the End of Democracy* (Noreena Hertz); *One World, Ready or Not: The Manic Logic of Global Capitalism* (William Grieder); *When Corporations Rule the World* (David Korten); and so on.[8]

Sociologically, economically, and politically, the diversity of peoples and cultures of the world have collapsed into a global system. Since the 1990s, and probably earlier, no analysis of contemporary life is satisfactory without acknowledging the enlarged context of our lives, that of connection and interconnection with countless spheres of influence and causality that exceed boundaries of nation-states. There is no way to understand our lives individually or together except in relationship to the whole of our planet and its peoples as the "local" context of peoples' lives is increasingly effected by nonlocal vectors.

We are intimately bound up with—connected to—all the inhabitants of the Earth. Indeed, it was recognized in the charter of the United Nations in 1947, more than fifty-five years ago, with universal and laudatory objectives.

> We, the peoples of the United Nations,
>
> Determined to save succeeding generations from the scourge of war,
>
> To reaffirm faith in fundamental human rights, in the dignity and worth of the human person, in the equal rights of men and women, and of nations, large and small,
>
> To promote social progress and better standards of life in larger freedom,
>
> And for these ends to practice tolerance and to live together in peace as good neighbors,
>
> To unite our strength to maintain international peace and security,
>
> To insure that armed force shall not be used, save in the common interest,
>
> To employ international machinery in the promotion of the economic and social advancement of all people,
>
> Have resolved to combine our efforts to accomplish these aims.[9]

Despite the good intentions of the founders of the United Nations more than half a century ago, the trajectory of global cooperation—in decreasing violence, improving the lot of the populations of the world, and developing a democratic system of international law and polity—has not advanced. Rather than progress, reports demonstrate we are only further along the path to a possible nuclear conflagration that will destroy life and the physical system that supports it here on Earth. The response of the National Security State of the United States to September 11 makes our nation's hegemony and devotion to unchallenged power and preeminence absolutely clear.

New Reality: Living in a Babylon of Global Culture

The root of the word religion, *religio,* means to bind together. In our twenty-first century world with a global and interdependent economy; worldwide organizations; diverse populations in most all countries of the world; the compression of time and space through Internet communication; and the rapid transport of people, capital, and material goods, we *are* bound together. Poets and prophets have expressed this concept for centuries. Today we live this reality; it is not a subtle abstraction. Wealth and power and economic and political relations are global, and important controlling institutions and their processes are global.

The *new world* has crashed in on us so to speak. Some, who recognize dramatic and qualitative change in the scope and quality of human relations and cultural values and principles, are like the ancient Jews crying in Babylon: "How could we sing the Lord's song" in global culture?[10]

Some people listened and began to work for peace and justice in the community; they struggled to bring the issues of social justice and the absence of wholeness in the national global society to the forefront of concerns among educated, privileged populations of the United States for decades. They protested: Things are not right! As the bumper sticker proclaims, "*If you are not upset, you are not paying attention*!" We moaned, "How can we sing in this strange land of global capitalism and empire?" How can we identify with or condone the violence done to other peoples, their lands and institutions, either directly or indirectly in the military-industrial-political system that exceeds our awareness, comprehension, and control? *Will we ever be able to sing the Lord's song in global society?*

The price of the new world order has been borne by human populations around the world. We speak of oil and resource wars in which people are killed and local governments are overrun. We speak of squandering national treasure on weapon systems and ignoring human needs. We speak of the diversion of human life and talent for war—the waste of personal and social and cultural well-being. John Pilger, a courageous investigative journalist, describes the motives underlying the killing of one million people in Indonesia in the 1960s as the Suharto government took power. Suharto, considered a model pupil by many in seats of power in the West, was supported by major corporations lining up to benefit from the legal framework drawn up for that country as a condition of that support.[11] This support translated into arms transfers from the United States and Britain. These were used against resistant and impoverished local populations while the elites profited. Western governments, policy makers, and economic reports identified Indonesia as a major international economic success story of the 1960s.

Scrutiny of the global economic system, its institutions and global actors—corporations, the World Bank, and the International Monetary Fund, and the ideology it enforces (for it will not tolerate dissent)—translates into what Walter Wink so eloquently developed as a description of the "domination system." Wink challenges us to interpret the gospel in light of that domination system and the web of violence it constructs and supports in all areas of life and human relationships across the globe.[12]

"Slavery and War on the Fourth of July"

Imagine celebrating freedom and the independence of the United States on the Fourth of July in 1852 as an African American, free or slave. "Sweet words them...but what do they mean for me?" In 1852, more than a decade before emancipation, the end of slavery, integral to the economic and cultural system in the United States, must have seemed as unthinkable to the majority population of the United States as the end of war sounds to people today. Less than 5 percent of churches were antislavery at that time.

In "What to the Slave Is the Fourth of July?" a speech given by abolitionist Frederick Douglass in 1852 to the Rochester Ladies' Anti-Slavery Society, Douglass quoted Albert Barnes, abolitionist author of *The Church: Bulwark of Slavery:* "There is no power out of the church that could sustain slavery an hour, if it were not sustained in it (the church)."[13] In other words, the compliant support of the church in maintaining the institution of slavery perpetuated the institution. If churches had objected, it would not have stood.

Abolitionism in the United States was an enduring social movement with a vision, the objective of ending slavery as well as the legal system that allowed humans to own others as property to be bought and sold as inanimate objects/subjects. The abolition movement prevailed and finally transformed American culture. However we assess its success today, in popular imagination, slavery is morally unacceptable, and, as Trent Lott learned at the end of 2002, so is praise for Jim Crow segregation.

Carol Hunter considered a parallel circumstance: the support of churches for slavery in 1852 and the support of churches for policies and uncritical patriotism that translates into support for the war system of today.[14] To claim an antiwar position today provokes doubt about one's patriotism. When it comes to the enemy and war, few churches take Biblical teachings to the extreme of preaching that "one does not kill"; "do not return evil for evil"; "we are the keepers of our brothers and sisters"; "do unto others as you would have them do to you"; "love one another."

About the same percentage of American churches are "peace churches"—churches that reject war and the culture of militarism it constructs—as were abolitionist churches. Churches may regret the suffering of the victims of 9/11 and appropriately officiate at their burials, as well as lead us through the grief and mourning for them. However, overall they fail to lead us into a relevant and radical understanding of the teachings of Jesus when they acquiesce and conform to the actions that bring more suffering, devastation, and chaos across the globe. Failure to challenge policies and caving in on basic democratic principles of governance and principles of human rights amounts to the sanctioning of killing and destruction, turning a blind eye to the suffering and circumstance of our fellow humans across the world.

> Most church members attend churches that fly the flag, sing patriotic songs and consciously or unconsciously lend support to the current administration's propensity to ignore diplomacy and promote decision-making by the defense department and to ignore treaties and internationalism in favor of dangerously unilateral positions.
>
> The anti-slavery Christians by and large had a simple principle—which should seem obvious to Christians, but seldom gets implemented. Jesus becomes the hermeneutic principle for interpreting any text. For example, Jesus taught "do unto others as you would have them do to you." By this principle, slavery as practiced in the U.S. is impossible, as no one wanted to be treated as a slave. Similarly, Jesus' teaching on resist not evil with evil (see Walter Wink's helpful exegesis of this in his book, *Engaging the Powers*) precludes a whole host of political options that the U.S. government is presently employing. I wonder what would happen if we printed Bibles with the gospel of John first (In the beginning was the Word...) to remind people that gospel precedes law.[15]

Jesus' life and ministry taught a universal message that human relationships are central in transforming the world. The stories in the Bible proclaim that in demonstrating caring and coming to know "others," upholding the value of each person, we ourselves, and the world, are transformed. Gustavo Gutierrez identified truths of transformation in "liberation theologies," elevating the poor for concern and, importantly, viewing their status and well-being as a measure of the ethics and justice of the entire society.[16]

We are at a time in history when the scale of violence and destruction is enormous. The prophetic message of Jesus the Christ calls us into the world and to a mission that can only be imperfectly fulfilled, but it is a vision that inspires us to construct an alternative to current realities in the world. "Another world is possible." The message and vision allows for purpose, direction, and hope in dark times.

The church can speak to building worldwide community by becoming peace churches for the abolition of war. The New Abolitionist Church would provide courageous leadership and witness by radical interpretation of Jesus' example, applying it to all areas of life—personal, social, cultural, economic, and political domains. The church can provide courageous leadership in all areas of social and personal ethics, affirming human rights and holding to strong principles of kindness, fairness, truthfulness, and consistency toward the world, its peoples, and the living things on the planet. Martin Luther King, Jr., reminds us: "Wars are poor chisels for carving out peaceful tomorrows."[17]

We were instructed to "love one another." It would be naïve to consider love as sentiment only for those people "like us." It is a way of living, demanding the full powers of intellect, self-discipline, and service. The challenge of our time, if we are to begin building worldwide community, is to live *nonviolently* in a manner leading to the spiritual, social, and cultural transformation of our world. As Mohandas K. Gandhi avers:

> *It Is Possible to Live in Peace*
>
> If someone with courage and vision can rise to lead in nonviolent action, the winter of despair can, in the twinkling of an eye, be turned into the summer of hope.
> It is possible to live in peace.
> Nonviolence is not a garment to put on and off at will. Its seat is in the heart, and it must be an inseparable part of our being.
> It is possible to live in peace.
> Nonviolence, which is a quality of the heart, cannot come by an appeal to the brain. It is a plant of slow growth, growing imperceptibly, but surely.
> It is possible to live in peace.
> The future depends on what we do in the present.
> It is possible to live in peace.[18]

"A home, a country, a planet free of fear, wars, and violence"—the vision of people gathered together to problem solve and work out a future for the world community. This is in stark contrast to the vision and grim prospect of continuous war espoused by the leadership of the United States.

Strange Land—A Different World

"How could we sing the LORD's song in a foreign land?" lamented Jews in Babylon 2,600 years ago. How could one be faithful and even joyous in the land of exile? How could they, as a community, be *whole*? They were on the banks of the Euphrates River, in a different geography—in what is present-day Iraq—separated from what they had known in the land of Palestine. The matrix of their community was displaced. However, with time the exiled remnant, "by the rivers of Babylon," adapted and even prospered. In this new place and context, they lived, often creatively. Here they produced the Talmud; they contributed to the larger society in service as physicians and to scientific discovery and philosophical discourse. They participated in building, along with others, legacies of human civilization in that strange land. They truly did learn to "sing the LORD's song" in the new place.

If our objective is to build global community, we must apprehend and understand the structures, institutions, and processes of the world order and its consequences such that we can discern how to sing the Lord's song in this new and strange land. The strange, new land is our highly interconnected global economic and cultural system, and it demands not just a personal faith and narrow theology, but a broad and humanizing enterprise and mission of building community among our brothers and sisters across the world.

The Twentieth Century—War Times

The United States is at the center of the dominance system. Its boundaries exceed lines drawn across geographically defined spaces. The field of action of the dominance system is global. Its posture toward the world is imperial, and total obedience and conformity are demanded.

In this system, there are huge differences in wealth, power, and prestige. These differences are embedded in different interests, different perceptions of justice, and what is the common good. Those who dominate are unable to "see" the consequences of economic and political processes they advocate for the others. For the most part, they live in a state of disconnect and denial, if not sheer hard-heartedness. They are out of touch with the realities of the majority, poor, and disenfranchised. They do not identify with those for whom medical care is not available or too expensive; they do not know about struggling to make a living wage, holding families together, and nurturing children in a fragmented political and economic system. Fear calls for abandoning civil rights and due process, roundups of immigrants and resident "aliens," for collecting information in a totalitarian society on all citizens who must now forsake precious anonymity for state security. Around the world, the bombarding of civilian centers with "state-of-the-art weaponry" does not carry compassion for the dead, injured, maimed, and those whose worlds and psyches will forever be terrorized.

Deceit and obfuscation—"good public relations"—have delayed popular awareness of the faithful response to destructive, immoral, and criminal actions in various places around the world. Looking honestly at the world and these actions, we see a web of violence at all levels of the biological, social, and cultural systems around us. This is apparent if we look closely. Yet one does not need to look so closely—as the gravity of potential collapse, more holocausts, and total destruction waft in the wind.

Resources, monetary and human, devoted to the creation, production, and deployment of instruments of destruction represent an insult to any conservative accounting system. The proportion of the U.S. budget devoted to the military outdistances the combined military budgets of the rest of the countries of the world combined. The United States markets instruments of death and terror to the tune of billions, more than any other country and the combined sales of other active weapons economies.[19]

Deterring democracy, engaging in covert actions and economic sanctions, "returning countries to the Middle Ages," and refusing to cooperate in international treaties to promote the common good are characteristic of the actions and reputation of the United States abroad. Policy makers in the halls of power have been known to evaluate the success of foreign policy in terms of whether or not they have succeeded in containing the threats posed by the legitimate aspirations of peoples around the world to pursue their happiness and freedoms as opposed to profit and power of the ruling clique.

Environmental degradation—pollution of earth, water, and sky—is a corollary of the processes transforming natural capital to profit for the few. As global capitalism has brought the world into a more tightly integrated economic and communication system, productive processes have impacted the physical, biological, and cultural environments of the entire world. Good public relations, default, and irresponsibility of a cowed media have blinded individuals from seeing the contradictions and unholiness of the pursuits of happiness sought by corporations, if not individuals.

Resources—physical, biological, and cultural—have been progressively commodified and made available for ownership and sale. What can one not buy today and what must one buy today? Who would have thought that Americans in the United States would be purchasing water? Twenty years ago, travelers to Europe found it quaint or strange to buy bottles of water. Today, this is common in the United States. Privatization of water resources is increasingly normative. Chief Seattle's question, "Can you sell the air we breathe?"[20] may soon be answered in the affirmative.

Increasingly, under the influence of globalization and its institutions—which are wealthier and more powerful than any one nation—we see that forces exerted from outside the country and local setting have the power to confine and constrain the options of actors in that society. This results in a diminishing and weakening of national sovereignty. The governments of countries are not able to protect their citizens from external political and economic powers and practices. As a result, populations around the world experience increased poverty and declining living conditions.

For example, political policies imposed by the World Bank's Structural Adjustment Regime may determine that paying a country's external debt must be of the highest priority. Therefore, a large percentage of the country's national income may be allocated to paying the loans secured through the World Bank and the International Monetary Fund that benefited a dictator who left the country ten years ago (or some other misappropriation). Children born in that society are then victims of a debt whose benefit they never realized and, furthermore, will suffer severe consequences. Perhaps the community will not be able to provide medical care or education for those children or even a politically stable environment. Victimization of individuals in these circumstances represents violence caused by social systems. This is what is termed "structural violence"—violence created because the economic and political institutions and policies in place create conditions of poverty, disease, fragmented and impoverished lives, and an impotent civil society that is unable to control the circumstances of the lives of its citizens.

Worldwide, political power has, like wealth, concentrated in the new "empire." Forty percent of the world's population is undernourished in food needs, let alone shelter, medical care, education, and human rights. Ideologically, idols have been erected in the public square: nationalism, chosenness and otherness, triumphalism, manifest destiny, patriotism, technological superiority, and progress.

Americans are separated geographically by oceans, and culturally by lifestyle, from peoples around the globe. At the same time, the global reach of the U.S. economic and military system has brought us into the lives of societies and individuals the world over. The economic and political policies that we enforce around the world benefit powerful interests and bring wealth to our society and to an increasingly narrow group of people, at great cost to and the impoverishment of others—their lives, well-being, and human rights. With the stock market crisis of 2002, some of the corrupt business and accounting practices have been revealed. Hopefully the populace will be less ready to accept the lack of responsibility and ethical standards that have operated for a long time.

Through the 1990s, as the conditions of life worsened around the globe, Americans preoccupied in their super-busy and super-full lives were disconnected. They did not have the information for putting the pieces together to understand the global economic scene. Media for profit and in the service of special interests meant that Americans remained ignorant of consequences and implications of their relationships with others around the world. Americans have been described as ahistorical and apolitical. This suits proponents of the status quo: This does not suit *perceptive faithfulness*. It does not suit the possibility of responsible stewardship and desire to establish a sustainable way of life that provides the promise of peace, democratic process, human rights, and justice—or wholeness for the whole.

The Challenge: Let Us Build Worldwide Community

"A home, a country, a planet free of fear, wars, and violence."

Loving and curious, open-minded Americans have learned about lives of human beings around the world and the events that effect their societies. They have moved beyond the opaqueness of media myth to learn of actions done in their name in various communities of the world. There have been countries invaded and governments overthrown—popular movements subverted in antidemocratic actions in pursuit of the interests of power and wealth. There has been escalating violence with weapons promoted by a prospering global arms industry. Poverty has brought destruction of lives as economies shifted to favor free trade agreements and the repayment of punishing debt through World Bank and International Monetary Fund policies and degradation of the environment, as well as social and cultural institutions around the world. If one is honest, if one is discerning, one recognizes that the cost of this global economic and political order is immense and hardly humane.[21] Is another world possible?

> When I listen to the news, the idea of a social transformation of the church of the magnitude it might take to transform the current unleashed monster of militarism into a force for justice in the world is pretty daunting. But I don't think the task looks any more daunting than that facing Douglass in 1852. Of the 140 million church members of the U.S., the historic peace churches don't have even half a million members combined. Separating costly discipleship to the Prince of Peace from powerful

> nationalism is not easy. The Civil War (or War Between the States) is a chilling and bloody reminder of what happens when a force as powerful as the church misses this call...The church could turn the world toward peace **if** every church lived and taught as Jesus lived and taught.
>
> As a member of September Eleventh Families for Peaceful Tomorrows—a group of family members of 9-11 victims seeking alternatives to war—I speak publicly about the loss of my brother. My witness of that day and the days that have followed are the only thing I have to share. Other members of our group bear witness to their winter visit to Afghanistan, where they learned firsthand the results of the U.S.-led bombing on its civilian population.
>
> Others hear their faith calling and are asking not to be forgotten. One religious assembly in my town, faced with the challenge of how people of faith are compelled to react to current events, have taken their testimony to the streets. They have declared themselves a "Just Peace Church," publishing a resolution and covenant stating, among other things, "Whereas we aspire to a prophetically critical witness in our community, in the face of our own uncertainty...we resolve to strive to bear witness to God's liberating, peacemaking, and justice-doing presence in the world..."[22]

Awareness and dedication to a social movement to bring about a humane and just world is formulated in the sacred space of human relationships through love and concern, sometimes in painful loss. Critical personal transformations take place in our relationships with other human beings, for it is here that we engage the world in a most powerful way.

Not all is new, for the values and practices encouraged in our traditions are reminders that we must rededicate ourselves to the wisdom of the beatitudes. We must feed the hungry; care for the sick; comfort those who mourn; visit those in prison; teach those who would learn; strengthen our moral resolve; encourage those who offer innovative solutions to our common problems; and celebrate the storytellers, the artists, the songwriters, and the peacemakers.

> But let justice roll down like waters, and righteousness like an everflowing stream. (Amos 5:24)

Those seeking worldwide community require an informed, objective view of the world. A comparative view of culture and a systems approach to today's global culture leads to "seeing" a "domination system" and its relationship to the "structural violence" around the world. This, of course, requires an informing media and educational system whose objective is to provide information that is both accurate and insightful. It involves honesty and integrity in establishing a posture of nondefensive evaluation of the world and the actions and policies of corporate institutions and groups. Without good information and a value on transparency and access to information, how are we to realize the stated mandate: "to love one another?" Problematically, however, these are the very tools for a "good society" that a society at war claims to be "security threats."

A nonviolent ethic in our interconnected world involves reaching out to all humans who share the planet. Understanding the circumstances of other human beings and their lives requires work. It involves identifying the forces that construct the realities of life for individuals and their communities. A nonviolent ethic involves political action and solidarity. Protests of the World Trade Organization in Seattle and Quebec, the World Bank in Washington, D.C., and the G-8 meeting in Genoa, Italy, are the expressions of rejection and resistance to the new order that those protesting have understood as the *dominance* system. Mainstream media presents these mobilizations as *misguided* individuals with violent tendencies. Those with access to information and profiles of the groups present will find that the organizational effort/objective of protesters was to challenge the structural violence that keeps people in unacceptable conditions around the world. Seeking "worldwide community" demands learning about and supporting the rights of people as they seek to bring about social justice.

Building worldwide community involves vigilance and seeking the truth. It requires engagement in challenging social and economic and political institutions and policies that do not build toward the vision of a peaceful world community based on democratic principles that recognize the worth of all human beings. It requires "knowing" people across the world, people who are not always like us. For it is in relationship with others—"strangers,"—that activists have learned about and become dedicated to "making another world"—"A home, a country, a planet free of fear, wars, and violence."

"Without Vision, the People Will Perish..."

What is our hope given the convergence of trends in the early years of the third millennium and twenty-first century? Truth-telling and iconoclastic boldness are required. An assessment of the realities that abound in our global culture is demanded: "Hard looking indeed!" This is the first part of "Singing the LORD's song in a foreign land"—and finding global community.

> Individuals have international duties which transcend the national obligations of obedience. Therefore [individual citizens] have the duty to violate domestic laws to prevent crimes against peace and humanity from occurring.[23]

> You do not truly believe until you want for others what you want for yourselves.[24]

> If I could have three wishes, world peace would be all three.[25]

How do we find our way through this labyrinth of woe that appears to have our world in a fatal tailspin? There are no givens. It may not happen; it may end prematurely, but then again we do not know all that is possible. It is the risk taking of those who hope and the support of human community that may determine the outcome.

The strategy for finding our way through the labyrinth of evil is presented to us in the example of the man Jesus: an example that elevates focus and tenderness on people with compassion and speaks with the grammar of reverence for life, respect for living things, and an awareness of the cosmic processes and particularity of our being on planet Earth.

To bring an age of universalism and inclusiveness, a system of international law is prerequisite. Equity and justice demand an operating system of law that works to insure the well-being of peoples and judges impartially and with consistency. This is a sacred trust of society. Law codes, even the earliest in the Ten Commandments, provide basic principles, for example, "Thou shall not…murder, steal, worship graven images" etc.

In response to the undeniable rending asunder of our worldwide society, Betty Williams reflected on the challenge of seeking worldwide community in our quest for peace with justice:

> We have a simple message for the whole world from the movement for peace. We want to live and love and build a just and peaceful society. We want for our children, as we want for ourselves, lives at home, at work and at play to be lives of joy and peace. We recognize that to build such a life demands of all of us dedication, hard work and courage. We recognize that there are many problems in our society which are a source of conflict and violence. We recognize that every bullet fired and every exploding bomb makes that work more difficult. We reject the use of the bomb and the bullet and all the techniques of violence. We dedicate ourselves

to working with our neighbors, near and far, day in and day out, to building that peaceful society in which the tragedies we have known are a bad memory and a continuing warning.[26]

Build Worldwide Community through Loving Rituals and Dialogue

At the end of the Gulf War in 1991, a local peace group held a memorial and prayer service. The peace group was Christian but not of my denomination. My Iraqi born Muslim husband and I attended. On the table at the center of the group was a plastic, three-dimensional globe floating in water in an even larger glass bowl. My husband had been asked to prepare some brief words about the people of Iraq; others spoke about the pain of war for people who oppose it. After a series of prepared remarks, all present were invited to come forward and touch the globe, think about healing our broken world, and use water to cool the pains of a particular location on that spherical map or its entirety.

No one in Iraq felt the coolness of the water, or the love my thoughts directed to them in the moment that was mine to stand at the table, feel the plastic world, and with loving hands lift water over that place on the map. This creatively conceptualized ritual was deeply meaningful; it was a tactile and a most intimate connection to a part of the world in which we had lived, still had family and could imagine the consequences of bombs and destruction of war. Being in the company of people who affirmed the humanity of "even Iraqis" in this act of witness was an act upholding the sanctity of the human beings our nation had been assaulting with weapons and violent destruction.

This ritual, communal and personal, impressed me forever with the power of shared and intentional rites in human experience, not as a memorial of a tradition, but as a live communion of spirit, our world, and *universal love* that is required in building community. Ritual has always been central in building community and must be used in new and creative ways to express ancient and profound truths of human experience and hope.

Interfaith dialogue has also played an essential and constructive role in building knowledge and relationships that are humanizing for people from different traditions. Religious language is "understood" and "routine" within the family of one's faith. However, the work required to speak across traditions and to develop a language of ecumenism is a special and important effort that must be continued. Such efforts allow for inclusiveness and comfortable mutuality in the pluralism of today's world.

Dialogue provides a beneficial and broadening activity that allows us to evaluate our relationships to people, to human beings with whom we share the planet and our future, if there is to be a future. Parker Palmer writes about the mandate of "hospitality" in his noteworthy essay, "In the Company of Strangers."[27] He describes the value of knowing strangers and tells us that unaware, in entertaining strangers, we may be entertaining angels. Palmer speaks of the posture of Christians in a diverse and pluralistic society—now a global and diverse society. He says that the rule of hospitality, of being open to the stranger, the one who is different, is imperative. He cites the example of Abraham, the patriarch of the three monotheistic religions, who entertained three strangers who announced that he would indeed have progeny despite his childlessness and advanced age.

It is from strangers, people from other traditions and experiences, that we will learn about ourselves and about our world and our connections to it. What might we learn from those now identified as the "enemy"? It is in knowing others that we are able to "humanize" people from around our world. In humanizing others we live out the witness inspired by Jesus in his example of engagement and demonstration of goodwill and transforming love. In our global culture, we must maintain *openness* to strangers and learn to decipher the messages they render in order to tear down walls, build community, and overcome our own shortcomings. Interfaith dialogue of recent years has yielded humanizing impulses and institutions and relationships that are of great significance in a worldwide community.

We live among people from diverse cultural experiences. Comprehending and developing an appreciation of other people living in adverse circumstances created by the global domination system and our interconnected global culture should force us to see ourselves. Intercultural communication skills are imperative in the new and global culture. It involves learning other ways of communicating. The three principles I routinely recommend for successful cross-cultural communication include (1) communicating respect (people can usually recognize sincerity and respect); (2) avoiding stereotypes (do not assume you "know" them); (3) expecting ambiguity (not everything will be immediately clear—there are many things you do not know and, indeed, may never know or comprehend). These are recommendations for interacting on a person-to-person level across cultures and in dealing with people from different social and cultural backgrounds.

Politicians and media pundits have bandied about the metaphor *Clash of Civilizations,*[28] made popular in a treatise by the same name, as an essentialist "principle" on how to understand the "global order." This metaphor continues to be used and is referred to by many apologists for the "war system." I see it as negative and destructive. As it is used to explain the current political crisis, it distracts people from substantive issues that can be understood, critiqued, and changed. It is a stone idol of convenience to the powerful in difficult times. It operates as a convenient simplicity to explain conflicts between populations with different histories and interests. It subverts engagement and the hard task of building positive intercultural exchange and trust.

It was formulated at the end of the Cold War when it appeared we lacked an enemy. It asserts that the seven major civilizations are destined to clash. It has an essentialist ring to its argument. Historians and other academics, who have evaluated and tested it as a social scientific hypothesis against the historical record, reject it. *Clash of Civilizations* is a crude deception. It justifies actions against a global order under law—international law—and justifies a descent into anarchy and unipolar power and unilateral actions. It is a self-serving reduction of all our human experience and wisdom about statecraft and governance and a system of international law to a "might-makes-right" imperial system. Peace seekers must reject and move beyond this destructive model for one that embraces global community and possibility.

Ancient wisdom guides us in establishing human relationships: Meeting and engaging people, importantly, people outside of one's own community, becomes a significant resource for educating and sensitizing ourselves to the world and building worldwide community.

> O humankind, we created you from a single pair, male and a female, and made of you peoples and tribes, in order that you might learn about each other. Surely the noblest among you is the one who is most righteous.[29]

"Wholeness in the Global System" and Peace on Earth

As has been noted, the word *religion* has as its base the concept of binding together, making whole. Today, however, religion often appears to be the basis for breaking our communities apart as opposed to binding our world together. Labels, categories of new distinctions, are elevated in new ways, including "cyberspace," to create walls between us, between persons of differing cultures.

Edward Said wrote in February 2002:

> I don't know a single Arab or Muslim American who does not now feel that he or she belongs to the enemy camp, and that being in the United States at this moment provides us with an especially unpleasant experience of alienation and widespread, quite specifically targeted hostility. For despite the occasional

> official statements saying that Islam and Muslims and Arabs are not enemies of the United States, everything else about the current situation argues the exact opposite.[30]

As this chapter goes to press, the situation has indeed become grave. Recent news events tell of

> the mass detention of hundreds of Middle Eastern and Muslim men and boys. "Given the evidence, there is no alarmism in saying this is a round-up," said Lucas Guttentag, Director of the ACLU's Immigrants' Rights Project. "Attorney General Ashcroft is using the immigrant registration program to lock up people who already have provided extensive information as part of their green card applications," he said. "Therefore the purpose is clearly not to get information but rather to selectively arrest, detain and deport Middle Eastern and Muslim men in the United States."[31]

Martin Luther King, Jr., identified the three large evils of his time to be "racism, militarism, and poverty."[32] In these grave times following September 11, 2001, are not all three of these evils raised to a new level?

The creation of cultural and religious barriers began much earlier than September 11, with the insistent labels "Muslim hijacker," "Islamic terrorist," or Arab this or that. Timothy McVeigh was not labeled as the Roman Catholic terrorist or Adolf Hitler as the Christian evildoer, and so on. Stereotyping and the creation of such constructs are in direct contradiction to "knowing" people as commended by Jesus. The so named "New Abolitionist Church" that will end war must also work to construct those things that make for peace.

What is spoken herein is a different approach, an approach that is critical but with the objective of promoting worldwide community and an effort to find peace, justice, and wholeness in a sustainable society. What is new is the context of a global cultural system and the challenge it poses for us—a challenge of apprehension, evaluation, and action.

The vision of worldwide community is not new; neither are its requirements. Knowledge is essential in building understanding and a rational position to evaluate moral action. Discussions in the process of our search for peace and the building of community among all people must include the issues of structural violence and how to create a just society. It is appropriate to discuss the "good society" and entertain critical debate. It is absolute neglect to leave these matters to a magical, hidden, mythical hand or naked force. Responsibility and stewardship make these matters central to living a faith that demands intellect, rationality, logic and dedication.

An engaged commitment to worldwide community can bind us together. In our stories and rituals we can share a message of peace and goodwill—and the possibility of transformation. Growth of a spirituality that serves to nurture rituals of confession, contrition, sacrifice, resistance, and celebration can sustain us with beauty, truth and freedom, humility, and strength. Only a network of mutuality can replace the destructive process we have created in the world. In the words of King:

A Network of Inescapable Mutuality

> We are caught in an inescapable network of mutuality, tied in a single garment of destiny.
>
> Injustice anywhere is a threat to justice everywhere.
>
> There are some things in our social system to which all of us ought to be maladjusted.
>
> Hatred and bitterness can never cure the disease of fear, only love can do that.
>
> We must evolve for all human conflict a method which rejects revenge, aggression, and retaliation.
>
> The foundation of such a method is love.
>
> Before it is too late, we must narrow the gaping chasm between our proclamations of peace and our lowly deeds which precipitate and perpetuate war.
>
> One day we must come to see that peace is not merely a distant goal that we seek but a means by which we arrive at that goal.
>
> We must pursue peaceful ends through peaceful means.
>
> We shall hew out of the mountain of despair, a stone of hope.[33]

Today, our challenge is to see the world, to evaluate what is happening in terms of our deepest values and ethics, and then act to resist what is wrong and destructive. Let us join in constructing a transformed world, one that operates differently, building rather than impeding worldwide community. Indeed, let us exert ourselves to our maximum, to secure "a home, a country, a planet free of fear, wars, and violence."

AND may it be so.

SECTION II
The Prophetic Call to Restore and Celebrate the Earth

5

Issues of Ecological Concern for the Church and Society

Charles McCollough

From the author's perspective, a chapter celebrating the prophetic tradition should start with a prophet, and a chapter on prophetic ecological concerns should start with a prophet who speaks to the ecology of God's creation. Many prophets in the Hebrew Bible did so, but Isaiah certainly did more than any other. Even in the sixth century B.C.E., Isaiah seemed to anticipate the ecological crises we face today. It takes some translation to connect Isaiah to today's world, a translation that requires a major change in our point of view toward the Earth. Without a change in our perspective, the prophet Isaiah sounds quite strange.

The bridge to and from Isaiah on ecological issues is a short one, not because he was short on ecological sermons and poems but because we are not educated to hear them. On the contrary, respect for creation was left out of virtually all theology in the West, but like justice for women, it is in the Bible, though hidden. And it is in the Judeo-Christian tradition, though also very hidden. We have to redo our theology to get to it. As in nearly all western education after biblical times, the Earth was viewed as something that was simply there to be used by people with no integrity of its own. This disrespect for the Earth must end or we will.

Something very dramatic will probably be needed to wake up people to our environmental crisis. As in California's energy crisis, the lights had to go out before the light bulbs came on. Here is a recent summary of ecological issues to which Isaiah speaks:

> Throughout the past century humanity did everything in its power to dominate nature. We dammed Earth's rivers, chopped down the forests and depleted the soils. Burning up fossil fuels that had been created over eons, we pumped billions of tons of greenhouse gases into the air, altering atmospheric chemistry and appreciably warming the planet in just a few decades. And as our population began the year 2000 above the 6 billion mark, and is still spreading across the continents, dozens of animal and plant species were going extinct every day, including the first primate to disappear in more than 100 years, Miss Waldron's red colossus.
>
> At the start of the 21st century, there were unmistakable signs that exploitation of the planet was reaching its limit—that nature was beginning to take its revenge. Melting ice in the Polar Regions suggested that the climate was changing rapidly. Weather was even more erratic than usual, giving some places too little rain and others too much. Fires raced across the parched American West last summer, and recent storms spread devastation from Britain to Taiwan...scientists say that in a greenhouse world, deluges and droughts will be more frequent and severe. Already the hotter climate has increased the range of tropical diseases such as malaria and yellow fever. Other ominous signals from an overburdened planet include falling grain and fish harvests and fiercer competition for scarce water supplies...[1]

This quotation is not from Greenpeace or Ralph Nader but *Life* magazine. Now listen and compare this to sections of Isaiah 24:4–12:

> The earth dries up and withers, the world languishes and withers; the heavens languish together with the earth. The earth lies polluted under its inhabitants; for they have transgressed laws, violated the statutes, broken the everlasting covenant. Therefore a curse devours the earth, and its inhabitants suffer for their guilt...The city of chaos is broken down, every house is shut up so that no one can enter...all joy has reached its eventide; the gladness of the earth is banished. Desolation is left in the city, the gates are battered into ruins.

The similarities between the *Life* magazine summary and Isaiah are evident, and it is like this all the way through Isaiah's sixty-six chapters—

all three "Isaiahs," before, during, and after the Babylonian captivity. It is not easy reading, but it is important to get behind the short readings from the lectionary and absorb it all.

Another block to getting inside Isaiah regarding our abuse of God's creation is that we have a lot more problems than he did in his time. Here is another list of ecological issues on the decline of the Earth's basic ecosystems as distinct from particular disasters. In *The People and Ecosystems: The Fraying Web of Life*, the UN Development Program, the UN Environmental Program, the World Bank, and the World Resources Institute reported the following statistics:

- Half of the world's wetlands were lost last century.
- Logging and conversion have shrunk the world's forest by...half.
- Nine percent of the world's tree species are at risk of extinction.
- Fishing fleets are 40 percent larger than the oceans can sustain.
- Since 1980, the global economy has tripled in size and population, growing by 30 percent to 6 billion.
- Dams and diversions or canals fragment almost 60 percent of the world's rivers.
- Twenty percent of the world's freshwater fish are extinct, threatened or endangered.[2]

In October 2000, the World Conservation Union reported that the endangered species crisis is

> more acute than everybody feared. Of the 18,276 organisms investigated, 11,046—including 24% of mammals and 23% of birds—are threatened with extinction. In the last four years since their last study, "the number of critically endangered primates has risen 50%." More alarming is that this list only comprises just a fraction of the world's 1.75 million known species—let alone the millions more that have yet to be discovered.[3]

Isaiah probably knew something about endangered species from the story of Noah. Fishing was not always great in biblical times, and forests were ravaged then, too. However, industrial pollution, chemical or oil spills, bleaching of coral reefs, expanding ozone holes, toxic dumping on the poor and people of color, SUVs, dirt bikes, jet skis belching toxic fumes, industrial hog farm lagoons overflowing on the poor, and global warming did not exist. How can we connect Isaiah to our present dilemma?

Biblical scholar Walter Brueggemann helps in his book on Isaiah, *Using God's Resources Wisely: Isaiah and Urban Possibility*. But even Walter Brueggemann apologizes for the rawness of Isaiah...twice! As I have similarly fretted a few times while preparing sermons, he knows the prophets are strong medicine for nice church people. He begins:

> I am not stupid. I know the best procedure is to be upbeat and to focus positively on what must be done and can be done. So forgive me this text. I start here not because I am angry or in despair. I start here because I believe, that the emergency is acute.[4]

And he also pleads:

> Forgive me for beginning as sourly as does this poet. It will get somewhat better, a lot better, as we go along. But it is important that we take unblinking stock of where it is that we live...and what it is that so ominously hovers all around us.[5]

It is essential, I think, to dig deeply for our theological basis for environmental action because the environmental movement has fallen on hard times since about Earth Day 1970 when, soon after, many decent environmental regulations were passed by the U.S. Congress. Before the radical right caught up, we had the beginnings of clean water, clean air, limiting CFCs to protect the atmospheric ozone layer, endangered species listings, and other standards. Even the churches started to eliminate foam cups from coffee hour. Recycling began and mainline churches developed programs such as the National Council of Churches extensive National Climate Change Campaign. Some important changes happened to start us on the road to a sustainable future before the radical right caught up in Congress, especially in the 1994 turnover in the U.S. House. Not only were no new and essential environmental laws passed since then, but Congress has recently sought to gut virtually every one of the decent laws on the books from the 1970s.

Likewise, the environmental efforts in the churches seemed to have slowed down after a few furnace audits and storm windows were erected. I take this as a sign that we have to dig deeper in the church and fight harder in Congress. For now, in the Bush White House, we have the three environmental departments filled with people with horrible environmental records. We have a president whose campaign was financed by the oil industry and is on record as determined to pump more and more oil whatever the environmental costs, including oil from the pristine wilderness of the Arctic National Wildlife Refuge.

So what happened? Why this slow down? For one thing we were not yet prepared in the church for the grand paradigm shift that is required. In fact, our theology of dominion over nature has held fast through the centuries. We took the first creation story in Genesis 1:17, subdued the earth and ignored the second in Genesis 2:15, forgetting to till and keep it. With all of the great rhetoric about stewardship, we could not elevate it and keep it much above money-raising. Of course, the Sabbath is meant, as Brueggemann says, to break "the vicious cycle of productivity that defined imperial life. Without a Sabbath, the busy scheme of production and consumption turns all of life, neighbor and self into a succession of commodities with only utilitarian value."[6] Rather than giving nature a rest on Sunday, we watch professional sports and its commercials or shop the malls. Instead of "blue laws," now defunct, we need "green laws" to give the earth a rest on the Sabbath.

However, some theologians and ethicists recently have been working away on environmental issues. Larry Rasmussen, for one, says that from the 1930s to the 1970s, Protestant theologians were "miserably deficient" in ways that "alienated us from the rest of nature..."[7] But now we have Pierre de Chardin, Thomas Berry, Matthew Fox, Brian Swimme, from the Catholic tradition, and Jürgen Moltmann, Sally McFague, John Cobb, Rosemary Reuther, Wendell Berry, Paul Santmire, and Jim Nash, who have been writing their creation theologies from the Protestant perspective. Nevertheless, it does not seem to be getting through to our pulpits, let alone our pews. The old paradigm of dominion over nature still undercuts our efforts to teach a respect for God's creation.

I think that there are two key parts of this old worldview that have blocked our vision and kept the domination of the Earth, rather than respect for it, as our ruling perspective. One is the notion of a curse on the Earth. The second is our dualism. The prophet Isaiah corrects this misreading of scripture and the Earth. The connecting bridge to and from Isaiah and our ecological crisis can be summarized as our need to overcome the ideas of the curse on the earth and our dualistic separation of body and soul. Isaiah says in 24:5–6: "The earth lies polluted under its inhabitants; for they have transgressed laws, violated the statutes, broken the everlasting covenant. Therefore a curse devours the earth." Note that *therefore* the earth is cursed *because* of human transgression. *Therefore,* all creation suffers, not because animals, plants, earth, water, or air have sinned. No, that is ridiculous. But Isaiah goes on: "Therefore a curse devours the earth, and its inhabitants suffer for their guilt." This is a very important distinction between why the curse was there and how it was removed. The curse goes all the way *back* to Genesis, and its misunderstanding comes all the way *forward* to the mischief of us and our lawmakers today *and* keeps our churches silent.

In Genesis 3:17 the ground or earth is cursed not because the ground did a bad thing but, as God says to Adam, "because you have...eaten of the tree…cursed is the ground because of you." We do not see that this curse has been lifted, even though it says so in Genesis 8:21, when God says to Noah, "I will never again curse the ground because of humankind." Now, as in the beginning, creation is good, very good. Creation, ground, nature, and the physical world are good—blessed. They are not condemned or cursed by God. Jürgen Moltmann says, "It is God's good pleasure to create a world with which he could be well pleased."[8]

Also note in the Hebrew Bible the direct connection between the moral-spiritual world and the physical earth. We do not talk or even think like that. Quite the contrary, for us moderns the moral world of guilt and responsibility is absolutely separate from the natural world of physical things. That is because we wear dualistic glasses. For us, science deals with the physical-body world, and theology with the moral, spiritual world, and there is little or no connection between the two worlds.

There is a history of this dualism that helps explain the way it blinds us to environmental destruction. Dualism works with the curse on nature to separate body and soul, matter and spirit, the physical and the mental, the temporal and the eternal, nature and history, the profane and the sacred, the natural and the moral. In dualism, the higher soul, spirit, mind, or moral being lives for a while in the lower body. So we moderns do not think or talk about the earth as a sentient being that is "languishing" and "mourning" as Isaiah does. We do not mix the two worlds of body and soul. This dualism started with Plato. He had Socrates say, "We ought to fly away from earth to heaven as quickly as we can; and to escape is to become like God, as far as this is possible and to become like him is to become holy, just and wise."[9]

The New Testament, especially Paul's writings, are a mix of Greek and Hebrew thought. Paul was a Greek-educated Jew who did not fully accept this Greek dualism, but, like Isaiah, mixed the body and the soul, the spiritual and the physical, even to the point of bodily resurrection. Creation itself waits in eager longing to be set free (Romans 8:21). The body/spirit were so connected in the Hebrew Bible that there is no separate Hebrew word for nature in it.

The drastic separation of body and soul was clear in the medieval mystics, but it really was made dominant in western thought in 1624 when Francis Bacon proposed his physical philosophy he called "science." In Bacon's utopia, *The New Atlantis,* the goal of science is "enlarging the bounds of human empire."[10] The modern world began with all the wonders of science quickly changing everything. It was called the Enlightenment because it removed the darkness of superstition, blind faith, and magic from the pursuit of knowledge. Very rapidly, the spiritual, moral, and sacred world was separated from the physical world by Bacon and Descartes, from pure reason by Kant, from the origins of human life by Darwin, from history by Marx, and finally, from the last holdout, human psychology by Freud. But this blind faith that was swept out was replaced by other blind faiths in abstractions such as "progress" and "expanding empire."

Following Bacon, the "bounds of human empire" were expanded—free now not only from the confines of ancient superstition but also (and here is the rub) from spiritual compassion and devoid of moral restraint. Such dualism helps explain our lack of moral restraint in our heedless destruction of God's creation.

It seems that people do not believe that our use of the physical world has moral limits or that it is good (blessed), or that the curse is lifted. On the contrary, from our pews to congressional committees, the earth gets no respect. Creation is there only to be used for human ends. The ground is dirty. It is at best an inferior and inert thing with which we have to live. We in the church have promoted this dualism and its rejection of the nature, the body, and the sensual, temporal part of being in which, regrettably, the higher spirit dwells until it is released heavenward. The battles in Congress over roadless forests, oil extraction, fuel efficiency standards, and toxic dumping on minorities and the poor are essentially theological battles. Those in power seek to use, mine, extract, and/or deplete nature of everything that is saleable and to dump the waste on the poor—all to benefit a very few corporations, campaign contributors, and stockholders. Meanwhile, a few remnant voices in the wilderness seek to save nature for its own sake, or at least for all of us and insist that polluters clean up their own waste. Those in power say, "Trust us; things will be ok." The remnant says, "Let us use the precautionary principle, for no human is infallible. Creation is a blessed gift, not a resource to squander."

At a seminary recently, I thought I would fill in a big gap in my theological education by studying mysticism. In my first seminary study of theology, I not only received no creation theology, I also missed the mystics and opted for the way of action over contemplation. Having been an activist for so long, I thought I needed to get more religion—less action and more contemplation. It was my attempt at extreme religion. So I audited a course on Late Medieval English Mystics and read the Neo-Platonists: Walter Hilton, Richard Rolle, and *The Cloud of Unknowing* (author, date written, national origin, and purpose for writing unknown). I had a terrible time reading these guys. They wanted to negate not only all of the senses but also anything you could touch, feel, or experience in creation. This negative way was how one searched for a higher spiritual being. They thought we should despise even *ideas* of physical things. One example is from *The Cloud of Unknowing*, in which "Mr. Cloud" teaches the novice contemplative who, in search of purity of spirit, finds himself a "foul and fetid lump, which must always be hated and despised and forsaken, if a man would be God's perfect disciple..."[11] In Walter Hilton's *Scale of Perfection*, "dying to the world" is the "gate to contemplation." Such dying to the world is the "luminous darkness" in which the world "forgets him like a dead man."[12] They took the curse on the physical world and the flesh to an extreme end. Other male religious leaders took this rejection of the earth into a rejection of women.

However, this mystics course was saved for me when we got to the fifteenth-century Anchorite woman, Julian of Norwich, who took all this rejection of the natural world and turned it around. With a hazelnut in her hand so tiny it could easily disappear, she said, "In this little thing I saw...that God made it...God loves it...God preserves it."[13] Julian is a part of that hidden tradition that did not buy the curse on the physical world. For if God made, loves, and preserves it, how can we despise it? God's creation is not cursed or condemned.

Let us get back to Isaiah, who presents two clear approaches to the curse on the earth in the example of Hezekiah, king of Judah, before the exile. One is free of the curse, and the other is under the curse. Isaiah was the court prophet who helped Hezekiah take a stand against what Brueggemann calls, "the military-industrial complex, greedy in its self-sufficiency, careless about creation, ready to use and abuse everything on which it can get its hands." In short, this is "military consumerism."[14] We call it the Pentagon, the CIA, and their corporate and political sponsors. The Bible called it Assyria under King Sennacherib. Assyria is about to invade Judah and lay siege to Jerusalem and its King Hezekiah.

Against this military consumerism, Isaiah railed and mocked. He organized Jerusalem women to demonstrate scorn against the mighty (185,000 strong) army of Assyria, wagging their heads behind the backs of the enemy. Isaiah charges Sennacherib:

> You have mocked the Lord and bragged about your many chariots and claimed, "I have gone up the heights of the mountains, to the far recesses of Lebanon; I felled its tallest cedars and its choicest cypresses." You have made cities "into heaps of ruins." And people like blighted plants. (Isaiah 37:24, 27; 2 Kings 19:23)

Against this ecological and military disaster, Isaiah, speaking for God while propping up Hezekiah, boasts to Sennacherib, "I will put my hook in your nose and my bit in your mouth; I will turn you back on the way by which you came" (Isaiah 37:29; 2 Kings 19:28). And so it happened.

Sennacherib retreated and Jerusalem was saved. Hezekiah stood up to this "military consumerism," and, by God, he prevailed...this time. Do we dare to stand up against the clear-cutting of our national forests and old growth trees, against militarism that pollutes the Balkans with depleted uranium, that teaches torture at the School of the Americas, and makes and leaves toxic dumps throughout the world, that lets big oil buy off our political campaigns? Like Hezekiah, we have a choice. And it takes all we have and more to reject the whole worldview of the empire that sits dualistically separated from the earth that is assumed to be cursed and condemned.

This courageous act took so much out of Hezekiah that he got sick. When he recovered, there was another empire of military consumerism waiting at his Jerusalem door, Babylon. These Babylonian ambassadors did not even have to threaten and seduce a spent Hezekiah this time. Hezekiah forgot how military consumerism had not saved him from Assyria. He forgot the blessings of God, and he bought into the real politic of empires. He gave the Babylonian envoys a military honor guard and showed off his treasury to them.

When Isaiah found out, he came storming into the palace to ream out Hezekiah for his capitulation to military consumerism. Then he predicted that Babylon would crush Jerusalem, carry them off to exile, and make their sons eunuchs in the court of Babylon. To this Hezekiah replied limply, "The word of the LORD you have spoken is good." But he thought, "There will be peace and security in my days" (Isaiah 39:8; 2 Kings 20:19). It won't be on my watch. It's not my problem. And so it was. Soon after Hezekiah, Jerusalem fell, and the exile began two hundred years of Babylonian captivity. Because of his moral failure, the curse fell on the land again.

How often have you heard people say, "Not in my time. What's the fuss? Global warming may actually help warm up our cold, northern states." Or, "Paper mill pollution is tolerable in our town as long as it keeps the jobs." Or, "Why worry about a few caribou in the Arctic National Wildlife Reserve when we need the oil and gas now?"

Hezekiah made two choices: The first was a trust in the blessings of God; the second was a trust in the curse of military consumerism. We are centuries away from his big decisions, but on these matters of faith, little changes over time. We have the same choices. We can believe we are condemned to a dualistic world that is an evil, accursed place so we have to keep giving the military consumer gods our taxes to do with as they please and keep ravaging the Earth for more and more consumer gadgets that go into landfills in a few months to make room for more widgets. Or we can follow Hezekiah's first choice against military consumerism and refuse to buy into the assumptions of empire and reject the need for excessive armies and a national missile defense system to keep a cursed world safe for just our time. Meanwhile, God's blessed creation deteriorates beyond recovery. The prophet's call to restore the Earth is clear and up-to-date in spite of the nine-thousand-year separation if we can overcome the false idea that the earth is cursed and if we can overcome dualism that isolates the moral-spiritual world from the physical earth.

But do not take my word for it. "God saw everything that he had made, and indeed, it was very good" (Genesis 1:31). And "the LORD said in his heart, 'I will never again curse the ground because of humankind...as long as the earth endures, seedtime and harvest, cold and heat, summer and winter, day and night, shall not cease'" (Genesis 8:21–22). Neither is creation nor are we cursed or condemned. And if we do not get it from the Hebrew prophets, it comes straight from Paul in Romans as well: "There is therefore now no condemnation for those who are in Christ Jesus" (Romans 8:1).

6

Becoming a Church for Ecology and Justice

Dieter T. Hessel

As planet Earth becomes hotter, stormier, less biodiverse, more crowded, unequal, and more violent, a growing number of scholars in theology and ethics as well as discerning leaders and members of churches on six continents are joining the ecojustice movement. It involves environmentally responsive Christians who seek the well-being of Earth and people through practices and policies that serve ecological wholeness and social justice together (ecology + justice = ecojustice). Participants engaging in this praxis can be instructed by decades of pioneering ecumenical journeying and should build on what churches, working together, have already been doing.

Stepping into an Ecumenical Stream

When cultural historians look back at the last third of the twentieth century with renewed appreciation for religion's ambiguous power, they may see that religious leaders, scholars, and organizations had to relearn from ecologists that, in addition to the human species and culture, *nature* in all its biodiversity is real and valuable. But historians should also see that twentieth century environmentalism often lacked passion for, or adequate principles of, social justice. So, it was left to working groups of ecumenical theologians and socially engaged laity—informed by the insights of environmental activists and social ecologists, as well as by the Hebrew Bible's Sabbath sensibility and covenant ethics—to emphasize that *there will be little environmental health without social justice and vice versa.* Once the ecumenical movement came to this realization, its gatherings and leaders began to express an inclusive vision of ecojustice that seeks what is ecologically fitting and socially fair through democratic decision-making for the common good.

The global ecumenical movement and its member churches began to address the environmental challenge in the mid-1970s, following the Stockholm Conference on Environment and Development (1972). In response, the Nairobi Assembly of the World Council of Churches (WCC, 1975) emphasized the need to establish a "just, sustainable, and participatory society."[1] In his address to that assembly, Charles Birch, an Australian biologist, explained:

> A prior requirement of any global society is that it be so organized that human life and other living creatures on which human life depends can be sustained indefinitely within the limits of the Earth. A second requirement is that it be sustained at a quality that makes possible fulfillment of human life for all people. A society so organized to achieve both these ends we can call a sustainable global society in contrast to the present unsustainable global society. If the life of the world is to be sustained and renewed...it will have to be with a new sort of science and technology governed by a new sort of economics and politics.[2]

After Nairobi, a 1979 WCC conference at MIT on "Faith, Science, and the Future" pursued the subject in more detail,[3] and the next WCC Assembly (Vancouver, 1983) focused on the theme "Justice, Peace, and Integrity of Creation."

Even with these prominent initiatives, it took at least another decade to gain wide ecumenical acceptance of a fulsome ethic of ecojustice that features basic moral norms of *solidarity* with other people and creatures; ecological *sustainability* in development, technology, and production; *sufficiency* as a standard of organized sharing that requires floors and ceilings for equitable consumption; and socially just *participation* in decisions about how to obtain sustenance and to manage community life for the good of all.

This, of course, is a postanthropocentric agenda. But not until the late 1980s, in a consultation at Annecy, France, did the WCC begin to address a theology and ethic for the liberation of life that demands respect for animals and preservation of species for their own sake, not just for their benefit to humankind.[4] That report informed the WCC's 1991 Canberra Assembly theme, "Come Holy Spirit, Renew the Whole Creation." Through the 1990s, the WCC mission in society unit developed an action/reflection emphasis on Theology of Life that has focused critical ecumenical reflection, including several WCC publications on environmentally and humanly destructive effects of economic globalization.

Similarly, in 1998, the World Alliance of Reformed Churches (WARC) issued a study paper to guide a "Committed Process of Recognition, Education, Confession, and Action Regarding Economic Injustice and Ecological Destruction" (*Processus Confessionis*). A paragraph in that WARC report said:

> It is not enough for our communities to denounce injustice and point to the seemingly irreparable damage done to the Earth [by economic globalization]. We need to travel further towards the embodiment of a just society living in tender relationship with the earth. We need to celebrate the "mustard seed" signs of the realm of God. We can give thanks for the ferment of the Holy Spirit in and through people who resist threats to life.[5]

Meanwhile, the WCC launched a climate change program led by David Hallman of the United Church of Canada. And in the late 1990s the Orthodox ecumenical patriarch Bartholomew received considerable media publicity for declaring pollution to be a sin against God. Nevertheless, concerns about violence, racism, and economic injustice have continued to elicit much more international and national ecumenical attention than has the ecological crisis.

The Roman Catholic story unfolded more slowly, beginning with the Pope's 1979 trip to the Americas (first Puebla, Mexico, and then Des Moines, Iowa), where John Paul II emphasized land stewardship. It took another decade for the Vatican to issue a 1990 message on "The Ecological Crisis: A Common Responsibility." Then, on Pentecost 1992, in Brazil, parallel to the Earth Summit (the 1992 UN Conference on Environment and Development), an inclusive gathering of Protestant, Orthodox, Roman Catholic, and Anglican leaders facilitated by the WCC issued a Letter to the Churches, which concluded its confession of complicity and expression of commitment with these words:

> The Spirit teaches us to go first to those places where community and creation are most obviously languishing, those melancholy places where the cry of the people and the cry of the earth are intermingled. [There] we meet Jesus, who goes before, in solidarity and healing.[6]

Coordinated Environmental Engagement by U.S. Churches

In the United States, ecumenical environmental response has exhibited five emphases:

1. Cultivating Quality Ecotheology and Ethics

It started with essays by forerunner Lutheran theologian Joseph Sittler and developed through a National Council of Churches (NCC) work group on "Faith-Man-Nature" formed in 1963–1964 by biologist Philip Joranson. Prominent theologians such as Daniel Day Williams, H. Paul Santmire, John B. Cobb, and Rosemary Radford Ruether soon added contributions. Roderick Nash tracked this early period in *The Rights of Nature.*[7] But Nash did not discern the beginnings of a theological bent toward ecojustice ethics and action, exemplified by the Friendship Press anthology, *A New Ethic for a New Earth.*[8] He also overlooked what the churches actually said and did in proximity to the first Earth Day and was unaware of extensive church engagement with hunger and energy policies from the mid-1970s forward.

Ecotheology and ethics languished in the 1980s but developed with vigor again in the 1990s. Now diverse voices representing both genders and a rainbow of people across the Christian spectrum are contributing to, and thinking about, well-rounded praxis, as can be seen in the literature on ecotheology and ethics.[9] Unfortunately, few theological schools feature this important advance in theology and ethics; most seminary and religious studies programs only offer electives on this subject. To refocus higher education to teach for the environment and to educate for sustainability is a more significant agenda.[10]

2. Fostering Sustainable Food Systems and Lifestyles

During the 1970s, progressive churches were prominently involved in struggles to protect the rights of farm workers. National boycotts of grapes and lettuce, spearheaded by the United Church of Christ (UCC), lent strong support to the United Farm Workers. Boycotts (selective buying) of other commodity producers to protest their violation of labor rights have also occurred with less fanfare in recent years.

Meanwhile, the churches working together in the NCC became quite knowledgeable about U.S. government food and farm programs as well as problems of international aid and trade. Churches invested considerable energy in leadership development for hunger education/action through new denominational initiatives and the ecumenical effort named WHEAT—World Hunger Education/Action Together (which I chaired). The hunger programs institutionalized by churches in the late 1970s gave some attention and project funding to the environmental dimensions of sustainable food systems—for example, how to decrease monoculture, pesticide use, export cropping, and grain-fed meat consumption while using appropriate technology for food production in poor countries. Today we face deepening problems of inappropriate technology in export crops, controlled by corporations that patent and produce genetically modified organisms such as pesticide resistant plants or "killer" seeds. So far, ecumenical critique of these ominous developments seems muted. Churches need to take seriously the assertion of Lester Brown (of the WorldWatch Institute) that what is needed is an environmental revolution powerful enough to transform the practices of agriculture and industry to conform with the goals of sustainability. Though Lester Brown would include agriculture in the following statement, Maurice Strong, Secretary General of the UN Conference on Environment and Development, captures this same perspective:

> The changes that come about as a result of the shift to sustainable development will have an effect as profound as anything that has taken place since the industrial revolution. Indeed, they add up to a veritable "eco-industrial revolution" in which environmental considerations will more and more drive economic policy and industrial transformation.[11]

As the crisis of family farmers deepened in the 1980s and 1990s, church groups, influenced by Wendell Berry, Wes Jackson, and Dean Freudenberger, began to focus on the need for sustainable agriculture, church- and community-based agriculture, and local food security. In the United States, much of the solid analysis, education, and advocacy has been led by creative clergy—often Lutherans—working with centers for land stewardship and rural life, especially in the upper Plains states. Roman Catholics have approached these concerns in a different style, featuring regional pastoral letters (drafted in both of the following cases by John Hart of Carroll College, Montana). In 1984, Catholic bishops of twelve Midwestern states issued *Strangers and Guests: Toward Community in the Heartland*. In February 2001, twelve Catholic bishops from the Northwestern states issued a pastoral letter on the Columbia River Watershed: "Caring for Creation and the Common Good." That international watershed is threatened not only by inappropriate dams and logging but also by water diversion for irrigated agriculture and a regional population explosion of high consumers.

Speaking of consumption, the pioneering work of campus minister William E. Gibson and the ecojustice project at Cornell University fostered quality education for lifestyle change as an emphasis of the church's hunger programs. It focused on reduced consumption, voluntary conservation, appropriate diet and recreation, plus public engagement. In the 1990s, education for lifestyle integrity returned to prominence, thanks to the initiative of another regional ecumenical project called Earth Ministry based in Seattle.

3. Advocating Responsible Energy and Climate Change Policies

Before the first oil shock from OPEC, U.S. churches were not involved in energy policy debates, viewing them as too technical or merely political. But in 1974, the Division of Church and Society of the NCC formed a committee of inquiry, chaired by Margaret Mead and Rene Dubos, on the use of plutonium as a commercial nuclear fuel. When, in October 1975, the committee proposed a policy statement condemning such use of plutonium, the nuclear industry and utility executives attacked the NCC for being irresponsible. A resolution calling for a moratorium was substituted for the policy statement. In the same action, the NCC mandated a broad study on "The Ethical Implications of Responsible Energy Production and Use," led by the late Chris Cowap, NCC Director of Economic Justice, who wrote a concise, instructive overview of that highly conflicted study for a book I edited.[12] Her description of the outcome of the three-year study, involving a panel of 120 knowledgeable persons, shows how intellectually demanding and politically sophisticated was this timely ecumenical endeavor.

The energy study impelled the ecumenical church to be powerfully present among competing interests with contradictory answers to the environmental challenge. The NCC energy policy study coincided with the decision of the grass roots movement to delegitimize nuclear power and to take a "soft energy path."[13] It was followed by interchurch programs to foster local energy responsibility, substantive denominational energy policy statements, and interfaith efforts to demand corporate accountability to communities on the part of utilities building power plants. Local congregations, however, tended to limit their participation to retrofitting their own buildings for energy efficiency.

Now, three decades later, the United States has come full circle to many of the same aspects of energy policy that the 1970s NCC study explored: fossil fuel dependence; reliance on dangerous nuclear and CO_2-emitting coal-fired generators; lack of public accountability by power companies; and lethargic federal support of renewable energy technologies, conservation incentives, mass transit subsidies, or carbon taxes to reduce consumption.

Moreover, the world now faces an urgent need to halt global warming, regarding which the United States—with 4 percent of the world's population, but responsible for 25 percent of the world's heat-trapping gases[14]—is dragging its feet. Ecumenical work on climate change—the world's most urgent moral issue—emerged through workshops in different parts of the world organized by Canadian churchman David Hallman as a way to focus on the links between economic injustice and environmental destruction. WCC workshops and its 1988 study paper on "Climate Change and the Quest for Sustainable Societies," plus reinforcing reports and statements by denominations, presented scientific facts about climate change, and theological-ethical reflections on social and ecological justice. This was followed by a worldwide petition campaign, involving the churches and other faith communities, that got the attention of government officials and positioned an ecumenical team of church representatives to become active advocates at climate change negotiations from Kyoto forward. Ecumenical advocacy on this issue emphasizes that the most industrialized countries must demonstrate global responsibility and show fairness to poor countries by making real cuts in greenhouse gas emissions rather than relying on "trading" emission credits. Toward this end, churches in the industrialized countries are engaged in advocacy work with public officials. Currently in the United States, this is done through Interfaith Climate Change Campaigns—occurring in over twenty states—coordinated by the NCC Eco-Justice Working Group (EJWG) working with state councils of churches.

4. Community Organizing for Environmental Justice

The U.S. churches' most distinctive involvement with the environmental movement has been to demand environmental justice. The UCC Commission on Racial Justice first prepared, published, and circulated documentation about severe racial and class inequity in locating toxic dumps and incinerators. The churches also took the initiative to contact community organizations fighting toxic facilities, to bring some of their leaders together, and to find funding that enabled community organizations to challenge unjust waste management. Though the Citizens' Clearing House on Hazardous Wastes (now the Center for Health, Environment, and Justice) deserves more credit for starting this kind of organizing, the ecumenical churches helped to make environmental justice more possible for communities of color, rural areas, and Native American nations.

By late 1987, these initiatives were being coordinated through the EJWG formed the year before, with Chris Cowap as staff director and myself as founding cochair. Support of community organizing for environmental justice led the EJWG to subsidize participation by leaders of community groups in the National People of Color Environmental Leadership Summit (Washington, D.C., 1991), at which it pushed the leaders of established environmental organizations to support basic principles of environmental justice and help "build a movement of all peoples of color to fight the destruction and taking of our lands and communities...and to secure our political, economic, and cultural liberation."[15] Lutheran layman Jim Schwab has pointed out in *Deeper Shades of Green* that this unique summit "drew more than 600 activists, combining the colors of the rainbow in one giant sharing and strategizing meeting that has literally and permanently changed the complexion of the U.S. environmental movement."[16] The environmental justice emphasis also strengthened collaboration between parachurch groups and nongovernmental organizations at UN forums such as the Rio Earth Summit (1992), the Cairo Conference on Population and Development (1993), and the Beijing Conference on Women (1995).

The environmental justice focus carried over into the work of the National Religious Partnership for the Environment (involving Christians and Jews), which provided funding for the NCC to hold special meetings with leaders of the black Churches and the Orthodox communions. But preoccupation with community organizing to combat toxic substances tended for a time to preempt other styles of engagement and to narrow ecojustice work to become a mere subset of economic justice advocacy.

5. Developing Leadership for Earth Community Ministry

At this point, the churches remembered that it is not enough to support grassroots groups of activists siding with the powerless in ecologically degraded urban and rural communities. A mature agenda of environmental responsibility is also concerned with preserving biodiversity and protecting special places. To grapple with this broad agenda, churches must continuously develop leaders and nurture members, gain a voice in the media and a hearing with public officials, and challenge indifferent or hostile institutions to care about the web of creation and human relations with others. In other words, for there to be significant implementation of a preferential option for the oppressed, there must be more pedagogy of the privileged and careful structuring of environmental ministry.

Undertaking Environmental Ministry and Doing Ecojustice Ethics Today

Since the mid-1990s, the EJWG and the U.S. Catholic Conference, utilizing generous foundation funding obtained by the National Religious

Partnership for the Environment, have concentrated on publishing educational resources and developing leadership to integrate creation-care into parish life—always with a strong social justice component. The NCC group now gathers its grassroots network annually to share the latest educational resources and to give focus to community engagement and public policy advocacy. Engaged congregations and ecumenical groups can move most effectively by not starting from scratch but by utilizing the ecumenical movement's resources for congregations and building on its pioneering work. The point just made is one of several guidelines to follow in building a local ministry for ecology and justice. (The next section of this chapter presents other guidelines.)

But many congregations are not even approaching this mission. Let us frankly acknowledge that *most churches and members remain indifferent to the ecojustice movement or ethic and are not yet involved in significant environmental ministry.* Compared to widespread church involvement in programs of social service and peace education/action, Christian communities have not institutionalized much care for creation. Church bodies and congregations continue to affirm and practice social "stewardship" apart from ecological responsibility. But they have yet to grasp the depth of the ecojustice crisis, nor do they see mission in terms of communing and suffering with creation or building sustainable community in healing and liberating ways. A third of a century after the first Earth Day, only a scattering of congregations cares for the place where they are as much as the people in their pews. Not many churches celebrate and minister to Earth community in worship, education, institutional practices, or public witness. Except perhaps for recycling some waste, talking about reducing unnecessary consumption, and planning to retrofit church buildings for energy efficiency, congregations typically conduct religion business as usual with little time for the most basic human vocation—seen in Genesis 2:15 as earth keeping.

Too many leaders of local, denominational, and ecumenical communities of faith still leave creation's well-being to environmentalists. Even where Christians do see ecological problems, church leaders display ambivalence about working with the environmental community. For example, the "Statement on Global Warming," issued by Oregon religious leaders in October 2000 when launching their interfaith campaign, declared: "We speak not as members of an 'environmental movement' but as people of faith giving thanks to God for the blessings of creation by working to preserve them for present and future generations." It is as if faith but no influence from environmental science and activism had led the Oregon religious leaders to begin a climate change campaign.

In contrast to such diffidence, the preceding story of ecumenical ecojustice journeying shows *that church leaders and environmental community leaders can positively influence each other in a reciprocal relation that needs to continue.* On the one hand, environmentalists have pushed ecumenical churches to rethink theology, ethics, and mission in light of the ideal of a sustainable society, to which churches have come slowly. While the ecumenical movement affirmed its social calling, in light of Jesus' public ministry, to care for and seek distributive justice to other humans, the environmental movement was focusing world attention on the plight and rights of the rest of nature, challenging the narrowly human-centered preoccupations of modern culture. Environmentalists, in addition to clarifying global ecological problems, contributed important concepts such as carrying capacity and interconnectedness. They defined the norm of sustainability in terms of ecological integrity, which forbids human activities that diminish Earth's biodiversity or life-carrying capacity. The environmental movement also demanded that humans are called to feel respect and show care for all forms of life, not just other humans—an emphasis that broadens the meaning of "solidarity."

Instructed by these ecological insights, as well as critical social analysis, ecumenical ethicists came to a holistic understanding of what ecojustice requires to meet the world's dual crisis: degradation of the natural environment and oppression of poor people. So, on the other hand, ecumenical ecojustice sensibility about human-Earth relations has positively influenced the environmental movement. It has pushed environmental organizations to explore beliefs about what is sacred and (moving beyond the insights of environmental philosophy and ecological science) to broaden their thinking about ecological sustainability in order to encompass principles of social and economic justice. That advance was demonstrated vividly in two events that bookended the 1990s: the October 1991 National People of Color Environmental Leadership Summit (discussed above) and the Earth Council's release in March 2000 of a peoples' Earth Charter text.[17] This global document actually illumines basic ecojustice values without using the term; the Earth Charter's four parts discuss principles associated with solidarity, sustainability, sufficiency, and participation—*in that order.* The Charter thus has the important effect of fostering an ecology of ethical values for Earth community.

In retrospect, a posture that first emerged to reconcile post-Earth Day competition between social justice and environmental action groups has turned out to offer much more than trade-offs. Ecojustice provides a dynamic framework for philosophical and theological study as well as environmental ethical reflection to meet the real needs of Earth community.

Ironically, environmental organizations have gotten the ecojustice message faster than have many in the faith communities!

The vision, values, and virtues expressed in ecojustice praxis give shape to a *contextual ethic* for church and society that applies at every level of moral agency—individual, institutional, and governmental. This contextual, nonabsolutist ethic informs immediate choices at any given time and place but does not tell us exactly what to do. In light of social experience and human reason, as well as scripture and tradition, the ethical task is to discern among real options the good to be achieved or the path of right relations, while expecting pluralistic solutions respectful of cultural and biotic diversity.

Solidarity with the Earth and people, ecological sustainability, basic sufficiency, and fair participation all matter as mutually reinforcing and correcting norms that inform and qualify each other. Full-orbed efforts to achieve just and sustainable community, therefore, encompass these deep, practical values as essential, interactive components of a healthy future—i.e., what Earth community requires. Also notice that the ecojustice norms are both ends-oriented and means-clarifying, illumining both where we want to go and how to get there.

Building an Earth Community Ministry

The ecumenical environmental responses reviewed in this chapter are aspects of *an historic movement toward the alternative paradigm of mutually enhancing human-Earth relations.* Congregations and larger church bodies, which think and act in terms of God's commonwealth or "kingdom," should appreciate and respond positively to these concrete signs of a better future. In other words, ecumenical examples of ecojustice journeying offer wisdom for ongoing efforts to embody the more appropriate paradigm of human-Earth relations that God intends. They express a vision of healthy Earth community that ought to catch every church's imagination. As that perspective and commitment grows, more churches will recycle theology and ethics, foster sustainable food systems and lifestyles, advocate responsible energy use and climate change policies, help to organize communities for economic and environmental justice, protect species, restore ecosystems, and develop leadership for Earth community ministry.

However, a congregation or ecumenical group that is just beginning to engage needs to go through a process of discernment to determine what it should and can best contribute. Following are several guidelines for building a meaningful ecojustice ministry.

First, build awareness by exploring the global/local environmental challenge and, by connecting with those in the know, do an ecosocial analysis. The experts you should consult include leaders of environmental and social justice organizations, residents of communities most threatened by toxic substances, independent students of these issues, and engaged religious groups. Discover how organizations in your area are acting to address urgent issues. In this discernment process, be sure to also connect with environmental policy advocacy networks to learn about the links between national, regional, and local public policies that affect the health of people and ecosystems. Join an ecumenical public policy advocacy network on environment/energy to receive pertinent alerts and briefing material.

Second, distill what you learn about the basic needs/issues that require engagement in your locale and about how other organizations are responding. Do not just tote up a bunch of issues, however. In your report, connect particular concerns with aspects of your overall ecosocial analysis so that you show the breadth and depth of the environmental challenge.

Third, offer solid opportunities for theologically grounded reflection by members of your religious community. Approach this educational task, with the help of theologically trained and engaged mentors, in ways that expose the roots of ecojustice ethics and action in scripture and tradition and that restate basic faith affirmations to meet the environmental crisis. Keep in mind that participants need more than information. Participants who live in a manifestly unsustainable society especially need to be nurtured spiritually for a tough struggle.

Fourth, determine appropriate emphases of your congregation or ecumenical group that will complement the work of others by filling in particular gaps. Identify the most likely partner groups in your area and announce who are the designated leaders of your congregation's involvement. Make your planning and action groups inviting.

Fifth, utilize all the basic modes of ministry in responding to the environmental challenge. What you intend to do and how you go about it should encompass various aspects of congregational and community life. Ecojustice ministry involves up to eight modes of engagement, each of which requires careful planning and good leadership.[18] The available modes of ministry are education; worship; community organization; lifestyle transformation; public policy advocacy; responsible property management and investing; pastoral care to foster authentic vocation; and coordinating/funding a response with local, regional, and global dimensions. Over a period of years, the congregation should utilize these modes of ministry in combination as a qualitative way to respond to a deepening environmental challenge.

It's Not Just Another Issue

Christians who journey with creation-awareness and ecojustice intention are contributing to something profound—the church's ecological reformation that promises to transform the human vocation to seek peoples' rights and otherkind's well-being together; to shift the axis of Christian ethics and liturgy; and to reshape/reconstruct the church's theology, worship, mission, and witness to meet the twenty-first century in response to our unique historical situation of real biophysical limits and threatened Earth systems. That comprehensive, long-term agenda is much bigger than taking concrete steps to deal with particular environmental issues or changing a few lifestyle habits.

Ecological reformation impels leaders in theology and ministry and alerts church bodies to make significant changes:

- *Abandon the bad theological habits* of separating history and humanity from nature and separating human redemption from creation.
- *Recognize that the web of life embraces distant galaxies* and that humans are an ecologically integrated, morally responsible species.
- *Utilize the relationality paradigm within current cosmology, ecology, process thought, and ecofeminism* to restore a sense of human-Earth unity. We also should reread scripture in trifocal perspective—combining the view from outdoors with the view from below and the view from abroad.
- *Represent theology in ecologically alert terms* and accordingly recycle traditional affirmations about God, Jesus Christ, the Holy Spirit, world, church, soul/body, sin and evil, redemption, and new Earth.
- *Redefine faithfulness in common life* in ways that *embody ecojustice ethics.*
- *Reshape liturgical life* so as to highlight God's loving and just relationship with habitat earth, not only human beings.
- *Remodel sustainability in individual and institutional practices* that are Earth honoring.

The needed transformation encompasses our religious convictions, consumer lifestyles, what and how we learn, the work we do, the way our organizations operate, and the networks we join for public engagement—all to strengthen sustainable community for creation's sake on and around this planet.

Though many churches and members still don't "get it," an ecological reformation has emerged prominently on the ecumenical agenda, and we can see its contours.[19] The question before each of us, then, is: "How alertly and energetically will we participate in this continuing eco-justice journey?" Or, as the prophet Ezekiel was asked, "Can these bones live?"[20]

Renewal begins by confessing our faults and asking for forgiveness in reliance on God's grace. Here is an example adapted from the Presbyterian *Brief Statement of Faith:*[21]

> **Prayer of Confession.** O God, in whom we trust, you have created the world good, and made each of us equally in your image. Yet, we rebel against our Earth-keeping vocation. Ignoring your commandments, we violate the image of God in others and ourselves, accept lies as truth, exploit neighbor and nature, and threaten death to the planet entrusted to our care. We deserve condemnation. Yet you act with justice and mercy to redeem creation. Reconcile us from sin, we pray, and set us free to serve Earth community.
>
> **Assurance of Pardon.**
>
> Leader: This we know: the earth does not belong to us.
> **People: We belong to the earth.**
>
> Leader: This we know: we did not weave the web of life.
> **People: We are merely a strand in it.**
>
> Leader: This we know: whatever we do to the web,
> **People: We do it to ourselves.**
>
> Leader: Let us give thanks for God's love shown in creation and by Christ.
> **People: Forgive us, redeem us, and help us to restore the earth.**

7

A Prophetic Vision of Restoring the Earth

David W. Randle

During the past few decades, scientists and theologians seem to be coming closer together in their reflections on the universe. Scientists have stated that a great fireball exploded some five billion years ago to form our universe; however, if that fireball cooled even a second faster or slower than it did, life as we know it could not exist. Some say that we might have lucked out. Matthew Fox is fond of quoting Julian of Norwich who said it this way: "We have been loved from before the beginning."[1]

Yet as great as this cosmic love has been, is, and continues to show itself through the wonders of God's creation, we are on the verge of an ecological crisis that may result in irreparable damage to the life sustaining process itself. At the root of this ecological crisis, many have come to realize that it is more of a subtle spiritual crisis. This spiritual crisis has been created in part due to our lack of connection with God's creation, and our turning away from the sustaining prophetic values of our various faith traditions to values of short-term greed and profit.

World scientists have issued a Warning to Humanity, yet their call goes unheeded by the politicians we continue to elect and/or who serve on our behalf. Warnings of the threats to human health, our quality of life, and even the future of our own children and grandchildren do not seem to be enough to heed the global Warning to Humanity.

The UN Environment Programme (UNEP) has gone a step further in its call for action to restore the Earth. It recently published *Earth and Faith: A Book for Reflection for Action.* In this book UNEP calls for an interrelated Earth Agenda:

Water
- Protecting freshwater resources
- Protecting oceans, coral reefs, coastal areas, and small islands

Land
- Conserving biological diversity
- Combating deforestation and decertification
- Protecting land resources from nitrogen overload

Health
- Protecting human health and the quality of life, especially the living and working environments of the poor, from pollution and environmental degradation

Air
- Protecting the atmosphere by combating climate change and transboundary air pollution

Industry
- Managing biotechnology in an ecologically safe way
- Managing hazardous wastes and toxic chemicals in an environmentally sound manner

Well-Being
- Examining and changing production and unsustainable consumption patterns
- Analyzing the effects of globalization on the environment, and take appropriate protective measures[2]

There is no shortage of knowledge of what needs to be done to restore the Earth. We have the science to at least point us in the right direction. We have the technology to implement many beneficial solutions. We have the understanding of the impact that a growing population has on our planet. We have the international structures to implement global international treaties to protect and restore the Earth. What we lack is the political will and the spiritual vision and leadership to take the necessary actions for what may be nothing less than our own survival as a human species.

For the past six years, I have had the wonderful opportunity to participate in the United Religions Initiative, an interfaith organization whose purpose is to promote daily interfaith cooperation and to build cultures of peace, justice, and the healing of the Earth. From these experiences I have found a source of hope in uniting people of faith traditions from all over the world to bring their spiritual resources together to create a new ethic for healing and restoration of the Earth.

Key to this new ethic seems to be the wisdom of many faith traditions from around the world found in sacred stories or sacred teachings. Some of the wisdom of sacred stories includes the Jewish story of Joseph and Pharaoh, the story of Noah's ark, and the Christian New Testament teachings of God's love. From other faith traditions we have stories and wisdom as well, such as the Dalai Lama's *Ethics for the New Millennium,*[3] as well as other sacred literature. Finally, we have the wisdom of indigenous and modern day theologians to guide our Earth restoration efforts.

In the story of Joseph and Pharaoh (Genesis 40—43), Pharaoh has a dream that Joseph is able to interpret. Joseph tells Pharaoh that after seven good years, there will be some severe climate changes that could bring about disaster if Pharaoh does not prepare. The story goes on to say that Joseph provides Pharaoh with a conservation plan. Joseph advises to save 20 percent of the grain that will be harvested during the seven good years, which will be used to make up for the shortfall during the seven bad years. It is interesting to note that Pharaoh decides to exercise the precautionary principle that is a key to our modern day challenge of restoring the Earth. The precautionary principle is, in short, to err on the side of environment vs. development if the information for a decision is incomplete.

I submit that dream interpretation in Pharaoh's day was not what we might call an exact science, and a 20 percent conservation plan certainly would impact the national economy of Egypt at that time. Nonetheless, Pharaoh decided to exercise the precautionary principle and implement the 20 percent conservation plan. The end result of this action was that not only was Pharaoh able to feed his own people during the famine, but he was also able to assist other nations of the world as well.

Let us suppose that Joseph was wrong and that the seven bad years never came. Pharaoh still would have had a grain reserve built up that could have improved his nation's trade balance, provided assistance to the poor, and provided security for disasters or difficult situations that might have occurred in the future. If world leaders would follow the example of Joseph's advice to Pharaoh and begin a strong conservation plan for energy, water, open space preservation, and so on (if they would follow the precautionary principle as they planned for the future), we would be making major strides toward the first steps to restoring the Earth.

A second biblical story that brings wisdom for restoring the Earth is the story of Noah and the ark (Genesis 6—9). Noah, like Joseph, was warned by God that there were going to be some severe climate changes ahead, that there needed to be a new order on the Earth that was not driven by greed and wickedness and so filled with violence. To make sure that the new order would succeed, God placed an extremely high value on biodiversity. God did not tell Noah to get as many humans into the ark as he could make room for. On the contrary, the humans were limited to Noah, his wife, his sons, and their wives. The priority after that was biodiversity, seven pairs of all the clean animals and one pair of every other living creature.

Somehow, God seemed to know that if the Earth was going to succeed in a new and restored way, with less corruption and violence, then there had to be the maximum amount of biodiversity to keep the integrity (or wholeness) of creation intact. We have learned today that biodiversity has served many needs: from food sources to balancing ecosystems, to assisting humans in their work and companionship, and to providing over 60 percent of all the medicines that we use today.

For Noah, the ark was the salvation of not only his personal family but also the family of creation. At the end of the flood, we find that God made it clear that God's covenant extended not just to Noah and his family but to all of the birds and animals that were with Noah on the ark as well. Thus, the idea of humans and nature sharing a covenant as one, the idea of birds and animals having intrinsic worth separate from humans, and the idea of our relations extending beyond just human beings set the foundation for restoring the Earth after the flood. If the world would adopt this type of respect for all life as being in covenant with God, of acknowledging the intrinsic value of preserving biodiversity in all of our decision making, we would again be going a long way to restoring the Earth.

Moving to the New Testament from the Christian tradition, we are given some valuable wisdom for restoring the Earth from a familiar passage in John: "For God so loved the world that he gave his only Son..." (John 3:16). The Greek word for world is actually *cosmos,* meaning "all of creation." So this familiar passage might be better translated: "For God so loved the cosmos and all of creation that he gave his only Son..."

Now this presents an interesting question and observation. If we as spiritual persons, no matter our faith tradition, claim that we love God, then should we not love the same things that God loves? If we believe that we should love the same things that God loves, and we know that God loves all of the cosmos and all of creation, then our spiritual practices cannot help but be directed in part to restoring the Earth, our part of the cosmos or creation that God loves so much.

Just as nations of the world and religions of the world have come to a consensus that things like sacrifice and slavery need to be abolished and that basic human rights need to be observed, so, too, do we need a new ethic that places love for the Earth as a priority in all nations and faith traditions of the world. As Jean Michael Cousteau has so often stated, "People protect that which they love."[4]

If the Earth is truly going to be restored, then it seems that we need to foster within our cultures and faith communities celebrations and adoration to show our love for the Earth. From this love an ethic of protection and restoration will flow.

From the Buddhist tradition the fourteenth Dalai Lama writes in his book, *Ethics for the New Millennium,* about the need to address environmental issues. The Dalai Lama makes the following key points:

- The best reason to care for the Earth may not be either that it is the ethical thing to do or the spiritual thing to do but that it is necessary for our very survival. He goes on to make the point that all young people are interested in their survival and thus this may be more engaging to them than either ethics or spirituality.
- Although a new spirituality by itself will not restore the Earth, without a new spirituality there is no chance to restore the Earth.
- The problems of the environment cross all national boundaries in a way that no nation can afford to ignore, thus bringing about an opportunity for international cooperation.[5]

The Dalai Lama advocates a strong focus on developing compassion for each other and the Earth as a key to restoring the Earth. The primary challenges that the Dalai Lama seems to be suggesting are whether the survival of our children will be important enough to counter the greed of their parents, whether nations of the world will come together to rise above national interests to solve global problems, and whether we can develop a new spirituality to help both of these things happen.

It is clear that ethics to restore the Earth are found in the major faith traditions of the world. In *Ethics for Agenda 21*, a companion document for the UN Agenda 21 adopted at the Earth Summit, Bahai, Buddhist, Christian, Islamic, Jewish, and indigenous writers all share their perspective on ethics to care for and restore the Earth.

- From the Bahai tradition, Peter Adriance reminds us of the need to "recognize the vital link between global transformation and spiritual principles."[6]
- From the Buddhist tradition, Samdhong Rinpoche reminds us that "the various lineages should strive hard for the unification of

humanity in a common bond of love and compassion and must not divide humanity in the name of religion."[7]

- From the Christian tradition, Sallie McFague reminds us that "The World Council of Churches says we must strive for peace, justice and integrity of creation." McFague goes on to say that "At this defining moment in history we have come to the realization that everything on our planet is interrelated and interdependent, and therefore, the well being of the parts depends on the well being of the whole and vice versa."[8]
- From the Islamic tradition, Mohammed T. Mehdi reminds us that under the Islamic tradition, a "human being is responsible not only for his fellow human beings, but also for all God's creation, animals, plants, and inanimate objects."[9]
- From the Jewish tradition, Bradley Shavit Artson reminds us that God's sense of wholeness and justice demands that

> ...specifically addressing the question of humanity's relationship to the ecosphere must, of necessity, speak also of the gap between the income of developing and developed nations, of the need to equalize the status of men and women, of the danger involved in the rapid rise in human population, the need to revise human consumption patterns, and the need to assert the unity of the human family.[10]

- Phil Lane, Jr., a Yankton Sioux chief says it this way: "Mother Earth is not sick. We are sick."[11] From the perspective of many indigenous people, it is the humans who need to change, not the Earth that needs to be restored. This means that humans need to be in right relationship with the Earth to see all things as being related. For many indigenous people this means that plants and animals are our brothers and sisters, the Earth our Mother, the Sun our Father or eldest brother.

In similar fashion Russel Train, former chair of the U.S. Council for Environmental Quality, pointed out that the Earth really does not need better stewardship. In fact, the Earth can and will manage itself quite well without human beings. Rather, it is humans who need to be managed better. This will only happen through a new reverence of life, a new paradigm of how humans see themselves in relationship to the Earth.

To be in relationship with the Earth, we need to also be in good relationship with ourselves. It is doubtful that we will be able to care for the land if we do not also learn to care for our bodies; that we will be able to have clean unpolluted rivers if we cannot stop polluting our bloodstreams; that we will be able to manage our energy resources if we do not learn to manage our internal energy; or that we will be able to clean up the air in our environment if we pollute our lungs or if we do not clean up our own spirit in our bodies. Living a wellness lifestyle can help us to build a consciousness that will, in turn, help us to live more in harmony with nature and thus better prepare us to restore the Earth.

Ethical Principles for Restoring the Earth

The United Nations recently released the book, *Earth and Faith: A Book of Reflection for Action*, which concludes with a statement of points of agreement in environmental ethics. Here is a summary of the eight points, along with some suggestions for implementation:

1. The natural world has value in itself and does not exist solely to serve human needs.
2. There is a significant continuity of being between human and nonhuman living beings, even though humans "do" have a distinctive role. This continuity can be felt and experienced.
3. Nonhuman living beings are morally significant in the eyes of God and/or in the cosmic order. They have their own unique relation to God and their own places in the cosmic order.
4. The dependence of human life on the natural world can and should be acknowledged in ritual and other expressions of appreciation and gratitude.
5. Moral norms such as justice, compassion, and reciprocity apply (in appropriate ways) both to human beings and to nonhuman beings. The well-being of humans and the well-being of nonhuman beings are inseparably connected.
6. There are legitimate and illegitimate uses of nature.
7. Greed and destructiveness are condemned. Restraint and protection are commended.
8. Human beings are obliged to be aware and responsible in living in harmony with the natural world and should follow the specific practices for this prescribed by their traditions.[12]

Actions to Support These Principles

- Seek out opportunities to celebrate Earth holidays such as Earth Day, the UN Environmental Sabbath, the equinox, the solstice, and so on.

- Support policy such as the Endangered Species Act; the UN Biodiversity Convention; and preservation of wildlands, wetlands, and forests around the globe.
- Take opportunities to experience nature through activities such as walks, outdoor activities, or just being outdoors.
- Practice your own "ecotherapy" by creating reminders in your home that nature is sacred and to be shown reverence, creating your own rituals that honor nature's inner healing qualities, and incorporating nature into relaxation and/or meditation activities.
- Make the sharing of sacred stories and wisdom related to nature a regular practice.
- Get involved with interfaith organizations such as the United Religions Initiative that are working on local, regional, and global levels to create cultures of peace, justice, and healing for the Earth.
- Provide environmental education within the context of your faith traditions and/or ecumenical or interfaith programs.
- Work to have your faith community be a model for conservation of energy, water, and land. As a group, practice sustainable living.
- Find ways to live in harmony with nature and to honor and respect other living beings.
- Practice a wellness lifestyle that allows for living lightly on the planet while improving health practices.

Moving Forward in Restoring the Earth

We are at a critical time in history where we must decide on actions that may determine the very survival of the human race as we know it today. To begin to restore the Earth, we must also begin to restore the wholeness of the human soul through a radical change of the heart and mind.

The choices we must make are numerous and include major decisions, for example,

- move away from fossil fuels to more conservation and renewable energy sources;
- improve efficiency of our use of energy, water, and other resources, including reducing our consumption, reusing products and materials, and recycling;
- stabilize and/or reduce the population, which by definition will require improved social and economic conditions and promotion of effective voluntary family planning;
- renew efforts to reduce poverty and improve health care for all of God's children; and

- provide for equality of all people regardless of race, sex, creed, or ethnic origin and to guarantee basic human rights for all.

Most importantly, we need to begin to live the spiritual wisdom of the faith traditions of the world so that we begin to live and work as one human family. There are groups such as the newly formed United Religions Initiative and other interfaith organizations that bring promise to work on the global agenda on local, regional, and international levels. It is up to each of our faith communities to become engaged with others to promote daily interfaith cooperation and build cultures of peace, justice, and the healing of the Earth if the Earth is going to be restored.

SECTION III
The Prophetic Call to Restore and Celebrate Justice

8

Issues of Injustice in the Church and Society

Cynthia Bowman

Throughout the country, our cities, and specifically the black community, the huge disparities that exist between the quality of life for blacks (and other people of color) and their white counterparts is inescapable. If you drive through middle class, (often white) neighborhoods, one sees a father, a mother, 2.5 children, a dog, and a picket fence—everything that epitomizes the American dream. While in poor neighborhoods (often black and/or Latino), you see women with children, or children by themselves—indicative of single parent families. You see neighborhoods that show signs of disinvestment and declining city services, run-down housing, no grass or trees, few banks or substantial businesses, and inadequate schools. You also see many, many churches, particularly black churches, churches that were ordained to be the leaves of hope.

In 2001, the Bush administration announced its new faith-based initiative, and churches throughout the country initiated, reassessed, or developed community development programs. Many of us in the church community believe the business of the church to be a ministry to the whole person and the whole community. We believe that the "spirit directed" faith-based community is the logical group to take a leadership role in fighting against injustice because we are those who profess a belief in "the assurance of things hoped for, the conviction of things not seen" (Hebrews 11:1).

Although this new interest in faith-based community development has caused an enormous amount of excitement, it has also raised many concerns and leaves room for cautious optimism. Is the church prepared to clean its own house? Is it prepared to fight against and correct the injustice that exists within its own walls as well as within the walls of the community? Is it prepared to break down the walls and hierarchical structures that exist so that all members of the body are affirmed, appreciated, and empowered? Is that not the true meaning of the gospel and what Jesus has called us to do?

The fight against injustice is both challenging and demanding. To be effective in battle, the church must be very clear about who it is and whose it is. The nature of the beast forces us to continually reevaluate and remake ourselves according to the beliefs that we espouse everyday, thereby enabling us to be true to ourselves and to the God whom we serve. A "teachable spirit" is a mandatory quality for those who heed the call of Jesus, for this teachable spirit allows us the freedom to grow and change, to conquer our personal shortcomings, and to become all that God intended us to be.

The church, as an institution, is not absolved from this continuous self-examination, for injustice in America has been hidden beneath the robes of judges as well as those of clergy. Consequently, the time has come for it to examine the role of its systems (institutions, traditions, and practices) in creating its own unique forms of injustice and sustaining the pervasive injustices that exist in society. The church must wrestle with and answer some tough questions. Is the church the servant or the master of the state? How can the church be the prophetic voice against injustice in the world when, inside its own doors, rigid adherence to traditional barriers prevent some of the body from experiencing true equality and justice?

The face of injustice takes various shapes, forms, and names throughout the world. In the United States, however, it is both impossible and meaningless to engage in honest discussion about injustice in church and society without addressing the subjects of racism, classism, and sexism. These three form the foundation on which all other injustice is built. While all injustice is deplorable and contrary to the teachings and ministry of Jesus Christ, there are particular types of injustice that are more prevalent, more elusive, more systemic, more deceptive, and therefore more destructive than others. Racism is a kind of injustice because it possesses a three-tiered power over all of God's people. At the first level, it unfairly oppresses blacks. Secondly, it provides undeserved power and privilege to whites. Lastly, it claims the power to name us all, thereby preventing us from being who we really are.

There have been many recent and passionate arguments and extensive academic discourse debating the relative significance of race vs. class in analyzing social injustices. Although many of the arguments focusing on class have been convincing, it is my belief that race still does matter. Until the issues of power, justice, and equality that divide blacks and whites are resolved, race will always matter. What else but racism can adequately explain the preponderance of statistical data that continues to provide quantitative evidence of the social ills that disproportionately plague the lives of African Americans everyday? Poverty, unemployment, poor housing and education, excessively high rates of incarceration, and nonaccess to capital and credit are all social conditions that have not decreased significantly for blacks and other people of color. Because of this belief, and the limitations of this chapter, the predominant focus here is on issues of racism, or more exactly, anti-black racism.

Since the events of September 11, or "9/11," some Americans have become more aware of and sensitive to injustice than ever before. Hardly a day has passed without some aspect of those tragic events being discussed, analyzed, or theorized about. The numbers 9/11 and the events of that single day will be forever engraved on their memories and the memories of their children and grandchildren. As tragic and memorable as those events were and still are, for others of us, they were not events that sensitized us to the nature of injustice. For some of us, our understanding of injustice began with events that took place hundreds of years earlier. The year 1619 was when the first enslaved Africans were brought in chains to the shores of this country to be traded so that others could prosper. The year 1619 began a chain of events specifically designed to permanently relegate people with black skin to the "bottom of the well" while simultaneously elevating the privilege of white skin. The year 1619 was the beginning of anti-black racism that began to weave itself into the moral fiber of our country's institutions.

The events that began in the year 1619 gave birth to racism and white supremacy. For almost 400 years racism and white supremacy have coexisted in this country and have prevented the United States from reaching its full potential. In 1903 W. E. B. DuBois predicted that the problem of the twentieth century would be the color line. In 2003 we have not overcome the divisions of the color line, but we are in the midst of a struggle in which the inquiries of the past continue to reproduce themselves. Racism continues to diminish the possibility of the realization of a "land of the free and home of the brave." Anti-black racism may have begun in 1619, but it continues today, although in different and sometimes barely recognizable forms. Yet, as pervasive and destructive as anti-black racism is in this country, it is still not an acceptable topic of discussion anywhere, certainly not across racial lines. Discussions about race still provoke intense feelings of anger, fear, and guilt and result in various levels of confusion for both blacks and whites.

Racism is a white problem, although it threatens the quality of black life. That is to say, although blacks are the victims of racism and white supremacist doctrines, only whites can be racist because they are the sole beneficiaries of systemic, institutional, anti-black racism. The collective church should be the conscience of the state and not only fight against racism but also fight to dismantle the systems and institutions that support racism. Because racism does not threaten the lives of white Americans, it has not been a primary issue for that segment of society. Initiatives and programs that have been geared to fight racism have essentially been measures to manage racism.

The concept of racism and the supporting doctrine of white supremacy have perplexed African Americans for centuries. James Baldwin gives an imaginary account of the first encounter between a white man and a black man that illuminates the absurdity of these phenomena.

> ...there was a day, and not really a very distant day, when Americans were scarcely Americans at all but disconnected Europeans, facing a great unconquered continent and strolling, say into a marketplace and seeing black men for the first time. The shock this spectacle afforded is suggested, surely, by the promptness with which they decided that these black men were not really men but cattle.[1]

Racism, for purposes of this discussion, is defined as racial prejudice supported by the power of systems and institutions. Racism is not merely personal prejudice or bigotry but a systemic power that, left unchecked, takes on an energy of its own. Consequently, the resulting injustice is pervasive, systemic, and ingrained into the very fabric of our institutions. Since 1619, instances of racial injustice pervade the everyday lives of black people regardless of actual or perceived economic status or class. Although significant gains were made during the civil rights era, fundamentally, little has really changed for African Americans. Today, we can learn to read, but the schools we attend have fewer resources, and higher education is becoming increasingly less accessible. We can usually vote[2] and eat at any lunch counter. We can sleep at night with relative certainty that we will not be dragged from our beds and lynched for delivering some perceived insult to a white person. But the memories of Amadou Diallo and Rodney King are still fresh in our minds, and so we must be concerned about "driving while black" or carrying anything that could be mistaken for a weapon. We no longer have to fear our loved ones being sold away from us, but the injustices of the penal system have already done significant destruction to black family structure.

While the face of racism manifests itself in countless ways and with varying degrees of subtlety, the primary systems that support racism and racial injustice are two: the legal system and the economic system. These systems are simultaneously the most destructive to black life and most supportive of white privilege.

Economic Injustice

The year 1865 marked the legal emancipation of enslaved blacks in America. Some four million men, women, and children who had endured the hardships of this dehumanizing institution for years were set free. Blacks were emancipated by their captors after almost 300 years of bondage in which they had been forcefully and systematically stripped of their names, culture, and dignity—their very identities. But freed to do what and with what? African Americans soon learned that freedom without capital and power was freedom in theory only.

In 1865 African Americans owned and controlled one half of 1 percent of all the wealth in the United States, and 50 percent of all blacks were paupers.[3] In 1965, 55 percent of all blacks still lived in poverty.[4] By 1990 the percentage of blacks living in poverty had decreased to 40 percent.[5] In 1999 African Americans owned and controlled .092 percent of all the wealth in the United States, and today 22.1 percent of African Americans live below the poverty line, compared to 7.5 percent of European Americans.[6] In 135 years we have made absolutely no progress in terms of wealth accumulation. Additionally, there are still huge disparities in the quality of life between blacks and whites which can only be explained by race. These disparities are evident in the following facts:

- African American homeownership is disproportionate to that of whites.
- African American business ownership is disproportionate to that of whites.
- The number of African Americans holding advanced degrees is disproportionate to that of whites.
- African American participation in the stock market is disproportionate to that of whites.

The social injustice that fuels these disparities is the unequal access to capital and credit that exists in the United States. This problem is a major concern because access to capital, in large part, determines one's ability to own a home, pay for advanced education, start a business, and invest in the financial markets that fuel our economy and create wealth. The inequitable access to capital that currently exists in this country is the primary contributor to the wealth disparity that exists between African Americans and whites. In this capitalistic society, one's inability to access capital and credit influences one's quality of life by limiting one's choices and opportunities. For most African Americans, the avenues of economic opportunity have been severely limited or destroyed.

A recent report issued by the Fannie Mae Foundation found that African Americans consistently pay higher interest rates on home mortgages when they are able to obtain them at all.[7] These higher interest rates result in diminished capacity to create wealth because the additional dollars used to pay interest are not available to invest in the stock market or other appreciating assets. The Fannie Mae report further stated that unequal access to capital has forced African Americans to disproportionately utilize fringe-lending institutions. These institutions include pawnshops, check-cashing outlets, payday lenders, and rent-to-own stores. Annually, approximately $5.45 billion are sucked from poor and disproportionately African American communities.[8] These dollars are in the form of revenues paid to these fringe lending institutions. The loss of these revenues serves to further strip the African American community of wealth-building capabilities.

Because this problem is so massive and impacts many levels of our existence, it must be attacked on many different levels. There has been some light shed on many of the problems resulting from unequal access to capital, and some changes have been made and are continuing to be made. Redlining and other discriminatory lending practices are illegal, at least on paper, but they must be abolished entirely. Legislation aimed at preventing predatory lending and fringe lending institutions is underway and must be pursued and supported. Affirmative action policies were instrumental in providing scholarships to African Americans for college education, but recently many of these policies have been dissolved all together or diluted by the inclusion of other minorities into the pot. African Americans are seeking increased financial literacy enabling them to more fully participate in the financial engines that drive this country.

How much has really changed for African Americans since 1865, the official end of slavery? Obviously, African Americans are no longer physically enslaved, but without the "forty acres and a mule" they worked, bled, and died for, they continue to be enslaved by the economic injustices that exist in this country.

Injustice in the Legal System

African Americans in this country consistently feel a sense of denied justice. A kind of tongue-in-cheek statement that is prevalent in the black community is that there is justice in the court for "just us," alluding to the fact that we are disproportionately arrested, tried, and sentenced as the result of legal infractions. In this country, there is a consistent inconsistency in the manner in which laws are enforced. Although laws are allegedly color-blind, those who enforce them are not. The question then becomes: "Can the law exist apart from the color-conscious society in which it operates or is it a reflection of the complex relationships that exist between and among its citizens?"

The disbelief and shocking sense of personal violation that white America expressed on hearing the O. J. Simpson verdict is the same sense of injustice that we feel and cope with every day. White America could not understand how blacks could possibly express joy and elation about the verdict. We were not celebrating the freedom of a guilty man, as O. J. was found to be not guilty. We were celebrating the fact that for once the legal system had worked for us. O. J. and his attorneys had used the rules of the American legal system and won.

During the first 200 years of African presence in America, those in power used the legal system to establish a complete, total, and permanent enslavement of blacks. In 1857, the Dred Scott decision provided the legal basis for intentional racial discrimination when it ruled that blacks were "so far inferior, that they had no rights that a White man was bound to respect."[9]

The motivation for this decision was economics. From 1619 until 1865, African Americans were physically traded so that others could prosper. While slavery required the psychological destruction of African Americans, their physical destruction would have been counterproductive to the purpose of exploiting their labor. Today, their physical destruction is counterproductive to the creation of wealth and maintenance of the economic status quo via, among other things, the prison system. The prison system is one of the fastest growing industries in America, and America's jails are rapidly becoming the plantations of the new millennium. Consider the following statistics:

- In 1984 nearly one of every two persons arrested for murder and/or manslaughter was African American.[10]
- *Ebony* magazine reported that in 1945 there were 13,207 blacks in federal and state penitentiaries, and that by 2000 that number had grown to 597,000.[11]

- Black men serve longer jail sentences for abusing crack cocaine than their white counterparts serve for abusing powdered cocaine.[12]

From the beginnings of slavery, through the Jim Crow period past the civil rights period to today, the law has contributed to perpetuating injustice toward blacks solely on the basis of color.

Conclusion

As the political and economic climates continue to change and the voices of the oppressed become louder and clearer, the response of the church will become more critical. We must press through the hypocrisy of the church to the liberating theology of Jesus Christ and reclaim our moral authority to effect authentic social change. We must understand that the gospel of Jesus Christ frees the oppressed as well as the oppressors.

Forrest Harris expressed it this way: "When theologically understood as God's call to Christian freedom and prophetically proclaimed as God's mandate for humanization, the gospel has salvific power for liberating not only the black community but this nation from oppressive practices and injustices that tend to destroy life."[13]

The church, particularly the black church, is a vital instrument for change in the black community, but we must be prepared. We must develop new attitudes, models, and strategies that affirm our belief in an omnipotent God, strategies steeped in our unrelenting passion for justice rather than in charity, patriarchy, or egocentricism.

The ministry of Jesus Christ requires that we, who are Jesus' disciples, be involved in the lives of the least, the lost, and the left out. We must know and respect but not be limited by the economic and political realities of the church, the community, and the world. As Jesus' disciples we are called to counteract the oppression and injustice inherent in the power systems. We must constantly ask, "Who am I called to be in this place and at this time?"

Andrew Billingsley stated: "The challenge is to make society more responsive to and supportive of all its members—ending racism in America will require vigorous, organized and persistent advocacy on the part of the collective community."[14] The black church must exercise its prophetic voice by teaching and preaching about and against all forms of racial and social injustices. The white church must accept responsibility for its participation in strengthening the powers that be. All churches that believe in the ministry of Jesus Christ and desire to contribute to the development of God's kingdom here on Earth must take seriously the challenge of the great commission: the dismantling of structures, powers, and principalities that create victims of us all, perpetuate crisis situations, and prevent us from being truly free and living in "the more."

9

Building a Justice-affirming Church

Jim Wallis

It was a Sunday evening some years ago, and the Sojourners Community had gathered together for our weekly worship. Our preacher was a young African American man who was codirector of the Sojourners Neighborhood Center. His text was from the Beatitudes: "Blessed are those who hunger and thirst for righteousness, for they will be filled" (Matthew 5:6). We had been doing a series on the foundational sayings of Jesus, examining one each week and asking someone who had a particular interest or experience with that saying to help us all understand what it might mean for us today.

In the Bible, righteousness is often synonymous with justice, and the two words are sometimes used interchangeably. Over the years, we had heard many sermons on justice and righteousness, but, nevertheless, I could feel the hunger growing within me as this young man began. As I listened to him preach, I realized that he was making his listeners hungrier and thirstier as he spoke. Why? Because he was so passionate, so hungry and thirsty himself.

The prophetic tradition insists that religion that does not manifest itself in action for justice is false religion. The Hebrew prophets boldly proclaimed that God rejected worship and prayers that ignored social justice. Jesus asked, "Why do you call me 'Lord, Lord,' and not do what I tell you" (Luke 6:46)? And the New Testament epistle of James insists that "faith without works is also dead" (James 2:26). What we see every day in our neighborhoods and cities makes us hunger and thirst for justice and righteousness. It is a holy demand for action, and that action is rooted in the hunger for justice.

When we are hungry, we become increasingly concentrated on relieving our hunger. When we are thirsty, we become more and more diligent to quench our thirst. When we are hungry and thirsty, the desire to satisfy our need seems to grow and grow. We are not easily distracted or drawn away by other things. We become single-minded, focused, and persistent. Are we hungry and thirsty enough to act for righteousness and justice? Or are we continually pulled away by other cares and concerns?

The movement from social concern to a hunger for justice has both spiritual and political significance. Our concern for the poor does little to bridge the enormous distance between us. Indeed, it creates the patronizing dynamics of some people "doing for" others, a pattern that can become destructive to everyone. But to become genuinely hungry for justice makes it more possible to join with the poor and oppressed in a common struggle. It is our own hunger, not somebody else's problem, that begins to drive us to action. Together we long for the day when we will all find satisfaction. When hungry people learn to share the bread of hope together, a new kind of community becomes possible, and the first fruits of justice can be enjoyed.

The day when a substantial number of middle-class Americans have moved from social concern to a hunger for what is right will be the day when justice becomes more possible in this country. As long as the poor are marginalized in their isolation and the concerned people are paralyzed in their guilt, no real action is possible. It is the hunger and thirst for justice, of which the fourth beatitude speaks that can bring us together and transform the political landscape. In the process, we might all find the healing and wholeness that have eluded us, the equality and mutuality that real human cooperation requires, and the dependence on God that could set our hearts free. Perhaps that is what Jesus was talking about. Justice is a sign of transformation.

Spiritual renewal will supply the energy for justice. Faith and spirituality could become the most powerful forces for social justice in the beginning of a new millennium. That would seem, to many, a bold and even unbelievable statement, given the common perceptions of religion today and the inward preoccupation of so much contemporary spirituality. During much of the twentieth century, religion was regarded as a mostly private affair and, at its worst, was a reactionary influence. With the great exception of the black churches, religion in twentieth-century America has not been a great force for justice. Likewise, so much of the resurgence of spirituality we have seen over the last several years has been successfully commercialized into mere self-help. Nonetheless, many factors now point to the probability that spirituality and faith will return to the dynamic social role they have often played before. The spiritual power of faith to change history is being rediscovered.

I believe in the linkage of faith and justice. As a new millennium has dawned, many religious people, having seen and felt the limits of purely private religion, are being drawn into the struggle for social change. At the same time, many people outside religion are hungry for the power and promise of spirituality.

The prophetic vocation is to challenge the old while announcing the new. Like the prophets, we must call certainty into question. The biblical prophets always had a twofold task. First, they were bold in telling the truth and proclaiming the justice that is rooted in God. They named the idols that led the people astray and unmasked their destructive reality. And they called the people to return to their true selves and purpose, to reject their false gods, and to remember who they were as the children of God.

In addition to truth telling, the prophets had a second task. They held up an alternative vision: They helped the people to imagine new possibilities.

Today, we need those who are willing to live as if an alternative vision is possible. Even when the possibility of real change seems quite dim—and especially then—history needs people who believe that change is possible and are willing to bet their lives on it. That often takes a good dose of faith.

Several thousand years ago, the writer of the Proverbs warned, "Where there is no vision, the people perish" (Proverbs 11:14, KJV). That ancient warning also applies to our contemporary situation. We need a new vision today. We need vision to provide us with a feeling of purpose, an assurance of meaning, and a sense of direction. Vision connects us to the past and points us toward the future, which is what gives the present its truest significance.

Vision is derived from understanding the connections between all the issues we face and the spiritual foundations that undergird them. Without this understanding, a vision that might empower restoration of the covenant we have lost with our neighbors on this planet and with creation itself would not be possible. With this understanding, which includes reaffirming our spiritual identity as the children of God, envisioning a new covenant not only becomes possible but also becomes a necessity.

In the age we now live in, characterized by hopelessness, an alternative vision leading to a new covenant by people of faith is needed. The new covenant must entail a message of hope for a better future. Our challenge is to live as if this new vision of hope is possible.

The world will not change until we do; personal and social transformations are inextricably linked together. That is the wisdom of the spiritual and social movements whose legacies endure. New politics and new spirituality can only emerge together. We must make that vital connection clear in a new movement for justice.

Why Faith Communities Can Lead

Social movements need a combination of spirituality and practical goals. The civil rights movement evidenced a powerful spirituality. It held out the promise of freedom for African Americans, a tremendous motivating force. It also promised whites the possibility of healing an uneasy conscience and fulfilling the ideals of the American dream. Dr. King used to say that he held the Bible in one hand and the U.S. Constitution in the other. The most successful movements must offer people the chance to better their lives *and* fulfill their deepest moral convictions and aspirations.

As well as responding to society's spiritual hunger, churches and faith-based groups have an advantage over many other institutions when it comes to the kind of community organizing and development most needed in a movement for justice today. It finally comes down to the question of social leadership: Who is best situated to offer critical components like vision, direction, credibility, longevity, trust, and, of course, organizable constituencies? Faith communities may be in the best position to lead in efforts for social renewal because of their inherent characteristics and commitments, enabling them to be community conveners in broad-based efforts involving many different kinds of organizations. There are three sets of essential ingredients that are at the heart of why it is so critical to tap the power of faith communities.

Message and Motivation

In a society where market values increasingly predominate, faith communities can offer a sense of meaning, purpose, and moral value that is increasingly missing in society. When people feel reduced to mere consumers and life is reduced to shopping, faith communities can speak directly to the deep spiritual hunger that so many people experience. In the community of faith, persons are more than marketing data for advertisers or polling data for politicians; they are the children of God with immense and sacred value, created in the very image of God.

Faith communities are also best situated to speak to the moral and spiritual impoverishment of the society, which others seem to accept as inevitable. They can help to reestablish a sense of ethics and values. The faith community makes it possible to do more than "look out for number one." Faith communities offer people practical opportunities to love their neighbors, serve their communities, contribute to a larger purpose, and sacrifice for something worth believing in. In the community of faith, the values of compassion, community, and solidarity have a theological foundation, not merely a sentimental one. Hope is more than an optimistic feeling; it is a firm conclusion drawn from trusting the promises of God.

The values you need for organizing are rooted in the very essence of the faith community. Rev. Eugene Rivers, pastor of the Azuza Christian Community in Boston, says that

> only the church has the moral authority and the vocabulary to introduce transcendent concepts of personal worth and the sacredness of life that will both inspire responsibility on a personal level and introduce purpose and definition to the role of civil government on a societal level.[1]

Thus, faith can be used to undergird, legitimize, and inspire social action.

Counterculture and Prophetic Voice

Faith communities are intended to be distinct communities, with ethics distinct from those of the surrounding society. The apostle Paul writing to the Romans says, "Do not be conformed to this world, but be transformed by the renewing of your minds..." (Romans 12:2). Alternative visions arise from alternative communities. Such communities can become support bases for nurturing and training, networking and mobilizing. The symbols and rituals of the faith community can become powerful educators and mobilizers for committed and even risky action. For example, black churches in the South constituted a coherent subculture in the midst of a white-dominated society. As such, they reminded their members who they really were and what they could really do. Churches became the practical place to organize car pools to sustain a bus boycott and the spiritual place to prepare oneself for nonviolent confrontations with police clubs and dogs.

A countercultural community can have a prophetic public voice. Here is where the authority and trust religious communities often enjoy in our society can be utilized for the common good. Who will tell the truth, or even try to find it, when falsehoods prevail? Who will stand up for those who are being left out and behind or whose human rights are being violated? Who will question the easy and hedonistic assumptions of the popular culture? Who will challenge the authority of the government when it becomes violent and abusive? Why did the government of El Salvador assassinate Archbishop Oscar Romero? They were afraid of his authority in challenging their political repression. And as a slain martyr, Romero gained even more authority. The faith community has the moral authority to make justice a priority.

Institution and Constituency

The most common institutions in local communities are the churches and the schools—and the churches are in much better shape than the schools. Churches have budgets, buildings, several kinds of meeting spaces, kitchens, nurseries, bathrooms, and parking lots, all of which are fundamental assets for organizing. They also have staffs, a cadre of professionally trained leaders, ties to larger denominational structures with greater resources, and a widely trusted historical tradition to build upon. Churches are the institution most commonly found in every kind of neighborhood—across all geographic, racial, cultural, and class boundaries. In some poor communities, churches are virtually the last standing institution. In those situations, it is often only the churches that have the moral authority and institutional presence to lead efforts for civic reconstruction. With proximity to the problems, churches can work from the bottom up, redeeming kids one by one, claiming whole blocks and neighborhoods for transformation—calling for moral, civic, and political renewal in the broader community, city, and nation.

And, of course, the churches have a constituency. They actually have members—another prerequisite for organizing—who can be mobilized and brought together. The very nature of a universal membership in the faith community can be instrumental in helping to overcome the divisions between people that are the greatest obstacle to organizing. And members of faith communities can be motivated to act not simply in their own self-interest but rather on the basis of the deeply held spiritual and moral values that undergird their faith. That faith can provide the staying power so critically needed for long-term campaigns. Religious institutions also have enduring power, as opposed to some other community institutions that are often here today and gone tomorrow. Most churches plan to be a part of their communities for a very long time, and therefore have a vested interest in their well-being.

Finally, because churches are built on relationships, they can provide a strong base for the kind of relational organizing style that is proving to be so effective around the country. Community organizer and sociologist

Marshall Ganz speaks of this as a "covenantal" organizing style. He contrasts it with "issue-based organizing," which is more "contractual": "It has a limited, short-term, outcome-based focus; it often brings people into coalitions that dissolve immediately after the objective is attained, or isn't." Ganz prefers "interest-based organizing," which is "covenantal." It has a longer-term focus of "identifying and developing those common interests that are affected by a variety of issues that come and go," Ganz says. "Interest-based organizing places a greater emphasis on building relationships as a way both to discern interests as well as to construct new interests which only emerge in the context of new relationship."[2]

Building a Movement for Justice: The Role of the Church

Enacting hope requires building a movement. Historically, social movements for justice seem to have several characteristics in common.

First, social movements are not just about self-interest but are about right and wrong. They raise moral issues, not just political ones. Movements involve people by appealing to their best selves, their best visions, and their best hopes for their children. They ask what is the right thing to do, the moral thing to do, the Christian thing to do, and so on. For example, the growing social inequality in America and the world does not just pose economic challenges but also raises fundamental issues of justice, a religious concern. A social movement to address those issues should make the moral questions clear. Recovering the transcendent character of moral values in a rights-based culture is key to the success of any social movement. Do not be afraid to raise the moral issues at the root of the questions you want to address and the things you want to change. It is the best way to mobilize people around a social movement.

Second, minorities, not majorities, always begin movements. Historically, it has usually been committed minorities, acting on moral concerns, who bring issues to public consciousness. Minorities catalyze the situation, establish new agendas, and finally succeed when majorities choose not to oppose them. If they win the majority's agreement, it is usually owing to the moral force as well as the political logic of their argument. Majorities seldom become involved, but they eventually agree to the proposed changes or at least decide not to resist them. It is minorities who change the terms of public debate; majorities just watch the discussion. The late anthropologist Margaret Mead said it well: "Don't think that small groups of people can't change the world; they're the only ones who ever have."[3] That means you do not have to convince the majority in your church, neighborhood, or nation before you begin to act. All you need is a committed and motivated minority in order to begin.

Third, action changes the terms of the public debate. Discussion is usually not enough. It takes action to get people's attention. From the biblical prophets to the great social movements we have discussed to the many examples I have cited of what people are doing today in their local communities, it is taking action that creates a new dialogue. After a public action has been taken, and people have seen it, the discussion about the issues at stake becomes a public one. Until that point, there might have been many private conversations, but nothing had brought the issue out into the open. Action has the power to do that. It often takes action on the part of some individual or group (much better if it is a group) to make a community or a society deal with something they have not dealt with before. So do not just sit around talking forever about your concerns. Find a way to take action—the more creative and courageous the better.

Fourth, movements make the connection between the personal and the social. In building social movements, it is not that self-interest is unimportant but rather that it gets redefined. Perhaps the most important question a movement can ask is who the "we" is. I preach a sermon entitled "How Big Is Your 'We'?" I ask the audience to consider how wide their circle is: Who is part of the family, who is in and who is out, and who is it that we are fighting for? These are critical questions. The best movements are those that enable people to connect their own self-interest to the interests of others. We are most satisfied when we feel part of something larger than ourselves. In a movement, self-interest becomes engaged in a larger common interest, and personal agendas become shaped by the common good. In your own situation, ask how you can connect people's personal interests to the problems at stake in the community. Find ways for the interests of the community to intersect with the personal and family concerns in people's hearts. You will give people a larger purpose and find it creates both satisfaction and fulfillment.

Fifth, movements develop inclusive agendas. For example, social inequality and the pressures of a global economy do not impact poor people only. There is enormous pain in our middle-class neighborhoods and churches where people are trying to hold their jobs and families together, not to mention finding time for significant involvement in wider community activities. We know that many single parents are not making it, but many two-parent families are also struggling just to keep up. Economics, family, and community are not coming together for millions of people in America today. A good society would want to support all three and keep them in balance. But we have lost our balance. Many people are hurting, and they are not all poor.

Taking seriously the depth of that social and economic pain is crucial to building a movement for economic justice. Calls to "help the poor" may sound like just another demand for time and money from people who feel they have less and less of both. People who feel squeezed normally do not feel generous. But if the call can be framed in the context of the common good, asking what we all need and putting forward a vision of economics, family, and community that might work better for everyone, including the poor, it will come across much more effectively. Ask yourself what some of the issues are that will bring in many people. How can we connect the needs of the poor with the needs and well-being of the wider community?

Sixth, movements are visionary. The role of a movement, especially one that is spiritually or religiously based, should be to offer a vision for what society should be or do. What kind of country do we want to be, and what should America mean to the rest of the world? Those are the kinds of questions a movement asks. Such questions also help people understand themselves as a democratic people, not just cogs in a world of economic determinism. We are asked to set aside the relentless demands of technology and the global economy for a moment in order to consider the larger questions of what we want as a nation as well as what quality and style of life we are trying to achieve.

Those seeking a new vision talk about "covenants," make "compacts," pledge "commitments." Movements speak a moral language that calls us back to the things we value most, helping us remember that there are things we regard as more important than the pressures of our daily lives. Social change movements do not seek volunteers just to make the present more tolerable; they recruit members who together take a stance for a better future.

Movements talk beyond the present and imagine a new future. The only way you can do that is to assert moral agency and responsibility in the midst of assumptions and structures that militate against both. Moral claims are made on social conditions, which becomes a matter of faith. While both secular therapists and religious pietists encourage their clients and converts to seek private solutions to social problems, movements invite people to find public solutions as well. So do not just spend your time volunteering and filling up your life with social service; instead, join with others around a real vision for changing something important.

Seventh, movements are prophetic. Religious communities and people of faith have played a key role in starting and sustaining social movements, as has been noted throughout this book. Abolition of slavery, civil rights, women's suffrage, child protection, labor laws, peace, and human rights were all movements that relied heavily on the participation of communities motivated by spiritual values. There are good reasons for that. Religious communities have the capacity to create movements precisely because of their belief systems. None of the above causes were ready to become part of the governing politics of their times when they first became social movements. In other words, movement politics never start with electoral politics. Rather, they begin to raise a public voice that, over time, politicians will be unable to ignore. Many social movements begin by asserting a moral claim or vision as an article of faith. Economic justice, for example, is a tenet of biblical faith, just as are many other religious doctrines. It remains a tenet of faith whether or not the economic boom pays any attention to it, or whether or not it is possible today to immediately create an economy that is more just and fair. If the Bible says that economic injustice should be corrected, and massive inequalities require periodic redistribution of wealth, that is enough to undergird and motivate a spiritual movement.

The civil rights movement did not begin in Selma, Alabama. Black churches were protesting lynchings at the turn of the century, developing leadership, protecting the community in numerous ways, supporting the legal battles of the NAACP, and much more. It was not a surprise when many black churches became the institutional support bases for the civil rights movement. It is the job of faith communities to put issues on the public agenda long before they can be achieved. But putting them on the agenda is the beginning of the long process that leads to eventual victory.

Our intuition tells us that the depth of the crisis we face demands more than politics as usual. An illness of the spirit has spread across the land, and our greatest need is for what our religious traditions call "the healing of the nations." The fundamental character of the social, economic, and cultural renewal we urgently need will require a change of both our hearts and our minds. But that change will demand a new kind of politics—a politics with spiritual values.

A vision of politics must be articulated that clarifies the essential moral issues at stake in any political discussion. Spiritual values must enter the public square. We are not calling here for the invasion of sectarian religion or theocratic grabs for power but rather for the contribution of neglected values to the political process. Most of us believe that institutional religion and the state must remain separate. But without values of moral conscience, our political life quickly degenerates into public corruption, cultural confusion, and social injustice.

We stand at a political crossroads, and critical choices must be made. Those choices are at heart religious, insofar as they will reveal our most fundamental values and moral sensibilities. The road we take will determine the kind of people we will become and the nature of the societies in which we will live. In short, the decisions we make will decisively shape the quality of life for ourselves, our children, and our grandchildren.

The Hebrew Scriptures say it well: "I have set before you life and death, blessings and curses. Choose life so that you and your descendants may live" (Deuteronomy 30:19).

10

From Empire to Common Security: A Prophetic Vision of Worldwide Justice

Joseph Gerson

> There is talk of a new American empire, of a world that presents the global superpower with a unique opportunity to exploit a victory in Afghanistan...to force decisions in every capital...and to rethink the principles around which nations cooperate.[1]

> The stability of the large world house which is ours will involve a revolution of values to accompany the scientific and freedom revolutions engulfing the Earth. We must rapidly begin the shift from a "thing"-oriented society to a "person"-oriented society.[2]

When we recall the horrifying images of passenger planes exploding into the World Trade Center and the Pentagon and the national shock that followed on September 11, 2001, the first word that comes to most minds is not *empire*. Yet, the attacks in the "Empire State" and against the Pentagon were targeted against the most impressive and popular symbols of U.S. power and preeminence. For Osama bin Laden and many in Arab and Islamic communities across the world, President George W. Bush is a modern day Pharaoh whose people and forces deserve "equal treatment" for the suffering we have inflicted from Palestine to Vietnam and Arabia to Afghanistan.[3]

The September 11 attacks plunged the United States into a dangerous identity crisis. For the first time in almost two centuries, the enormity of the oceans failed to protect us. As U.S. Americans began to experience the tiniest, but infinitely painful, portion of what our nation has visited upon others from Hiroshima, Vietnam, and Iraq, we were traumatized and became vulnerable to exploitation of the crisis by politicians, political forces, and vested interests with their own agendas.

September 11 was certainly a "day of infamy." With the surprise attacks and the fact that they came at the peak of nostalgia for the generation that had defeated Japan and Germany, it was natural that many associated September 11, 2001, with December 7, 1945. Propaganda systems designed to "manufacture consent" and mobilization were soon working on a scale not seen since the Second World War.[4] Lost to George Orwell's memory hole was September 11, 1973, the searing date in Latin American history when General Pinochet, with the support and encouragement of President Nixon, Secretary of State Kissinger, and the CIA, overthrew the democratically elected government of Salvador Allende in Chile, ushering in an era of deadly dictatorships, disappearances, and impunity across Latin America. Also lost in the tidal wave of "United We Stand" patriotism[5] was memory of U.S. support for the Taliban during its rise to power and its first years of abusive rule; decades of U.S. support for repressive Arab monarchs and dictators to guarantee privileged access to Middle East oil; U.S. support for the Israeli military occupation and colonization of territories conquered in 1967; and the Clinton-Bush U.S. "Full Spectrum Dominance" military doctrine.

The September 11 attacks were not primarily responsible for the majority of the subsequent changes in U.S. military, foreign, and domestic policy wrought in the name of the "war against terrorism." Before assuming power, the leading figures of the second Bush administration had clearly identified themselves with the imperial ambitions and revolutions in U.S. military thinking of the late nineteenth century—U.S. imperialists including Alfred T. Mahan, Henry Cabot Lodge, and Teddy Roosevelt. Only months after assuming office Vice President Dick Cheney affirmed that "the arrangement [for] the twenty-first century is most assuredly being shaped right now," to ensure that "the United States will continue to be the dominant political, economic and military power in the world."[6] Cheney and others in the Bush administration were not shy about their commitments to accelerate development and deployment of new generations of high-tech weapons, the abrogation of the Antiballistic Missile Treaty, deployment of offensive first-strike "missile defenses," and monopolization of the militarization of space. Their goal was to create "a whole new world."[7]

This was not an aberration. Their antecedents lay in the Constitutional Congress of 1789, which laid the foundations for a new empire based on the models of its Greek, Roman, British, and French predecessors.[8] The Monroe Doctrine in 1823 demanded that Europe respect U.S. hegemony in the Americas. Seward's Folly, the U.S. purchase of Alaska, secured the northern route to Asia as a step toward replacing Britain as the world's dominant power. And, even before big business and finance capital pressed the conquest of Asian markets as the best means to end the economic depression and social unrest of the 1890s, the "forty acres and a mule" given to Civil War veterans created overproduction of wheat and other grains and demands that Washington conquer Latin American and Asian markets for this produce. Admiral Mahan, Henry Cabot Lodge, and Theodore Roosevelt were the nineteenth century intellectual and political fathers of the Great Navy with which the United States did replace Britain as the ruler of the seas. And, on the eve of the 1961 U.S. invasion of Cuba, Secretary of State Dean Rusk explained that the United States could legitimately use force because we had done it before. To prove his point, Rusk cited 127 U.S. military interventions between 1798 and 1945, from Libya to China.[9]

Only a decade ago, in the aftermath of the Cold War, Bush the Elder launched the Gulf War, despite massive national opposition,[10] not only to "liberate" the sheikdom of Kuwait but also to create a hegemonic "New World Order" in which "What we say, goes."

The second Bush era has been marked more by continuity than change. Despite the end of the Cold War, one of President Clinton's first commitments was a vow not to reduce the military budget. During the Clinton years, the military budget grew to $300 billion, equal to the United States' NATO and Japanese allies, Russia, China, and the so-called "rogue nations"—*combined*! President Clinton prepared and threatened to initiate nuclear war against North Korea, Iraq, and Libya, and it was during the Clinton administration that "Full Spectrum Dominance" became the Pentagon's mission.

Consider what it means for other nations to be "full spectrum" *dominated* on a daily basis.

Empire

Until recently, there was a powerful taboo against the use of the word *empire* to refer to what the Council on Foreign Relations once described as the United States' "grand area."[11] Henry Kissinger and more scholarly analysts occasionally appropriated a concept from Marxism, but few wished any association with Lenin's belief that "imperialism is the highest (and final) stage of capitalism." With exceptions that proved the rule, violation of the taboo guaranteed marginalization, ridicule, and job insecurity. Among the exceptions were high school and college texts with chapters titled "The Age of Empire" that provided sanitized sketches of the U.S. conquests of Cuba, the Philippines, Puerto Rico, and Guam between 1898 and 1900. Another exception was the 1960s–1970s school of revisionist historians who mined deep veins of U.S. imperial history. Two significant anomalies were Zbigniew Brzezinski and Walter Russell Mead. The former was the founding Director of the Trilateral Commission and National Security Advisor for President Carter. The latter was an independent scholar who became senior fellow at the Council on Foreign Relations. Both thought it necessary to use honest terms of analysis to describe, maintain, and expand the U.S. imperial system.[12]

With the end of the Cold War, which left the United States as the "sole remaining superpower," mainstream and right-wing foreign policy journals affirmed the "hegemonic moment" and debated how best to extend it. They were following the lead of the Reagan and first Bush administrations, whose strategic doctrines were explicit about ensuring U.S. global dominance for the long term. Perhaps as a subconscious way of explaining why the September 11 attacks were targeted against the United States, in the months following the terrorist attacks, the press and many "national security intellectuals" legitimized and modeled the use of the imperial frame of reference. They told us that we live in the most powerful empire the world has seen since imperial Rome; unlike Rome, "our" empire is global.

As Joseph Nye, the leading imperial strategist associated with the Democratic Party, put it, "Not since Rome has one nation loomed so large above the others." Although formerly Assistant Secretary of Defense (War), Nye's approach is more complex and nuanced than his Bush administration successors. Anticipating UN Security Council debates over the Bush administration's war against Iraq, Nye argued that relying solely on overwhelming U.S. military power was likely to speed the development of a countervailing alliance that could include Europe, Russia, China, and other nations. Instead, Nye and his acolytes advocate complementing U.S. military power with greater reliance on corporate globalization and the "soft power" of U.S. popular culture, the media, higher education, and values to co-opt other nations.[13] The major differences within the U.S. elite are thus over means, not ends. They agree that the goal must be to preserve and expand U.S. global dominance—its empire.

People who live at the receiving end of Full Spectrum Dominance imperialism have fewer inhibitions about describing reality in unvarnished terms. Thus, the Japanese scholar Muto Ichiyo reminds us that "American hegemony, unlike the preceding British hegemony, was originally meant...to integrate the whole world as a single American market." After the diversion of the Cold War, the United States "has come back as the full-fledged Empire...The U.S., without ceasing to be a nation state, has appointed itself, even within the global center, an entity beyond a nation state and claims its right as such." Today, Ichiyo writes, "International laws, the UN Charter, the Hague and Geneva treaties and conventions do not apply, as America is the law. And America enforces the law with its nightmarishly colossal military machinery."[14]

The United States is also wearing out its welcome in Europe. Edy Altes, the former head of the Dutch Foreign Ministry, spoke for many Europeans when he said:

> The National Security Strategy of the United States of America, recently presented by President George W. Bush to Congress...lays down the claims of the U.S. for world hegemony, based on unparalleled military strength and great economic/political influence. From now on the U.S.— and the U.S. alone!—aspires to lead the world...The UN is relegated to a marginal role...The document shows no velvet on an iron fist...Unilateralism—now presented as American Internationalism—is bound to lead to deep irritation, yes stubborn resistance, even from traditional allies...The proclaimed 'Pax Americana' will not enhance security but instead endanger world stability and be fraught with a great deal of turmoil and suffering.[15]

The Bush administration's abrogation of the Antiballistic Missile Treaty; its rejection of the Kyoto Protocols on Global Warming and of the International Criminal Court; and U.S. unilateralism in its wars against Serbia, Afghanistan, and Iraq are but a few of the instances cited by Ichiyo, Altes, and others around the world.

It can be painful to look at root causes. Doing so can challenge the assumptions on which we base the ways that we live. In the case of this Bush administration's global military crusade, the causes lie more in the nation's European colonial and crusader Christian origins, in the creation of a continental and (later) international empire, and in what Hannah Arendt depicted as the "banality of evil," than in Islamic fundamentalism or a desire to prevent proliferation of weapons of mass destruction.

George Kennan, author of the Cold War containment doctrine, named and helped to create a major cause of today's international crisis when, in 1948, he advised President Truman that:

> We have about 50 percent of the world's wealth, but only 6.3 percent of its population...In this situation, we cannot fail to be

> the object of envy and resentment. Our real task in the coming period is to devise a pattern of relationships which will permit us to maintain this policy of disparity...We need not deceive ourselves that we can afford today the luxury of altruism and world-benefaction...We should cease to talk about vague and...unreal objectives such as human rights, the raising of the living standards, and democratization. The day is not far off when we are going to have to deal in straight power concepts.[16]

The commitment to "this policy of diversity" has been bipartisan and enduring. Half a century later, long after European and Japanese postwar reconstruction, President Clinton paraphrased Kennan, saying, "We have 4 percent of the world's population and we want to keep 22 percent of the world's wealth."[17]

A Whole New World

The indiscriminate September 11 terrorist attacks provided the Bush administration with political cover to, as Secretary of State Colin Powell put it, "set the reset button" on U.S. foreign and military policies. With the terrorist attacks opening the way, the Bush administration proclaimed its preemptive military doctrine, increased its military budget by approximately $100 billion, expanded discredited alliances and created new ones, disciplined client states, published its terrorizing Nuclear Posture Review, withdrew from the Antiballistic Missile Treaty, sabotaged the Kyoto Protocols and the Biological Weapons Convention, enlarged its global network of foreign military bases (especially in oil and gas-rich Central and Southwest Asia), advanced the encirclement of China, subverted constitutionally guaranteed civil liberties, and largely abandoned international law.

The Bush administration's unprecedented National Security Strategy attempts to defy the forces and lessons of history. It commits the United States to developing overwhelming military power to ensure that no rivals ever emerge to challenge U.S. power or the "free-trade" capitalist economic order that it dominates. Essential to this vision are first-strike nuclear capabilities, monopolization of the militarization of space, and deadly demonstration wars, like those in Iraq and Afghanistan that communicate Washington's will to use its intimidating arsenals not only to win wars but to ensure that, as Deputy Secretary of Defense Paul Wolfowitz said: "Other nations fear us."

There is also the matter of oil. Former Chairman of the Joint Chiefs of Staff Maxwell Taylor once described Middle East oil as "the jugular vein of Western capitalism."[18] With the subsequent rise of the Japanese, Korean, and Chinese economies, Middle East oil reserves have become the jugular vein of global capitalism.[19] At the turn of the twentieth century, when internal combustion engines began to dominate military and industrial life, privileged access to Middle East petroleum became "the prize" of World War I, with Britain and France carving out their Middle East spheres in the secret Sikes-Picot Treaty. An oil embargo imposed on Japan after its invasion of French colonial Indochina precipitated Tokyo's fateful decision to attack Pearl Harbor and oil-rich Indonesia. And, during the Cold War, as Noam Chomsky explained, "Axiom One of International Affairs [was] that the United States will take any possible steps to ensure that its allies do not gain independent access to these resources to any significant degree, and surely that the Soviet Union does not." And, today, Full Spectrum Dominance is more than a military concept. At the economic level, it includes reconsolidation of U.S. domination of the world's energy supplies, especially Middle East and Central Asian oil. To these ends, the United States threatened to *initiate* nuclear war at least eight times.[20]

Control of oil was a factor in the Bush administration's U.S. regime change war in Afghanistan—a war that might have been averted had the Bush administration not disdained the Taliban's request for evidence linking Al Qaeda to the September 11 attacks. The war provided the occasion for Washington to establish alliances and to construct a new network of military bases across the region. It was the hope of building a pipeline from Turkestan, through Afghanistan, to Pakistan and the Indian Ocean—free of Russian and Iranian influence—that initially led to U.S. support of the Taliban's rise to power and to its early tolerance of the Taliban's brutal excesses. Few noted that after the Taliban was ousted, the first foreign trip taken by the U.S.-installed Afghan president was to Turkestan—to reopen negotiations for the construction of the pipeline.

The new Central Asian military bases and alliances also advanced U.S. efforts to encircle China. The United States also used the cover provided by the "war on terrorism" to reinforce its alliances with Japan and across Southeast Asia, deepening the encirclement of China. U.S. forces returned to the Philippines, with the ostensible goal of carrying the war on terrorism to a small band of Mindinao bandits, while U.S. military forces returned to Guam in considerable numbers. These alliances and deployments placed the United States in better positions to intervene in the potentially oil-rich South China Sea, to control the Malacca Strait choke point through which the Middle East oil that fuels East Asian economies must flow, and to influence developments in Indonesia—the resource-rich and most populous Islamic nation.

Nuclear Terrorism

Ten months after the September 11 attacks, Senji Yamaguchi, a leading Japanese A-bomb survivor (*Hibakusha*) who suffered exposure to 3,000 degrees of radioactive nuclear heat in the 1945 atomic bombing of Nagasaki, described the atomic bombings of Hiroshima and Nagasaki as the single worst acts of terrorism in human history.[21] Even General (later President) Eisenhower was clear: "The Japanese were ready to surrender, and it wasn't necessary to hit them with that awful thing."[22] It was pursuit of strategic advantage over the USSR in the Cold War that had already begun that led the Truman administration to require that the A-bombs' targets be war-related cities with "a large number of workers and closely surrounded by workers' homes."[23] With two primitive bombs, Washington demonstrated to the USSR the cataclysmic power of nuclear weapons, and Washington's will to use them. It simultaneously brought the war to an immediate end so that the United States would not have to share influence with the USSR in Asia.[24]

Since then, led by the United States, governments in Moscow, London, Tel Aviv, New Delhi, and Karachi have also threatened to initiate nuclear war. The nuclear powers, led by the United States, have also refused to implement UN General Assembly resolutions and their Nuclear Nonproliferation Treaty commitments to eliminate their nuclear arsenals. Added to the ranks of the *Hibakusha* who continue to suffer and perish from A-bomb inflicted wounds and illnesses are a host of "global Hibakusha": "Downwinders," miners and "atomic veterans" from across the United States and their counterparts in other nuclear nations.[25]

The United States now goes to war so often that patterns in its routine of war fighting have emerged. The United States now regularly threatens nuclear attack to ensure that those it is targeting are not tempted to use weapons of mass destruction to defend themselves.[26] This nuclear bullying grows out of a long tradition of escalation dominance. As Harold Brown, Jimmy Carter's Secretary of Defense (War), testified a generation ago, the U.S. nuclear arsenal ensures that U.S. "conventional" forces remain "meaningful instruments of military and political power."[27] This approach has since been reified by successive U.S. presidents, most recently in George W. Bush's Nuclear Posture Review.[28] These threats provide nuclear umbrellas protecting U.S. aggressions.

The Bush administration has taken this practice to new heights. Not since the first years of the Reagan presidency has the United States placed such great emphasis on nuclear weapons in its military strategy as the Bush administration does today.[29] And, contrary to popular belief, even with the Bush-Putin nuclear arms reduction agreement, the United States plans to deploy "not 1,700 to 2,200 nuclear weapons, but as many as 15,000"[30] in the coming decades.

The Bush administration is also deploying "missile defenses" designed to augment first strike nuclear war fighting preparations. If there was any lesson from the September 11 attacks, it was that suitcase bombs and other smuggled weapons pose far more immediate threats to the United States than other nations' missiles. Yet, because the Bush administration sees China as a long-term "strategic competitor," it has abrogated the Antiballistic Missile Treaty and begun construction of missile defense bases targeted against China and North Korea. By threatening to "neutralize" China's comparatively small arsenal of missiles with theater missile defense systems, both the Clinton and Bush administrations have sought to coerce China into negotiating a "grand bargain" to ensure China's integration into the U.S. dominated global system on U.S. terms.

Beijing, not surprisingly, sees missile defenses as a shield to complement the United States' first-strike nuclear sword. Chinese leaders are clear that they will not return to the humiliations that prevailed following the Opium Wars. They insist that China will build as many missiles as necessary to overwhelm U.S. missile defenses. Washington's pursuit of nuclear superiority is thus about to trigger a catastrophic nuclear arms race in Northeast Asia.[31] Spending tens or hundreds of billions of dollars on missile defenses also advances the campaign for U.S. monopolization of the militarization of space; it will fatten profits of the military-industrial complex, and it is financing a revolution in military electronics.

As the United States bullies the United Nations and the world's nations with the ultimatum that "You are either with us or against us," it is clear that our political leadership and its supporters are dangerously intoxicated with what was once termed "the arrogance of power."[32] As the United States now reaches for near-totalitarian power through control of the world's essential resources, the ability to strike any place on earth with space-based, high-tech and nuclear weapons, to monitor global telecommunications, and demonstrates its disdain for international law and democratic civil liberties, European political leaders and diplomats are increasingly drawn to making comparisons between the United States and the first years of Nazi rule in Germany.[33]

Toward Common and Human Security

What then must be done?

Martin Buber, the Jewish philosopher answered this question with the commandment: "Do not withhold yourself," that liberation requires drawing on the fullness of our human capacities. At about the same time, Karl Jaspers, the German existentialist, reflecting on the question of German guilt, taught that "There exists a solidarity among men [and women] as human beings that makes each co-responsible for every wrong and every injustice in the world..."[34] There is also, Jaspers wrote, "a sort of collective moral guilt in a people's way of life which I share as an individual, and from which grow political realities."[35] The world's social and political realities are human constructs. Humans can change them, and it is the responsibility of humans to do so.

History teaches us that actions across a broad spectrum can prevent or mitigate particular atrocities in the short term (for example, playing a cello in the bombed and targeted Sarajevo marketplace to illuminate the madness of war, students doing the painstaking research needed to exonerate men and women wrongfully convicted of murder, or lobbying members of Congress to prevent funding for production of new nuclear weapons or to ensure access to medical care for all). More fundamental change takes place across longer planes of historical time. Here a challenge is to create alternate visions of possible social structures, values, and politics so that they are in place when "hinge moments" of history provide openings or when corrupted structures of power collapse and fall away.

It was a seamstress, Rosa Parks, whose community organizing and personal resistance galvanized the southern Freedom Movement by refusing to walk to the back of a bus. Religious leaders and congregations played essential roles in ending U.S.-style apartheid and the Vietnam War. A letter written by ten-year-old Samantha Smith to Soviet Premier Yuri Andropov contributed to the environment that made ending of the Cold War possible. Folk singers and graphic artists write the songs and provide the images that reflect and inspire popular movements, and a book by Rachel Carson played a seminal role in launching the Western environmental movement. Each of us has as many roles to play as we can imagine or present themselves to us.

At this writing, our most urgent tasks are to stop the Bush administration's disastrous global military crusade, to reverse the assaults on constitutionally guaranteed civil liberties and essential social services, and to heal the profound wounds that gave rise to deadly terrorist attacks.

Nonstate terrorism does pose dangers to Western societies and to the repressive regimes in which they have gestated. As we can see from the enduring popularity of the Taliban among a minority of Arab and Islamic peoples, resistance to U.S. Full Spectrum Dominance and Western-dominated "globalization" is deeply rooted. Stella Rimington, the former head of MI5, the UK security service, is clear that war is not the answer.

Instead, terrorism is successfully countered through sound police work within legal and constitutional limits, through internationally coordinated intelligence work, diplomatic initiatives that address the root causes of terrorism, and patience.[36] Thinking historically, we do well to remember that wars have rarely defeated ideas and belief systems.

Four Grievances

In the diplomatic realm, there are four profound grievances that the United States must address:

(1) Arab and Islamic peoples are painfully conscious of the diplomatic, financial, and military support the United States has provided for Israel's decimating occupation and colonization of Palestinian lands and communities conquered in the 1967 war. They identify with the beleaguered and desperate Palestinians. The glaring double standard of the United States going to war and imposing deadly economic sanctions against the people of Iraq because of Saddam Hussein's many violations of UN security resolutions, while financing the Israeli destruction of Palestine in violation of three decades of UN resolutions, common decency, and international law understandably fuels sometimes violent anti-Americanism.

Were the United States to implement calls from progressive Jews, Arab-Americans, and sectors of the U.S. establishment to use *all* of Washington's diplomatic leverage to force Israeli withdrawal from the occupied territories—including the threat of ending military, economic, and diplomatic aid to Israel until the withdrawal has taken place—while reiterating its support for Israeli survival, both Israelis and Palestinians could live with greater security, and enormous reserves of rage that have given rise to militant anti-Israeli and anti-U.S. actions would be dissipated.

(2) The second diplomatic initiative requires a turn away from empire. Beginning in the 1950s, the United States constructed a network of foreign military bases across North Africa and the Middle East to guarantee privileged access to Middle East oil. As long as the United States insists on maintaining these bases across the Arab world and near Islam's holiest cities, it will breed resentment and resistance. Removing these bases would ease U.S. pressure on the "jugular vein" of world capitalism and weaken the artificial supports that Arab petrodollars provide to the U.S. economy through massive investments in U.S. bonds, banks, industry, and real estate. But the withdrawal of U.S. troops and bases could contribute to U.S. and world security by removing a cause of Arab and Islamic rage and speeding conversion from the profligate consumption of the fossil fuels that endanger the survival of future generations.

(3) The third great grievance is the thirteen-year war in, and now continuing occupation of, Iraq. From the "turkey shoot" on "the highway of death" in the last days of the 1991 war, through the sanctions with their toll of more than a million innocent Iraqi lives, to George W. Bush's "regime change" war that was launched on false premises and brought greater insecurity and fear to ordinary Iraqis, to the heinous and inexcusable torture of Iraqi prisoners by U.S. troops, successive U.S. governments have brought enormous pain and suffering to the Iraqi people. Our governments have betrayed the values that the U.S. people hold dear and that our leaders have sworn to defend, marking our country as a pariah nation.

Like many other U.S. clients, Saddam Hussein was a brutal and aggressive tyrant. The 1991 U.S. Gulf War to oust Iraq from Kuwait was fought with U.N. approval, but only after Russia's vote was purchased with a U.S.-brokered gift of billions of dollars from Saudi Arabia and Japan, and after China was bullied to abstain from voting rather than cast a veto. While the U.S. media focused on missiles flying down warehouse chimneys and into ministry windows, others were targeted to destroy Iraq's electrical grid and water purification systems, planting the biological time bombs that the U.N. later estimated to have claimed a toll of 200,000 civilian lives in the first years following the war.

Then came the decade during which the U.S. taught that when a tyrant is targeted, it is his people who suffer. In the most comprehensive economic blockade imposed on a nation in modern history, economic sanctions—initially designed to force Iraqi military withdrawal from Kuwait—were extended to ensure Iraqi disarmament and then to win "regime change." Water purification equipment was proscribed, ostensibly because it could also be used for making weapons of mass destruction. As a result, contaminated water became the number one killer of Iraqi children for most of the 1990s. The Iraqi health care infrastructure, once a model for developing nations, was decimated by lack of essential medicines, ambulances, and X-ray machines that were categorized as forbidden dual use items.[37] Even pencils and other essentials for education were similarly banned. By the late 1990s, Iraq was under assault from multiple directions,[38] and UNICEF reported that sanctions had caused the deaths of more than half a million children under the age of five.

George W. Bush's invasion and occupation of Iraq were the final catastrophe. The war was launched in defiance of the United Nations Security Council and on patently false premises. Like the United Nations' inspectors, those dispatched after the invasion by the Bush administration discovered no evidence of an active Iraqi nuclear weapons program or other weapons of mass destruction projects. The Bush administration was forced to admit that before the war there were no ties between Saddam Hussein's regime and Al Qaeda, and—in fact—the invasion and occupation transformed Iraq into a haven for, and new source of, terrorism. The failure to plan adequately for the occupation left Iraqis more fearful and insecure than the vast majority had been during the Hussein dictatorship. And the photographs and reports of U.S. troops torturing prisoners in violation of international law and common decency betrayed the false promises of exporting democracy at the end of a gun (or a cruise missile).

(4) The fourth grievance is nuclear terrorism, practiced most frequently by the United States, emulated by other nuclear powers, and now feared from nonstate forces from Chechen rebels to Al Qaeda terrorists. The United States remains the only nation to have detonated nuclear weapons on targeted populations during wartime. Despite repeated condemnations by the world's nations, the UN, and the World Court, the United States continues to insist on preparing for and threatening the decimation of nations with nuclear weapons. While insisting that the U.S. nuclear arsenal is in "responsible" hands, every president since Truman, with the possible exception of President Ford, has threatened to initiate nuclear war during crises and wars.[39] Efforts to offset this imbalance of terrorism spurred the Soviet nuclear weapons program and later China's. The desire to deter or emulate the United States has thus become the principle force driving nuclear weapons proliferation.

Compounding the situation is the refusal of the nuclear powers, led by the United States, to abide by the Nuclear Nonproliferation Treaty. The essence of that treaty, negotiated in 1968, is that nonnuclear nations renounce the possibility of developing nuclear weapons in exchange for the nuclear powers committing to "good faith" negotiations for the "cessation of the nuclear arms race at an early date and to nuclear disarmament..." and to making nonmilitary nuclear technology available to nonnuclear nations. Three decades later, with the United States having pressed the pace of the nuclear arms race and resistance to nuclear disarmament, its nuclear arsenal and those of the declared and nondeclared nuclear powers are larger than they were in 1968. This is no accident. As former Deputy Secretary of Defense and CIA Director John Deutch explained in 1998, "The United States never intended, nor does it now intend, to implement Article VI of the Nuclear Nonproliferation Treaty."[40] This hypocrisy and the hierarchy of nuclear terror weapons now fuel increasingly dangerous nuclear weapons proliferation.

Calls for verifiable nuclear weapons elimination have been repeated since the first UN General Assembly resolution. In recent years, the Nuclear Nonproliferation Treaty was reaffirmed in a 1995 Review Conference, and the World Court's 1996 advisory decision condemned the use and threatened use of nuclear weapons and reiterated the legal necessity of achieving complete nuclear disarmament.[41] Meanwhile, there have been a growing number of nuclear weapons abolition initiatives: the UN General Assembly annually and overwhelmingly endorses a resolution introduced by Malaysia calling for the elimination of nuclear weapons. The Report of the Canberra Commission initiated by the Australian government provided a road map to nuclear weapons abolition. The New Agenda Coalition of "middle powers" has pressed for implementation of Article VI of the Nuclear Nonproliferation Treaty; the Tokyo Forum provided a second road map. Furthermore, disarmament and legal scholars drafted a model Nuclear Weapons Convention in 1997. During the 2001 Nuclear Nonproliferation Treaty Review Conference, these and other pressures forced the nuclear powers to make an "unequivocal undertaking" to achieve "total elimination" of their nuclear arsenals. Yet the Bush administration remains committed to an arsenal of 15,000 nuclear weapons.

Before nuclear weapons are completely eliminated, a number of intermediate goals can be pursued. They include making nuclear weapons more difficult to use by "de-alerting" them (decoupling nuclear warheads from missiles), negotiating a treaty to halt production of fissile materials, establishing a world inventory of nuclear weapons and materials, adopting the no-first use and no-use declarations by nuclear powers, and creating new nuclear-free zones and reinforcing existing ones.[42]

Common Security and the World House

Change is the constant of the universe. Like the tides, all empires rise and fall. Every empire, like the tides, rises and falls. For better or worse, a new era will follow this one.

The Bible reminds us that, "Where there is no guidance, a nation falls" (Proverbs 11:14). Whether the U.S. empire has a comparatively soft landing like those of Britain and France, or whether it will be a painful collapse like those of the Ottoman and Soviet empires, depends in large measure on our visions and actions. We can continue to gamble on Full Spectrum Dominance, assuming that we can bear the costs and losses from the armed resistance, lost social services, decimated democratic values, and environmental degradation. Or, if we have the vision and will, we can build on our understandings of Martin Luther King, Jr.'s, warning that "Oppressed people cannot remain oppressed forever," and that "we must learn to live as brothers or together we will be forced to perish as fools."[43]

Long before the revolutions in telecommunications and computers, Martin Luther King, Jr., understood that we had inherited "a great 'world house'" in which, despite differences in religion, wealth, and culture "we have to live together, because we can never again live apart, [that we] must learn somehow to live with each other in peace."[44] Anticipating the critics of Promethean Western materialism,[45] King taught, "We have allowed the means by which we live to outdistance the ends for which we live. So much of modern life can be summarized in that suggestive phrase of Thoreau: 'Improved means to an unimproved end.'"[46]

Alternative visions can also be found in the realms of real politik. The end of the Cold War was in considerable measure a consequence of the alternative vision of "common security." That idea had gestated on both sides of the Iron Curtain and was crystallized by the Independent Commission on Disarmament and Security Issues, which included senior Russian, European, U.S., Asian, and Third World diplomats, and is remembered as the Palme Commission. The Commission's core warnings and recommendations remain timely today: "The costs and dangers of the arms race—the acceleration of political tension and instability, the persistence of conventional military conflicts, the rising danger of nuclear war, the growing economic and social burdens of military spending—will not be eased if the nations of the world persist in pursuing security along familiar avenues...So long as [the great powers] insist on trying to protect national interests unilaterally, behaving as if their security can be gained at the expense of others, they will fail."[47]

The Commission's alternative vision was as radical as it was ancient: Common security, the idea that one person or nation cannot be secure if another is not, that "There is one overriding truth in this nuclear age—no nation can achieve true security by itself...security in the nuclear age means common security." The Commission based its recommendations on six principles:

1. All nations have a legitimate right to security.
2. Military force is not a legitimate instrument for resolving disputes between nations.
3. Restraint is necessary in expressions of national interest.
4. Security cannot be attained through military superiority.
5. Reductions and qualitative limitation of armaments are necessary for common security.
6. Linkages between arms negotiations and political events should be avoided.[48]

The Commission was also clear that "The United Nations must, and does stand at the center of the international system," even if "governments have not permitted the UN to function as it should."[49]

How do we transform U.S. values, policies, and politics to become and remain consistent with these principles? The recommendations that follow are framed along lines of a framework for analyzing civilizations through six interdependent dimensions. It should be borne in mind that in different historic periods, different dimensions play more or less decisive roles, for example, the role of European muskets in the late fifteenth century and of U.S. information technologies at the dawn of the twenty-first century.[50]

1. Spiritual/Values

U.S. society remains profoundly influenced by traditions of Crusader Christianity and colonial Puritanism. As we see in the pronouncements of President George W. Bush and powerful televangelists, these values continue to lie close to the mainstream of U.S. culture, which believes in the superiority of Christianity and its right to dominate, subjugate, and even kill those with lesser beliefs (and darker skin). These are the same spiritual values that served the genocide visited on Native Americans, the enslavement of Africans, discrimination against Asians and Jews, and today's dehumanization of Muslims and Arabs that makes discrimination and war possible.

There is an interesting parallel between Martin Luther King, Jr.'s, and Karl Jaspers' critiques of "thing"-oriented faith,[51] in which humans dominate nature for our own ends, and non-Western resistance to corporate globalization and the culture it represents. Although industrialization and postmodern culture have increased our comfort and extended life expectancy, there is no denying that human devastation of nature—the ground of our being—has placed human survival in jeopardy.

What other spiritual values do U.S. people learn from the popular culture? Watching television for hours on end, we learn the legitimacy and centrality of violence, and we are inculcated in the values of materialism and consumerism. Enticing advertisements teach that "living life to the fullest" means buying a stylish and expensive automobile, drinking beer, or saving money on nail polish so that more can be spent on chocolates.[52] Through television, the market and its values have penetrated, and often dominate, family life and values.[53]

National flags and anthems are not omnipresent in most other societies. Yet here in the United States, from cradle to grave, they are used to inculcate unquestioning nationalism and militarism. In nearly all school classrooms children daily pledge their *allegiance* to the *flag* and to the "nation for which it stands." Ostensibly objective TV news anchors wear stars and stripes lapel pins, much as brainwashed North Koreans wear Kim Jong Il buttons. As Dan Rather has confessed, they are afraid to pose the most challenging questions to our national leaders.[54] U.S. flags often adorn churches and synagogue altars. Like those in the Kaiser's Germany, they inculcate the message that "God is on our side," that "we" are better than "they." And what would a World Series game or Super Bowl be without the ear-shattering blasts of jet fighters screaming over stadiums, legitimizing the military and the wealth of our athletic heroes and their bosses?

Ambassador Edy Altes reminds us that whether one's spiritual path is Einsteinian metaphysics or traditional religious beliefs,

> Spirituality can be of crucial importance for establishing a creative relationship with the origin of our existence...It makes an end to the fragmentation of the personality in providing an integrating magnetic force for living...a meaningful life. Through it we discover our true identity.[55]

Individual and moral identity are essential to democracy. It is here that we develop the ability to draw lines, to create moral limits and boundaries. As James Carroll has written, if we fail to develop moral identities, "we are like leaves in flowing water, drifting along toward whatever the future brings."[56]

2. Economic

As the inequities of the U.S. and global economies increasingly resemble those of the age of Robber Barons, John Rawls' theory of justice and the worldwide movement against corporate globalization are increasingly valuable. Rawls discovered that if he asked his students to describe a just society without knowing their status in it beforehand, overwhelming numbers opted for societies that measured their success on their treatment of the least privileged.[57] Such a society reflects the value of, and a commitment to, each of its members. Yet, it does not require absolute economic equality. Such a just society would not tolerate debilitating inequities of wealth, but it would provide greater economic security for children, health care providers, students, industrial workers, and artists than does our own.

A society committed to human solidarity could not have a military-industrial complex as one of its central pillars. It could not devote fantastic amounts of the nation's limited wealth and resources to the Full Spectrum Dominance of others or to production of munitions designed to destroy human lives and creations. Economic conversion from capital-intensive and toxic military production to labor-intensive models addressing human and environmental needs would provide more jobs and economic security than our militarized economy does.

A common security political economy could not tolerate energy policies based on oppression of people or devastation of the global environment. It would embrace and build on the Kyoto Convention—to reverse global warming. It would emulate policies of other nations that enjoy essentially the same standard of living that we do but that consume half the energy on a per capita basis.

How to get there? Reintroduce the Carter-era tax credits designed to encourage conversion from fossil fuel consumption to greater reliance on sustainable, nonnuclear, energy sources. Tax gasoline purchases as they do in Europe and East Asia to limit fuel consumption. Construct modern mass transit systems along the lines of those in Western Europe and Japan that provide efficient train service to every city, town, and village.

Recognizing human interdependence, a common security society would not maintain high tariff walls against agricultural, clothing, and textile goods produced by our impoverished Third World sisters and brothers. It would understand that "maintaining this position of disparity" creates oppressive environments in which people understandably learn to hate and sometimes consider acts of violence and terrorism against those they see as their oppressors. A common security society would not rank last among industrialized nations in providing development assistance to the world's poorest nations. It would also understand that for most people the act of migrating from one's homeland to a largely unknown nation is not something undertaken lightly. Mass migrations are acts of desperation resulting from economic despair, severe discrimination, famine, and war, all of which can be rectified by justice and human solidarity.

3. Intellectual

A year into the U.S. war against the Taliban and Al Qaeda, a freshman Congressman uttered a revealing remark. He had been "surprised," he said, to learn that "people from other countries have different values and sometimes think differently than we do." He had always thought that other people were "just like us."[58] Unfortunately, this reflects geographical and cultural illiteracy that are characteristic of our culture. With 10 percent of U.S. people having been born abroad, we do not need to travel far to find people who can teach us about other cultures and the wider world. Another approach is to get a passport, travel, see, and *listen*. A recent visitor to Berlin learned an encouraging lesson from his experiences there. "Berliners of all ages," he wrote, "leave an indelible impression of broadly humanistic and progressive values…many Germans…have responded to Nazism and its legacy…with an indivisible commitment to oppose all forms of oppression."[59]

That Germans had changed so much in fifty years was not an accident of history; it was largely the consequence of the combination of international pressure and the struggle of conscientious intellectuals who honored their fundamental responsibility: naming reality, imagining alternatives, and working to bring them to fruition.

We have many models for such integrity in the United States. At the height of the Cold War, C. Wright Mills challenged intellectuals to examine their co-optation and their roles in preparing the world for a nuclear World War III. He inveighed upon his peers to "fight against the doctrine that...there are no alternatives...We should take democracy seriously and literally...We must," he urged, "attempt to educate, and then again to impute responsibility...we must reveal by our work the meaning of structural trends and historic decisions...we must state what we have found out concerning the consequences of the decisions of the high and the mighty."[60]

Confronting what Senator William J. Fulbright called the failure of scholars "who ought to be acting as responsible and independent critics of the government's policies but who instead become the agents of these policies," Noam Chomsky skewered the "mandarins" of the U.S. imperial establishment. In *American Power and the New Mandarins,* he described how, as U.S. intellectuals achieved the status of a doubly privileged elite, the "inequities of society" recede from vision. Chomsky wrote that, "It is the responsibility of intellectuals to speak the truth and to expose lies." Chomsky modeled such teaching by deconstructing and rewriting histories of the Spanish Civil War and the U.S. invasion of Vietnam.[61]

The nation's intellectual life begins in elementary and secondary schools that increasingly resemble the rigid class hierarchies and undemocratic values of the Pakistani educational system. Elite private schools serve the wealthy and the fortunate few who win scholarships and then must navigate the shoals of alienation on a daily basis. Public schools in U.S. cities and rural areas are often woefully underfunded and frequently lack essentials: books, paper, and dedicated and well-educated teachers. Finally there are the U.S. versions of madrassas—religious schools that inculcate fundamentalist and authoritarian values. Even in many U.S. public schools, religious fundamentalists, like the Taliban, seek to prohibit the teaching of evolutionary science. Democratic alternatives have long been known. They begin with ample funding for public education and move through updated and multicultural versions of the pedagogy described by John Dewey in *Experience & Education.* Dewey understood that teachers should be constantly re-creating learning environments to provide opportunities for learning and openings for engagement with a variety of aspects of the subject at hand. While urging structured flexibility, Dewey insisted on honoring the continuity of learning, building on what is known, and has captured the learner's interest.[62]

4. Social-Cultural

Kato Miki, the celebrated scholar who played a pivotal role in U.S.-Japanese postwar intellectual and cultural exchanges, observed:

> While we in Japan may err on the side of communalism, individualism is a great problem for you. In the U.S., people are anxiously looking out for themselves with 100 percent of their energy. It is exhausting. If you learned to trust others at least 30 percent of the time, you would be happier people.[63]

Like Japan, ours is a capitalist society, but there are profound differences in the two countries' dominant values. While ostensibly honoring the Golden Rule, U.S. culture places greater value on social Darwinism in which "rugged individualists" prevail. The dominant Calvinist belief is that the rich have earned their right to be rich, while poverty and economic hardship reflect laziness and an unwillingness to take risks. We are a nation of Horatio Alger "winners" and Willie Horton "losers" and are taught to "look out for yourself." We see the consequences in vast and growing income inequities, in the numbers of homeless people and the lack of respect shown to them, and in the warehousing of children in inadequate day care centers and the unemployed in prisons.

Meanwhile in Japan, traditional values of communal solidarity have led successive governments to resist pressures to reuse U.S. means to vitalize their stagnant economy by multiplying the number of bankruptcies, unemployed workers, and imperiled families. Differences in U.S. and Japanese values are readily apparent in daily life. In Tokyo, when people drink together socially, a person does not fill his or her own glass. Instead, a friend or colleague fills it; everyone is expected to look after the needs of others in the group. Like the traditional tea ceremony, this reflects a profound social commitment to caring for others, even if it is at times debased.

Economic policy differences resulting from differing cultural values are also evident between the United States and Europe, even as both have been deeply influenced by Protestant values. In Europe serfs served their lords, but the feudal lords were responsible for the overall security of the estate or community. In contrast, U.S. traditions of frontier individualism and resistance to oppressive British colonial governments created a culture in which people are socialized to expect less of our government and to give scant attention to the truism that a rising tide lifts all ships. It is thus more difficult to fire or lay off workers in many European nations than in the United States. Western European unemployment and social welfare benefits are not as punitive as in the United States. And, in many European nations higher education and health care are seen as social goods paid for by the national budget.

The Horatio Alger and Willie Horton analogies also reflect the continuing power of racism in U.S. culture. Jim Crow may be dead, and Condoleeza Rice and Colin Powell may serve the Bush dynasty, but with affirmative action, multiculturalism, and government social service and economic programs all on the defensive, race and racism remain defining realities for U.S. Americans. With exceptions that prove the rule, the ways that we are racially identified play determinant roles in where we are born, our chances of surviving infancy, how we are perceived and treated by others and ourselves, the quality of education that we receive, whether we face daily insults and harassment, and the job opportunities and thus the life options that are open to us. While much has changed since the Jim Crow days of legally mandated apartheid, we do well to remember that the Republicans' "Southern strategy" did not end with Senator Trent Lott's confessions and fall.

The essential elements of a U.S. culture based on greater human solidarity and common security have long been known, yet, with the exceptions of the Great Depression of the 1930s and the Freedom Movement of the 1950s and 1960s, we have lacked the sense of urgency and solidarity needed to defend essential victories or to make further progress.

Our ability to commit ourselves to common security, domestically and internationally, will be severely limited until we overcome the racism integral to our society. Although it will take generations for the United States to fulfill its destiny as a multiracial/multicultural society, the essential steps toward eliminating racism have long been known.

Multicultural education and training are essential antidotes to the parochial foundations of racism, enriching us with the extraordinary histories, wisdom, and cultures of the people with whom we share the United States and the world. Affirmative action has been undermined by people, as well as political forces, who are either blind to the long-term wounds and structural inequalities resulting from slavery, Jim Crow, and more subtle forms of racism or who have simply and selfishly sought to preserve their privileged access to education, jobs, promotions, and wealth. As even Trent Lott now claims to understand, it is time to reaffirm affirmative action to equalize the playing field and opportunity for all.

A second path toward overcoming racism was intimated in President Clinton's failed national dialogue on race. Like many Clinton initiatives, the national dialogue was long on image and short in substance. Nevertheless, a combination of social forces and those willing to expend their political capital could create the political environment in which we could, with comparative safety, reimmerse the nation in the tumultuous and ultimately liberating exploration of crimes and wounds of racism and of alternatives that are possible in the United States. One model is the South African Truth Commission, presided over by religious and other widely respected leaders, coupled with a prior commitment to legislate necessary changes.

5. Political

It is not yet clear if the U.S. people's commitments to Republican forms of government will prove more persistent than the temptations of consumerism or the demands, hierarchies, and repressions of Empire.

It was almost half a century ago that outgoing President Eisenhower warned about the dangerous power of the military-industrial-complex. This vast economic, political, and coercive leviathan has grown exponentially in the succeeding decades. The vast majority of Congress has been co-opted, as contracts and subcontracts for major weapons systems are strategically allocated to ensure that most states and congressional districts receive their portion (or more) of the military pork. Boeing, Lockheed, Raytheon, General Electric, and other major weapons makers are among the largest financial contributors to election campaigns, Republican and Democratic, making much of Congress dependent on—if not fully accountable to—the weapons industries.

In addition to the military-industrial complex, democratic practice and structures are under assault from at least two other subversive forces: "money politics" and the consumer/celebrity culture. It is common knowledge that free and fair elections are being sacrificed on the altar of wealth. Rarely now can a nonmillionaire gain access to the funding needed to run for higher elective office, and at all levels of government elected officials are increasingly beholden to those who pay for their campaigns. Then there is the Republican-dominated Supreme Court that has decided that money is not simply a commodity that facilitates economic transactions. It has transformed itself into a constitutionally protected form of speech. It cannot be helped, it is argued, if some are more equal than others, with the wealthiest having amplified powers of speech. No wonder populist critics complain that the country has become a plutocratic kleptocrisy!

Few would have predicted that the democratic values and practice could have become so corrupted that people would quietly tolerate the outcome of the 2000 presidential election that (1) turned a deaf ear on the systematic disenfranchisement of African Americans, (2) rigged ballots that led Jews to vote unintentionally for an anti-Semitic third party candidate, and (3) was decided by the Supreme Court that includes judges appointed by George W. Bush's father, with family members of two judges on the Bush transition team's payroll. Democracy may be more alive in the Philippines, where political corruption has sparked two nonviolent "Peoples Power" revolutions.[64]

The alternatives are well known: moving toward publicly funded elections with spending limits that equalize the playing field, returning to the wisdom that money is not speech, eliminating the electoral college, removing legal obstacles that make it almost impossible to run successful third-party campaigns, and making election day a holiday to increase participation.

It has become a cliché that democracy is not something that can be owned or passed from one generation to another, but this is also a fundamental truth. Democracy is a human construct that must be nurtured, sustained, and not infrequently re-created or resuscitated by successive generations, or it ceases to exist.

The democratic rights we have inherited and won, and the culture we have created, are jeopardized by more than money politics and the "bread and circuses" of U.S. consumer culture. The Bush administration's post-September 11 assault on constitutional civil liberties and unprecedented military spending are tearing the nation's social and political fabric. It was President John Quincy Adams who long ago warned that if the United States succumbed to the temptations to "become the dictatress of the world, she would be no longer the ruler of her own spirit." More recently, the journalist Michael Ignatieff put it more bluntly: "What empires lavish abroad they cannot spend on good republican government at home: on hospitals or roads or schools. A distended military budget only aggravates America's continuing failure to keep its egalitarian promise to itself."[65]

Defending participatory as well as electoral democracy requires a willingness to engage daily in their practice. It necessitates the courage to name and debate the perilous choice between republic and empire. It means that citizens must remember that elected officials—including the president—put their pants or pantyhose on one leg at a time. People must be willing to engage, lobby, and, as necessary, confront them. It means risk taking to organize and to speak out in workplaces, schools, places of worship, and elsewhere in our communities, and organizing or participating in vigils and demonstrations. When necessary, it also means being willing, like Rosa Parks, Daniel Ellsberg, and tens of thousands of others, to commit nonviolent civil disobedience, risking imprisonment in the name of democracy, justice, and real security.

6. Military

Several nations have achieved complete disarmament. Costa Rica abolished its military, and Iceland's language, despite its Nordic and Viking roots, has no words that mean military strategy. This, however, is not the goal of common security, which is better understood as but a step in the direction of a world without war. Although numerous common security techniques have been integrated into many militaries' practices and doctrines, having served its Cold War era purposes, common security no longer plays the central role once assigned to it. Yet, in this period, when U.S. national security strategy again threatens to ignite new races, spurs nuclear weapons proliferation, and generates terrorism, it is well past time to consider about common security alternatives to Full Spectrum Dominance.

By definition, common security cannot be achieved unilaterally. To build the necessary trust, it must be negotiated and phased in through stages and over time. In addition to obvious steps such as renouncing its first-strike nuclear warfare and aggressive military doctrines, it will require commitments to the phased withdrawal of foreign military bases, and serious reductions in U.S. military spending.[66] A number of the essential elements of an enduring common security system are also clear. These elements include

- a recommitment to the United Nations, international law, and arms control treaties;
- regional negotiations and confidence building measures; and
- fulfilling the "unequivocal undertaking" to negotiate the "total elimination" of their nuclear weapons.

Conclusion

With the terrorist attacks of September 11, people in the United States began to appreciate realities that people in many nations have been waiting for us to learn: The world is not Disneyland. The United States is not universally adored. U.S. invasions and Full Spectrum Dominance give people reasons to hate us. There will be no peace without justice.

This is a "hinge moment" in history. The Bush administration may be overreaching with its campaign to reconsolidate the U.S. empire along neocolonial lines. Although no individual nation has the resources to directly confront and challenge the hegemony, Washington's increasing reliance on its military "big stick" may so alienate the rest of the world that essential cooperation is reduced or withdrawn: intelligence, diplomacy, crime fighting, and economic and environmental cooperation. This would seriously isolate the United States, making our lives and communities much less secure than they are today. Similarly, as the Bush administration raises the costs of empire through unprecedented military spending, unprecedented police state surveillance and repression, and intolerable civilian and military casualties, we may choose republic and common security over empire through demanding struggles comparable to the Abolition, Freedom, and Vietnam era peace movements. Hopefully, the prophetic voice of the churches will provide leadership.

The future will be what we make it.

SECTION IV
The Prophetic Call to Restore and Celebrate Peace

11

Issues of Peacemaking in the Church and Society

Richard L. Deats

Cold War tensions and fear were at a peak in 1982. The United States and the USSR were locked in a deadly nuclear arms race, and the insane policy of Mutually Assured Destruction was firmly in place. The two superpowers were on a collision course that led many people to think that World War III, and the possible end of civilization, were edging closer and closer to reality.

At the same time, there was paradoxically a growing sense of the church's calling to follow Jesus Christ as the Prince of Peace and a willingness to challenge the dominant governmental and societal mind-set of a never-ending arms race and the continuing possibility of all-out war.

When the United Nations convened its 1982 Disarmament session (June 7–July 9), that event became the occasion for concerted, unprecedented peace activities by a broad-based coalition of many organizations that included churches, religious orders and communities, and peace groups. The Cathedral of St. John the Divine in New York City was the site of an international religious convocation that gave voice to the prayers, hymns, scriptures, and messages of the sacred call to peacemaking. Together the worshipers affirmed:

> We declare we are at peace with all people of good will. We need no leader to define for us an enemy nor to tell us what we need

> security for, or defense against...We choose to be peacemakers rather than peacekeepers, we choose a nuclear-free future, and we will settle for nothing less...Before us today are set life and death. We choose life, that we and our children may live. Let it be so. [1]

Thousands marched in the streets with their banners and posters. Over one million people gathered in Central Park in a giant rally to "Freeze Nuclear Weapons/Fund Human Needs." Never in the history of the United States had there been such a public outpouring for peace. The day after the giant rally, hundreds gathered at the diplomatic missions of the five nuclear powers (France, Great Britain, the USSR, the United States, and China) and sat in as acts of peaceful civil disobedience to protest policies that were threatening the future of humanity. Typical of the events at the five missions, the protesters in the Chinese mission sat down in front of the police cordon while spokespersons of the peacemakers took to representatives of the Chinese mission a bouquet of flowers and a freshly baked loaf of bread, along with a message stating: "To the Chinese people: you are not our enemy. Nuclear weapons are the enemy of us all. Disarm now." [2]

A people's peace movement that included many Christians continued to grow, giving impetus to the ending of the Cold War. Although the East/West conflict had been the stated reason for the decades-long arms race and consequent neglect of human needs, the end of the Cold War did not reverse the dominant military policies in the United States. Even though the USSR collapsed, leaving the United States as the only superpower, the bloated military budget continued, and the long-promised peace dividend never materialized.

Disarmament has remained a critical issue for the church. A decade after the end of the Cold War, with the United States unrivalled militarily anywhere in the world, according to the 2000 budget, $291 billion went to the military as compared to $35 billion for education, $36 billion for children's health, and $7 billion for the Environmental Protection Agency. Russia's military budget, by comparison, was $55 billion, China's was $38 billion, and the total of those labeled as "rogue states" (Iran, Iraq, Syria, Sudan, Libya, Cuba, and North Korea) was $14 billion. [3]

The preponderant military expenditures that overshadow our priorities as a nation are nowhere more critically seen than in the continued reliance on nuclear weapons as the cornerstone of U.S. foreign policy. Although the public has been lulled into thinking that the nuclear terror is over, this is by no means the case.

Nuclear proliferation has continued as more and more nations join the nuclear club. India and Pakistan have added to the lethal tinderbox of the world's nuclear arsenal. Their hostile relations to each other, additionally fueled by the war on terrorism, is an ominous example of the danger of nuclear proliferation. The conflict in Kashmir could easily escalate into a full-scale war, in which the use of nuclear weapons is a real possibility.

Russia and other nations of the former USSR still possess thousands of nuclear weapons in a situation that is highly unstable, with nuclear materials so poorly safeguarded that accidental use is a troublesome and even frightening possibility. In addition, there is the real possibility of theft or purchase by nations or individuals with hostile intent for their use. The policy of Mutually Assured Destruction, as insane as it was, prevailed between two superpowers that recognized the threat posed by their adversary. Now even that diabolical stability is no longer present.

Although the American public widely supports the elimination of nuclear weapons, this has not been translated into policy, nor have the churches made it a high priority. Both major political parties support hawkish policies as the United States seeks to advance its nuclear capability even further by working toward new generations of nuclear weapons with the use of high-tech subcritical tests and computer simulations of new nuclear prototypes. The United States retains the right to a first-use policy even as it preaches to the world the danger of nuclear weapons and their proliferation. The Comprehensive Test Ban Treaty was not ratified by the U.S. Senate during the Clinton administration, and under the Bush administration, our "go it alone" approach has been manifested with the world's superpower assuming it is a law unto itself.

This is particularly seen in the decision to deploy a national missile defense system and to terminate the Antiballistic Missile Treaty, which was painstakingly negotiated between the United States and the Soviet Union in 1972. Although unproven and unimaginably costly, the Bush administration is pushing ahead with a national missile defense project that is likely to trigger a new arms race with China and destabilize relations with our allies. In addition, the this project has no relevance in dealing with the looming threat of the individual terrorist carrying a nuclear bomb in a suitcase or placing such a device in a container entering a major city. Like the Maginot Line built by France before World War I, "Star Wars" is a monument to the past and irrelevant to the present.

The 2002 Moscow Treaty between the United States and Russia perpetuates a highly dangerous situation. The agreement to limit deployed strategic weapons to 2,200 is not the breakthrough it appears to be because the treaty does not provide for the dismantling of even one nuclear warhead.

The weapons are only to be *stored*—available for some future use. Hence, the world is left with the specter of the United States and Russia each possessing over 10,000 warheads, leaving open the possibility of nuclear war either by intention or accident.[4]

The irony of these developments lies in the fact that the support for the abolition of nuclear weapons has never been more widespread and more substantial.

"Abolition 2000" represents over one thousand organizations in seventy-five countries. A surprising number of retired generals and admirals have come out strongly for nuclear abolition. The former commander of the U.S. Strategic Air Command, General George Lee Butler, has become a crusading abolitionist. In departing from his former position, he said:

> What is the measure of civilization? What is the test of morality? What are the scales on which, ultimately, the capacities of mankind to live in peace on this planet will be measured? Isn't it, in fact, not only highly to be desired but also likely that someday we will come to understand that the distinctions upon which, until now, we have based our assessments and calculations regarding the prospects of peace—considerations of culture, religion, color of skin—have been entirely superficial, and simply recognize that fundamentally we are—all of us—of a piece? That, at the level of our DNA, we are indistinguishable, and that, given the opportunity, we all aspire to common values, including the right to live in peace and harmony, free from fear, and with the opportunity to realize all of the talents with which our Creator endows us? Why would we cut off those prospects, which are set forth in the founding documents of our democracy, by embracing a creed which accepts that, given certain provocations, we will resort to methods which will extinguish the lives of tens of millions of people? That's barbaric. In face, it is more barbaric than, perhaps, any measures for survival that you'll find in the animal kingdom. I have arrived at the conclusion that it is simply wrong, morally speaking, for any mortal to be invested with the authority to call into question the survival of the planet. That is an untenable allocation of authority, and yet it has become the central feature of the nuclear age...There is no security to be found in nuclear weapons. It's a fool's game.[5]

This clear abolitionist stance is really quite extraordinary and indicates the sobering logic that objectively examining the nuclear threat can have. And General Butler is by no means alone. In June 2000, twenty-one national religious and eighteen military leaders released an unprecedented Joint Nuclear Reduction/Disarmament Statement that said, in part:

> We deeply believe that the long-term reliance on nuclear weapons in the arsenals of the nuclear powers, and the ever-present danger of their acquisition by others, is morally untenable and militarily unjustifiable. They constitute a threat to the security of our nation, a peril to world peace, a danger to the whole human family...This is the situation today despite two truths—first, that the most commonly postulated threats to our national security are not susceptible to nuclear deterrence; second, that our nation's efforts to provide effective leadership in opposing the growing threat of nuclear proliferation will be credible only if our policies and those of the other nuclear powers demonstrate a commitment to the universal outlawing of these weapons. We also believe that reliance on a nuclear deterrent in the long run calls into question our stewardship of God's creation. In the short run, effective diplomacy may well require reciprocal and phased reduction of nuclear weapons over some period of years. [6]

A related and critical issue is the neglect of human need occasioned by the priorities demanded by the military budget, in particular that of funding the nuclear weapons industry in all its aspects. This linkage is inescapable.

In November 1998 a number of religious peace groups, including the Fellowship of Reconciliation, Pax Christi USA, Sojourners, the New Call of Peacemaking, and World Peacemakers, issued a New Abolitionist Covenant in which they stated:

> The maintenance and development of nuclear arsenals is a sin against God, God's creatures, and God's creation. There is no theology or doctrine or spiritual tradition that could ever justify the use or the threat of nuclear weapons. Whether one begins with nonviolence or with the just war doctrine, nuclear weapons are morally unacceptable.
>
> The God of all life, who is revealed through holy scriptures and the wonder of creation, loves the poor and demands justice for the oppressed. To continue to spend tens of billions of dollars on nuclear weapons every year while millions go hungry is a grievous failure of compassion and an affront to God. But by God's grace our hearts can be softened. It is time for all religious traditions to bear witness to the nonviolent and benevolent essence of all faith which is finally our only hope. [7]

While the average American assumes that the United States is the most generous nation in the world and is even profligate in aiding other peoples, the fact is that the percentage of the gross national product of the United States channeled into foreign aid ranks last among the world's twenty-one richest nations.[8] Since 1985 there has been a steady decrease in the real U.S. aid extended to other nations.

Even in the matter of foreign aid, approximately half of that aid is of a military nature. And it should be noted that 40 percent of U.S. foreign aid goes to two countries, Egypt and Israel, two staunch allies who are among the leading purchasers of U.S. arms.

These priorities mean not only neglect of the world's poor, but they also skew our ability to creatively respond to the new challenges and possibilities of the post–Cold War world. With most conflicts in the world today being within rather than between nations, there has been a growing involvement of the member states of the United Nations in peacekeeping activities and the nonviolent resolution of conflict. This is a new field where the global community has much to learn but where there is enormous potential for the building of a just and peaceful world. Yet the United States has been involved in only a tiny percentage of UN peacekeeping operations. Despite the low priority this has had in U.S. foreign policy commitments, powerful members of the U.S. Congress oppose such efforts and even oppose the payment by the United States of its UN dues and assessments.

This has not stopped important initiatives by citizens' groups and churches that are working to build a nonviolent future. The Christian Peacemaker Teams of the historic peace churches go into areas of conflict to monitor and publicize what is happening and to stand for justice and peace. Peace Brigades International sends international volunteers to accompany and thereby protect endangered persons in places of war and violence. The Fellowship of Reconciliation and other groups provide nonviolence training to those working for justice, liberation, and reconciliation. The Global Peace Force is imaginatively working to build a standing volunteer force prepared to go into areas of conflict and unrest. Churches can do much to build awareness and support for such efforts.

A legacy of the Cold War is the military projection of U.S. power with American troops stationed in places as varied as Japan, Okinawa, the Philippines, Saudi Arabia, Germany, and South Korea.

Even where troops are not stationed, foreign military and police forces receive training from U.S. institutions such as the notorious U.S. Army School of the Americas in Ft. Benning, Georgia. Although the ostensible aim of the School of the Americas is the strengthening of law and order to enhance democracy, in actual fact over sixty thousand Latin American soldiers have been trained in commando tactics, military intelligence, psychological operations, and other civilian-targeted warfare practices. Graduates of the School of the Americas have committed many atrocities, including torture, rape, "disappearances," and massacres. Nineteen of the twenty-six Salvadoran officers cited by the UN Truth Commission for the 1989 assassination of six Jesuit priests and their housekeeper and her daughter in El Salvador were trained at the School of the Americas, as were the assassins of Archbishop Oscar Romero, murdered while he was celebrating mass.[9]

Each year people of faith gather in Ft. Benning to call for the closing of the School of the Americas. (The School of the Americas was recently renamed The Western Hemisphere Institute for Security Cooperation in a cosmetic change to divert the protests.) Thousands make the trip to Georgia with their petitions, banners, crosses, and other symbols.

Speeches, songs, and prayers outside the gate of the School of the Americas characterize the weekend gathering. To the solemn beating of drums, a funeral procession, with participants carrying coffins and wooden crosses on which are painted the names of victims of School graduates, slowly crosses onto the School grounds, thereby breaking the law and risking arrest. All who risk arrest must have taken careful nonviolence training with the following discipline:

- At all times, we will use our anger at injustice as a positive, nonviolent force for change.
- We will refuse to return the assaults—verbal or physical—of those who oppose or disagree with us.
- We will refrain from insults and swearing.
- We will protect those who oppose from insults or attack.
- If arrested, we will behave in an exemplary manner. We will not evade the legal consequences of our actions.
- As members of a nonviolent demonstration, we will follow the directions of the designated coordinators. In the event of a serious disagreement, we will remove ourselves from the action.
- Our attitude as conveyed through words, symbols, and actions will be one of openness, friendliness, and respect toward all people we encounter, including military personnel, police officers, and members of the larger community.
- We will not damage property.
- We will not use any drugs or alcohol.

- We will not run or use threatening motions.
- We will carry no weapons.[10]

Before they cross the line, they are commissioned (first in Spanish, then in English) with these words:

> **Leaders:** By participating in this memorial funeral procession, you honor the lives of those who have and continue to suffer because of the School of the Americas. Like so many before you, you go as emissaries of peace to confront violence with nonviolence. Will you commit yourself to be nonviolent in your spirit and action today as you join this solemn funeral procession to the School of the Americas? And in the months to come, will you continue to work to close the School of the Americas and encourage others to do likewise?
>
> **Response:** In the nonviolent way of Dr. Martin Luther King, Jr., Dorothy Day, Gandhi, and Rosa Parks, I will be nonviolent in my spirit and action today. And as an advocate for peace, I will continue to work until the School of the Americas is closed. By presence, word, and action, I will honor those who have suffered and those who continue to put themselves at risk for justice.
>
> **Community Blessing:** (unison) May love and mercy go with you as you speak for those who cannot speak. Through your witness may their voices be heard here at the School of the Americas, in the White House, in the Halls of Congress, and in the hearts of the US citizens across this nation so that the School of the Americas will be closed forever.[11]

Thousands have been arrested yearly as the funeral processions have entered the school. Those with multiple arrests have been sentenced to heavy fines and months in prison.

Supporters of the movement have succeeded in winning growing congressional support for cutting off funding for the School of the Americas. Lobby days bring thousands to Washington, D.C., to work for its closing.

The celebratory activities of the protesters are a powerful witness by people of faith to the nation and its institutions. Another example of the way peace witness is expressed as an integral part of Christian faith is the ongoing witness at the Nevada Test Site on Western Shoshone land near Las Vegas, where over one thousand nuclear weapons have been detonated. Fasting, prayer, processing, worship, and civil disobedience give expression to a transformative faith that calls Christians to stand with determination against the principalities and powers and point toward a more excellent way—the way of God's peace.

There are a multitude of other peace-related issues demanding attention, such as the manufacture and trade not only of weapons of mass destruction but also of small arms including landmines; the use of child soldiers in many countries; the militarization of space; a decade of sanctions against Iraq that are devastating an entire people and their society; and support for the United Nations and its peacemaking efforts. From these international issues we see a parallel in our communities where handguns, largely unregulated and easily obtainable, bring widespread suffering and death; where violence is glorified in the media; and where capital punishment is the capstone of a racist and class-based prison system that neglects rehabilitation and emphasizes punishment.

The very pervasiveness of violence in the twentieth century, continuing now into the twenty-first, has begun to awaken a renewed sense of the importance of peace and the search for nonviolent alternatives to the present path we are on. This awakening is seen in the appeal of all the living Nobel Peace laureates for the first decade of the twenty-first century to be the Decade for the Culture of Peace and Nonviolence for the Children of the World. Particularly through the efforts of Nobel laureate Mairead Maguire and the French visionary, Pierre Marchard, and with the support of the International Fellowship of Reconciliation and others (along with a parallel effort by UNESCO), the appeal was passed unanimously by the UN General Assembly on November 10, 1998. [12]

At the same time, similar efforts were developing among the churches, so that from January 29 to February 6, 2001, the Central Committee of the World Council of Churches (WCC) in Berlin launched the Decade to Overcome Violence. In a pledge to work for reconciliation and peace, the emphasis was on love and faith applied within families, neighborhoods, communities, and churches. The message coming from Berlin was for the churches to

- work together for peace, justice, and reconciliation as a visible sign of the churches' unity in life and witness;
- repent together for our complicity in violence;
- engage in theological reflection to overcome the spirit, logic, and practice of violence;
- embrace creative approaches to peace-building within the Christian tradition, local communities, secular movements, and other loving faiths; and
- stand alongside victims of violence to seek to empower those people who are systematically oppressed by violence. [13]

The WCC launching of the Decade to Overcome Violence was concluded with a candlelit march to the Brandenburg Gate where Konrad Reiser, General Secretary of the WCC said: "For us, the Decade journey must start with repentance for the violence that Christians and churches have tolerated or even justified. We are not yet the credible messengers of nonviolence that the gospel calls us to be." He concluded with Hebrews 12:1–2: "Therefore, since we are surrounded by so great a cloud of witnesses...let us run with perseverance the race that is set before us, looking to Jesus the pioneer and perfecter of our faith..."

From the General Assembly of the United Nations to the Central Committee of the WCC, we are being encouraged and strengthened to become effective peacemakers in a world that may, at long last, be ready to do the things that make for peace.

12

Building a Peacemaking Church

Jay Lintner

Identity is perhaps the biggest key to building a peacemaking church. When a local church or denomination views itself as a peacemaking church and cultivates this perspective as central to its identity, it affects all church members and gives impetus to many peacemaking acts.

Is our church a peacemaking church? Probably not too many churches think of themselves this way. What is your image of your church? We are the historic first church, a living and important part of our community. We are the radical and vibrant new church at the edge of town. We are a loving community. We are a community attentive to the Word. We are a community of Word and Sacrament. We are the Body of Christ. We are a community celebrating the love of God and called to glorify God and love our neighbor. All of these images have, as one of their components, the identity of peacemaking. Each church is a community of peacemakers, celebrating and acting to embody God's peace.

Three denominations in the United States are very conscious of this image and are known as historic peace churches: the Quakers (Society of Friends), the Mennonites, and the Church of the Brethren. Central to their identity is that they will not participate in war, will seek nonviolent alternatives to conflict, and will, as members, seek the role of active peacemakers. Individual members may sometimes choose to go to war to defend their country, or even engage in violence to defend their families, but when they do, they know they are going against the teachings of their church.

Many other Christian denominations as well as other members of various churches must sometimes think: If these are the peace churches, what are we? Are we the war churches? And, of course, many churches have mixed records on supporting or opposing war. The churches of New England, for example, generally supported the Revolutionary War as necessary to achieve freedom in the Thirteen Colonies and end the colonial domination by England. They generally supported the Civil War as necessary to end slavery and maintain the unity of the country. But they also generally opposed the War of 1812 and the Mexican-American War of 1845. Other churches in different parts of the country might have had different reasons for supporting or opposing specific wars. Does this mean that only a few churches should be considered peace churches? Or does it mean that the search for peace is complex and confusing, with the reality of peace being elusive? Does it mean that the search for peace and the search for justice and an end to oppression are hopelessly intertwined?

As some churches have sought to engage in the quest for world peace, they have encountered neighboring churches, or strong voices within their denominations, who have criticized their peacemaking activities by reminding everyone: "There is no peace without justice." Churches in South Africa, for example, that condemned violence in the struggle against apartheid were reminded that living under apartheid was itself a condition of violence. The Kairos Document, issued in 1985, was critical of what it called "church theology" for condemning violence in a way that seemed to speak against the violence in the streets without responding adequately to the systemic violence and brutal oppression of state violence. The debate, which existed in churches during the Revolutionary War and the Civil War, was in many cases exactly this debate between peace and justice.

I have photos on my bedroom wall of my great-great grandmother, Rose Emerson Blake, and my great-great grandfather, Ashel Blake, who lived in Massachusetts at the start of the Civil War. One of their conversations, according to my grandmother, went roughly like this:

> Ashel said, "I have to go free the slaves. The war has started and I have to go fight to free the slaves."
>
> Rose responded, "I don't believe in war. If you go join the army, I won't let you back in this house."
>
> Ashel persisted, "I have to go do my part to free the slaves."
>
> So Ashel left and spent time guarding a prisoner of war camp, being too old to fight. When he returned to Massachusetts after

the war, Rose would not let him back in the house, and he moved to Michigan.

The tension that existed between Rose and Ashel is a real tension within families, congregations, and individuals. Ashel was a man of principle who felt he had to take a stand to end slavery. Rose was a woman of principle who felt her commitment to pacifism had to be absolute. Did either struggle long enough to find a way out of this conflicting set of positive values? Did they have time, given that war was upon them and Ashel felt compelled to act?

The struggle between peace and justice can be very personal. What is the path to true peace? Does it sometimes lead through war or should we opt out of fighting all wars? I respect both Rose and Ashel as justice advocates and peacemakers. I have no idea who was right, and the fact that they could not work out the differences of their strong and unbendable convictions is painful. It is also a challenge for us to work them out.

Many mainline Protestant churches, over the past couple of decades, have come to consider themselves as "just peace" churches—a conscious attempt to balance the passion for peace with the passion for justice, recognizing that there is no peace without justice and no justice without peace. The quest for peace and the quest for justice are intertwined. It is a false peace, the false peace identified by the prophets, that tolerates unjust domination and oppression, crying "peace, peace," when there is no peace.

So for mainline Protestant churches, evangelical churches, Catholic churches, all churches that do not belong to the three historic peace churches, how can the identity of the peacemaking church be claimed? This theological struggle is difficult for people to understand.

Documents written over the past generation have attempted to clarify this struggle. The U.S. Bishops' Pastoral Letter on War and Peace, issued in 1983, helped position the Roman Catholic Church against war generally and the Cold War in particular, even as it left plenty of room to continue the struggle against Communism and the aggressive tendencies of the USSR. It brought new life to "just war" theology, which was central to Catholic peace theology since St. Augustine and St. Thomas Aquinas, updating it to cast serious doubt on whether a nuclear war could ever be justified under just war theology and placing just war theology into a larger theological context that in many ways is more compatible with just peace theology.[1]

The United Church of Christ (UCC) convened a Peace Theology Development Team of fourteen people who spent four years reflecting together and writing papers before issuing *A Just Peace Church*.[2] As a part of this effort, the General Synod of the UCC passed a Pronouncement in 1985 declaring the UCC to be a just peace church. It defined *just peace* as the interrelation of friendship, justice, and common security from violence and placed the UCC General Synod in opposition to the institution of war. In the years immediately following this action, some 200 local congregations studied the issue and took congregational votes to declare themselves to be just peace churches, greatly contributing to their identity as peacemaking churches, still an important part of their identity years later.

Similarly, the United Methodist Council of Bishops issued *In Defense of Creation* in 1986. In it, they say, "We seek to keep the just-war tradition alive, even as we seek to keep the pacifist tradition alive, each serving as a partial but vital testimony to the requirements of justice and peace."[3] The document goes on to lay out the principles of just peace theology and provides the larger context in which pacifism and just war theology are to be understood.

Seven Strategies for Building Identity as a Peacemaking Church

How is this identity of peacemaking developed in the local parish? A wise (and active) parish may have a number of strategies in motion at the same time to strengthen its peacemaking identity or peacemaking capacity. Seven strategies might be employed to strengthen the overall strategy of creating a peacemaking identity at the parish level and developing real capacity for becoming a significant peacemaking force. The leadership of the church needs to nurture and set in motion these strategies.

There should be strategy for (1) peacemaking in the worship life of the congregation, (2) theological reflection, (3) peace education, (4) building a peaceable community within the parish, (5) community action or witness, (6) peace political advocacy, and (7) peace funding.

1. Worship as Celebrating God's Peace and Our Peacemaking Role

The worship life of the church community is, of course, central. Hence, the God who gives us peace and the response of the community in peacemaking should be celebrated frequently in worship. Calls to worship can be calls to the peacemaking community and calls to celebrate the God whose gift is shalom. Prayers of confession can center on our failures as peacemakers and provide insights into the tensions we face that tempt us away from our roles as peacemakers, confessing even our complicity in the forces that make for injustice and separation and violent conflict. Most hymnals are filled with hymns celebrating peace and peacemaking.

Scripture has numerous passages that point to the vision of peace, the gift of peace, the way to peace, and the challenge of bringing peace. Sermons, even when they are not addressing peace as the central focus, can touch on different dimensions of peacemaking. The pastoral prayer can be an excellent opportunity to name the places that need prayers for peace, the issues that are being fought out between those who seek peace and those who have other, and often more selfish or nationalistic, motives. While celebrating peacemaking can be present frequently during the year, a few services can provide special focus.

2. *Thinking Theologically about Peace*

Achieving peace is a difficult task, requiring the balancing of different values. Through sermons, educational forums, and the reflective media of the church, the congregation needs to be encouraged to think and reflect theologically about what just peace is and how to achieve it. Because theology is so central to the meaning and mission of the church, more will be said about this later. For now, the point that needs to be made is thus: Encouraging the congregation to think about peace theologically is critical to any strategy for building a peacemaking community in the church.

3. *Education for a Just Peace*

Adult forums provide an excellent time to look at issues and strategies for peacemaking. Differing points of view should be encouraged. If people are not disagreeing about the best way to achieve peace, they are not being honest. Until a climate is developed in which differing points of view can be expressed, people treating each other respectfully and learning from each other, one of the basic ingredients of a peacemaking church is missing. Should serious conflict break out, this should be viewed as a good opportunity to test conflict resolution skills.

At any given time there are countless conflicts around the world. What is the path to peace in the Middle East? Should U.S. policy be based on strategic competition or strategic partnership with China and Russia? Why are North Korea, Libya, Iraq, and Iran sometimes called "rogue nations"? How can we develop new relations with these countries based on just peace? If sanctions seemed to work when applied to South Africa, why are they not working when applied to other countries, such as Cuba and Iraq? How can the United Nations be supported and strengthened? Is the U.S. policy in Colombia, aimed at stopping the drug trade, working? Can international terrorism be stopped with the use of the military? What role should the United Nations play?

These and many more questions are in the newspapers constantly. Often they are discussed by politicians who distort the issues, more intent on making themselves look good and their opponents look bad than on clarifying what is really at stake. Superficial and dishonest dialogue results. Hence, forums are desperately needed where experts can look beneath the conflicts in the headlines and where church members can share and discuss different points of view, helping each other understand which U.S. and global policies to support and which to oppose, which U.S. and global policies need strengthening and which need correcting.

Adult education is vital, but children and youth peace education should not be neglected. A number of denominations and organizations have excellent resources.[4] The best resource is the peacemaking convictions of the teachers.

4. Building a Just Peace Community

The community life of the congregation needs to nurture and reflect peaceful community. The congregation should be a model to the world, an example to the world of how Christians live. Care and love need to be felt by all members. Justice needs to be a living reality. This does not mean that fighting within the congregation is not going to happen. Conflict within the congregation is normal, as different people express what is important to them, what is valued, what needs should be addressed. Conflict should not be repressed. That is the false peace of the false prophets, who cry "peace, peace" when there is no peace. Rather, it is how the congregation handles conflict that marks it as a just peace church.

There is a rich literature on conflict resolution and the processing of conflict. As church fights develop, using these conflict resolution skills can provide members with a laboratory for learning to deal effectively and fairly with conflict. Polarization within the church—the development of hardened positions—can provide opportunities for utilizing the skills of identifying interests, brainstorming options, and finding mutually enriching solutions to conflict. Members should not be afraid to express different opinions, and both members and pastoral leadership should be sensitive to those who are silent, who are not expressing themselves. All need to be nurtured to participate and to work through differing feelings and visions in order to reach common ground.

The ability to forgive, the ability to create reconciliation, the ability to spot injustice and unintentional or intentional cruelty and reach out to those hurt and those doing the hurting—all these are basic, and ancient, Christian skills critical to peacemaking. The healthy church community is one that participates in a widespread effort at community building and community rebuilding.

5. Organizing for Just Peace

The first four strategies are aimed at life within the congregation. However, in every healthy church there is an inward dynamic to the Christian life and an outward dynamic. Is your congregation known in the community as a peacemaking congregation? Is your congregation connected to active peace movements?

Gaining consensus around various peacemaking issues and strategies can be controversial. Not everyone in the congregation may agree that pressure needs to be applied to Israel to stop building settlements on the West Bank. Not everyone may agree that defense spending is too high or that specific weapons systems are not only not needed but also may provoke other nations into an arms race. Not everyone will agree on the best ways to respond to terrorists.

Occasionally, there may be enough of a consensus to take various public stands in the name of the congregation. This consensus might be tested at an annual meeting or in some other way, and proposals for action can be voted on at the annual meeting or by the church council or a committee. Taking public stands as a congregation can create an identity for the church in the community as a just peace church. As the congregation becomes known in the community as a force for justice and peace, making a difference in creating just peace, new members, especially those who want to make a difference, may be attracted. But achieving this ability to act in the name of the church will require all the skills at group process and conflict resolution in order to make sure there is a working consensus or comfort level with this public stance.

Various just peace organizing possibilities can be presented to the congregation as action or mission opportunities. Petitions can be circulated and signed at the fellowship coffee hour. Letter writing tables can be set up. Announcements of marches or community meetings can be made. These can be organized either formally by a committee responsible for just peacemaking or informally by a few people who follow issues of peacemaking closely. As violations of justice and peace occur in the community, the congregation should be quick to act. Has a mosque or have members of the Muslim community been threatened? Has a synagogue been attacked with anti-Semitic graffiti? Has racial conflict occurred in the school system? Are gays and lesbians being attacked? Every week there are opportunities for the church to speak out and to act.

6. Advocating for Just Peace

Almost every week that the U.S. Congress is in session, political decisions are being made that threaten or enhance justice and peace. Many denominations have Washington offices that track these issues and share information with congregations and church members regarding the background of the issue, what is at stake, and when the critical decisions will be made. Church-related organizations also track these issues, often focusing on specific areas of peacemaking. Numerous peace organizations are set up that are actively engaged in lobbying for just peace issues. All of these organizations are desperate to increase their mailing lists because all of these organizations know that letters and phone calls from constituents do make a difference. If your congregation is not connected to a peace advocacy network, it is missing a critical opportunity to witness and work for a just peace.

This is particularly important if your representatives or senators in Congress are in "swing" districts or "swing" states. Many churches are located in districts or states where the representatives and/or senators have firm and unshakeable attitudes toward issues of justice and peace. In Massachusetts, for example, it is the rare representative who does not question the need for massive investment in a new weapon system, or why a quick bombing run is a better solution than more diplomacy. In Alabama, on the other hand, there has been a generally firm commitment to an expensive military and a tough foreign policy. Hence, when votes are taken that decide which policy our country will follow, the decisive votes are often cast in swing states and districts in Maine, North Carolina, Pennsylvania, and Oregon, states that could vote either way on these issues.

Congregations in these states and districts have a particularly important role to play in national issues of war and peace. However, because there is divided opinion in these swing states and districts, it is sometimes harder for churches to enter the political process for fear that the congregation will be divided or polarized. Where the need is greatest, the fear is greatest, and the tradition of silence on the great issues of war and peace can be strong. The peacemaking congregation is the one that can cut through this fear and silence.

7. Funding Just Peace

Developing peace worship resources and peace education resources costs money. Organizing for peace costs money, particularly the ongoing support of peace organizations. Political strategies, if they are to be effective, cost money. Sustained effort always takes money, and permanent peacemaking will always require sustained effort and money.

One method of organizing for peace is to take a special offering for a specific just peace cause or organization. A just peace offering provides the opportunity to create congregational awareness about the issue and the organization or organized effort to bring about peace. Since peace efforts are seriously underfunded, those engaged in these efforts will certainly appreciate the money, and contributors will know they are making a difference through their stewardship.

Whether peace funding is done through special offerings, the interpretation of the peacemaking work of regular budgets, through dedicating part of the regular church budget to various aspects of peacemaking, or all of the above, the conscious collection of money for the sustained work of peacemaking is central to creating a strong peacemaking community.

Stewardship is, of course, all about creating identity and sustaining ongoing institutional work. If peacemaking identity is to be developed in the congregation, and if institutional support for just peace strategies and institutions is to be maintained, the stewardship program of the church needs to be examined for what it says or does not say about the church as a peacemaking community.

Tactics for Institutionalizing These Strategies

Each of these strategies are ways in which just peace identity is created. As a peacemaking identity is developed and reinforced, these seven strategies are strengthened in turn, until the congregation is a real and active force creating peace in the community and in the world. In order to accomplish this, the seven strategies need to become institutionalized. Here are two simple suggestions: (1) form a committee and (2) take a vote.

The committee is so obvious it perhaps does not need to be mentioned. Certainly any sustained effort at peace organizing and peace advocacy will require a committee. To figure out how to institutionalize all these strategies, or to set priority among different strategies at any given time, it is wise to gather a group to reflect on this together, to take action, and report back on how things are developing. Regular lines of communication need to be established between the peacemaking committee and the governing board so that the work of the committee is seen as a key part of the life of the congregation.

Scheduling a vote at the annual meeting to declare the congregation a peacemaking community or a just peace church is a significant way to get this critical dialogue into the life of the whole church and encourage action and the creation of identity on the part of the whole church. Congregations that have taken this vote find that the vote helps them to sustain identity as peacemakers over time.

Just Peace Theology and Pacifism: A Continuing Dialogue

As peacemaking strategies are set in place in the local parish, it is almost inevitable that a real dialogue, perhaps even tension, will develop between classical pacifist thought and other forms of peacemaking theology, including just peace theology. The wise parish will make sure that this continuing dialogue is real within the life of the parish as a part of the theological strategy mentioned previously. It is within this context that core convictions are formed and real identity developed. For this reason, the rest of this chapter is devoted to this theological task.

Roland Bainton, in his classic study *Christian Attitudes toward War and Peace*, identified three different Christian peace theologies: pacifism, just war, and crusade.[5] Pacifism has proved to be a popular peace theological paradigm because of its refreshing simplicity. Individuals can understand its implications immediately and what it means for them personally. Just war theology has also proved a popular and enduring paradigm because, while individuals may have a more difficult time applying it to their individual lives, nations have an easier time applying it to the concrete situations and policy options they face. Crusade theory, certain that it knows which side God is on in any given struggle, is the most popular theory of all, adopted as theology by Communists, anti-Communists, liberation struggles around the world, and patriotic people everywhere.

Twenty years ago I served as staff to the UCC Peace Theology Development Team. After four years of meeting, our team concluded that we need a fourth theological paradigm that would incorporate elements of the other three peace theology paradigms but would attempt to place them within a broader framework.

In 1981 the UCC produced a Peace Futuring curriculum, working with staff of the World without War Council.[6] One session of this curriculum spelled out four different strategies (or ethical stances) for achieving world peace: peace through strength, peace through pacifism, peace through world law, and peace through revolution. People were then asked to choose their favorite of these four strategies and to write scenarios on how they thought an enduring peace would be achieved through the strategy. Traveling around the country in the early 1980s, I conducted many workshops, getting people to choose their strategy and think through where it might lead. This gave me a significant feel for what people in the UCC believed about the theology and ethics of peacemaking.

Peace through strength, of course, is the motto of the military and congressional hawks. Of those who came to workshops on peacemaking, this was the least popular. In fairness, however, the scenarios developed by church members affirming peace through strength did not differ very much from some of the other strategies.

Peace through pacifism was chosen by a small but committed group of UCC members, and the emphasis was never on the negative command of pacifism ("I will not go to war") but always on the positive commands of pacifism:

- "I will find an alternative to violence that resolves conflict and brings justice."
- "I will perform surprising acts of love that transform situations and open new possibilities."
- "We as a nation can put more resources into diplomacy and conflict resolution."
- "We as a global community can put more trust and resources into creating new global institutions that can replace the institution of war."

In many specific situations leading to war over the last twenty years, pacifists and just war adherents have found themselves on very similar ground. In the Persian Gulf War of 1991, and in the terrorist attacks on the World Trade Center and the Pentagon and the subsequent war against the Osama bin Laden network and the Taliban, pacifists insisted that an alternative way to military bombing and invasion must be found to force Iraq to leave Kuwait and to bring bin Laden and his followers to justice. Just war adherents always view war as a last resort and so joined pacifists in seeking to exhaust all means to secure justice before military force was used. The pope and a U.S. Lutheran bishop did say, however, that force could be morally justified in pursuing bin Laden, but the emphasis was in moving to diplomacy and the use of international institutions as soon as possible.

Peace through revolution is one variation of crusade theology. Our Peace Theology Development Team and the peace-futuring workshops surfaced a fair number of UCC members who chose this path to peace. Crusade theology got a very bad name a thousand years ago when crusaders invaded the Holy Land, and Muslims have responded with their own form of this theology: *Jihad* or holy war. But crusade or holy war theology reemerges any time one side is convinced that all truth and all goodness is on their side, that God is on their side, and that all evil resides with the enemy who must be defeated and banished before peace can be restored.

And since once a war starts both sides inevitably demonize the other side, most wars slip into crusades.

Liberation theology, with its profound and blanket statement that God takes sides in human history with the poor and the oppressed who engage in the struggle against their oppressors, was the basis for many UCC members adopting the stance of peace through revolution. Many UCC ministers, particularly those in urban and African American settings, thoroughly believed that peace was not the absence of conflict but the presence of justice and were highly suspicious of efforts at arms control and other peace strategies that took energy away from the struggle for racial and economic justice.

However, the most common peace strategy chosen by members of the UCC, when given a choice of the four options, was peace through world law. Fifty percent or more of the workshop attendees chose this option. From this perspective, the alternative to war as an institution is law. Just as crime within a nation is now handled, not with vigilantes and shootouts at the OK Corral but with police force and criminal courts, so world law and a world police force must some day soon replace war as an institution. Given the constant escalation of weapons of mass destruction, if we delay too long in bringing these changes about, our planet may not survive.

Pacifism and just war theory both point in this direction. It is particularly ironic that the George W. Bush administration rejected any consideration of an International Criminal Court in the months before the most horrendous criminal acts at the World Trade Center and Pentagon. As the war against terrorism continues, it is important that the United States reconsider its opposition to joining the International Criminal Court (now a reality), greater use of the United Nations, and the search for other new international mechanisms. Otherwise, the unfortunate phrasing of President Bush, insisting that every nation must decide whether they are for us or against us, and his unfortunate use of the word *crusade* in the early days following the attacks, will turn the struggle against terrorism into a U.S./radical Islam holy war.

Since we are in need of but have not yet developed adequate global institutions, we are at a vulnerable point in human history. The new war against terrorism will hopefully speed up their development. The four strategies for peace from the Peace Futuring curriculum and the historic three theologies (or ethics) of pacifism, just war, and holy war/crusade, when laid out for a congregation, can provide a basis for a rich dialogue among members. Hopefully, the fourth theological paradigm, just peace, can also add to this conversation. All of this should be in the context of what church people perceive God is doing in the world. As stated earlier, the Peace Theology Development Team and the fifteenth General Synod of the UCC defined *just peace* as the interrelation of friendship, justice, and common security from violence. This definition grows out of an understanding of God and what God is doing in the world.

What is God doing? God the Creator is still creating, still struggling to bring order out of chaos, still creating salvation experiences out of which community is formed and laws develop. God the Creator is in the struggles of nations to bring just community and security for people, free from the chaos of criminal violence and war. God the Creator is in the struggle of nations to develop international institutions, which will bring to all people and nations the justice and security and friendship that is shalom, peace. God is in the midst of the force nudging the new just global order into being. It is this vision, this hope of shalom, that pulls all creation toward a time when weapons are put down and all creatures lie down together without fear. The church is called to join the political struggle to create a new global order of justice, friendship, and common security from violence.

God the living Christ, the eternal force of reconciliation, urges us to love our enemies, even when that seems totally inappropriate, bringing us to unity against all our human determination to remain divided, creating cosmic unity against all our human divisions. We will be one. We will overcome our divisions. And so the church, the Body of Christ, is called to be agents of reconciliation, breaking the rules of the world, reaching out, transforming the situation by reckless or unwise love. We are called to love our enemies. We are called to work through conflict, resolve conflict nonviolently, accepting differences, and building a multiracial, multicultural world where people can affirm their unique heritages even while embracing and being embraced by a more basic unity beyond all diversity.

God the living Spirit, the eternal force for justice, the justice advocate, is turning the world upside down, insisting on justice, in the midst of the struggle for the liberation of women, oppressed races and groups, and poor and exploited nations—in the struggle for class justice and equity and an end to homophobia and sexual discrimination. God is the mighty stream, the rushing wind, the spark for freedom and justice and community empowering change that cannot be overcome. The rich and mighty will be cast down and the oppressed liberated. All people shall own their own fig tree and dwell secure from want. And so the church is called to stand in solidarity with the oppressed, with the marginalized, the poor, joining the struggles for liberation and addressing the structures of oppression on behalf of all God's people.

God the Creator is bringing order out of chaos. God the Christ is bringing unity and love out of division. God the Holy Spirit is empowering justice to end oppression. But, of course, God is one. God the Creator creates love and justice. God the Christ is passionate about justice and a just social order. God the Holy Spirit brings love and a secure community along with justice.

Similarly, in defining a just peace as the interrelation between friendship, justice, and common security from violence, there is the recognition that one of these qualities cannot be present without the other two. People have struggled for centuries to understand how God can be one and the Trinity at the same time. Perhaps it is just as difficult to hold a theology of peace that balances three concepts and attempts to insist that they are, in fact, one reality, even as they remain in tension.

It is a struggle to balance acts of friendship, acts of justice, acts leading to common security from violence. Nevertheless, it is this struggle to which the church and the world are called.

13

A Prophetic Vision of Establishing Worldwide Peace

Hugh Sanborn

Prior to the September 11 terrorist attacks and the war in Iraq, a story was told of a Christian layperson from a West Coast church, who got the president's attention in a letter requesting to speak with him about an urgent matter in her community. Thinking this woman might serve as one of those concerned citizens honored at the State of the Union address, the president had her flown to the capital for a ten-minute appointment in the Oval Office. She told him that she was deeply concerned about the terrorism that had occurred recently in her northern Oregon community. The water system had been poisoned, the electricity generating plant had been bombed, telephone wires were cut, and the one grocery store in her rural town had been burned. Many residents had died or were hospitalized as a result of the poisoned water supply and the grocery store fire that had spread to nearby homes. She asked if the president could provide some much-needed assistance. The president was alarmed and outraged. Why had he not been informed about this tragedy before now? Whoever was carrying out this terrorism on American soil should be found, tried, and executed. He assured her that he would make sure the FBI was working on finding the guilty party, no doubt Arab terrorists who had infiltrated the country. "You are the guilty party," she replied. "What you have been doing to my brothers and sisters in Iraq is ten thousand times worse than what I just described to you."

Although this is a fictional story, one wonders why more churches in the United States have not been providing leadership in confronting our elected officials for pursuing policies that have resulted in terrorism directed at innocent civilians.[1] Some have written letters and spoken out against such policies as continuing the war in Iraq during the 1990s (a topic that will be examined more closely later in this chapter), maintaining the Cuban embargo, teaching methods of terrorism to Central American military personnel at the School of the Americas in Georgia (recently renamed the Western Hemisphere Institute for Security Cooperation), selling military hardware throughout the world, declaring a war on terrorism, supporting Israel's attacks on Palestinians, and carrying out a preemptive strike on Iraq. The vast majority of churches, however, have professed ignorance of, remained silent about, or given their blessing to these policies, muting the prophetic voice of the Body of Christ.

The word *terrorism* is used here advisedly as the only word that adequately describes the modus operandi of U.S. policies that are illegal, immoral, and devastating to the civilian populations of other nations. Pursuing policies that result in the impoverishment and death of civilians, even when those civilians are citizens of nations considered to be enemies of the United States, negates what most Americans deeply affirm: the Universal Declaration of Human Rights; the UN Charter; the International Covenant on Economic, Social, and Cultural Rights; the Convention on the Rights of the Child; and the Declaration of the Right to Development. To do so is to act illegally and immorally and attempts to place our nation above international law. The results of these policies are no more acceptable than the terrorist attacks on our country on September 11, 2001.

It should be noted that the United States is one of two nations (the other being Somalia) that has refused to ratify the Convention on the Rights of the Child and stands alone as the only country voting against the UN Declaration of the Right to Development.[2] It should also be noted that the United States rejected the jurisdiction of the International Court of Justice when condemned for illegally employing military force via the contras against Nicaragua and in 1998 voted, together with Iraq, against the establishment of the International Criminal Court for dealing with war crimes.[3] Furthermore, when the Court recently became a reality, ratified by all NATO members except the United States and Turkey, the United States announced on May 6, 2002, its policy of remaining opposed to and separate from the Court and nullified its signature of the Rome Statute.[4] Such policies, as well as the arrogance underlying them, leave little doubt as to how the United States is making use of its superpower status in the world. Its policies, shaped to maintain domination,[5] are deleterious to the promotion of worldwide peace.

At the time that the Berlin Wall fell and the Cold War with the USSR ended, the hope that a new age of peace was dawning swept over the American people and most of the world. It soon became clear, however, that the power vacuum resulting from the breakup of the USSR allowed unresolved conflicts that had remained largely dormant during Cold War years to resurface. These conflicts in Eastern Europe, together with continuing conflicts in the Middle East, Africa, and parts of Asia and Central America, were impeding movement toward a peaceful world order. Furthermore, nuclear weapons, rather than being eliminated and universally outlawed, were being developed by more nations convinced that the United States and its allies, together with Russia, had no intention of completely destroying their nuclear arsenals. Wealthy nations continued to grow wealthier, in part due to the increase in the sale of armaments to poorer nations seeking to resolve internal and external conflicts militarily.

Perhaps as insidious as the proliferation of nuclear weapons and spread of armaments have been the exploitation of cheap labor and disregard for the environment on the part of many expanding multinational corporations. Capitalism in its worst form (e.g., the domination of resources, the accumulation of wealth, and the disregard for human need and the environment) has become a major export coupled with military hardware. What this has meant, of course, is that the largest flows of capital from wealthy nations are channeled into the exploitative control of capitalism and militarism and away from humanitarian concerns such as providing for the basic needs, education, and rights of the world's population.[6]

When the wealthiest nation in the world spends more on military armament and personnel than on education and assistance to the poor, provides corporate welfare during times of high profits and stagnation in labor income, and promotes the use of violent approaches for resolving conflicts, it should not be surprising to find that the public education system has suffered, the gap between the rich and the poor has increased, and violence has become a daily occurrence.

While the United States continues to express concern about the threat of terrorism from abroad, the populations of most poor nations view the United States as the chief source of terrorism in the world due to its exports of abusive capitalism and its twin, military might. At times it appears that all of the generosity and constructive programs, sponsored by Christian churches and other benevolent groups attempting to ameliorate human poverty and suffering, are dissipated by the destructive forces of the domination system, herein used to refer to the socioeconomic, political, and military-industrial complex of power.

Given this socioeconomic and political context, the need for a prophetic vision and voice is a major challenge for the Body of Christ. While it would appear self-evident that the Christian church, in faithfulness to Christ, is committed to the task of establishing worldwide peace, the complexity of what peace actually means and requires (i.e., the nature and cost of fulfilling this form of discipleship) results in considerable resistance. Use of the word *prophetic* is instructive in this regard. For the Jewish prophets through Jesus were constantly calling for faithful living that required major changes in socioeconomic and political structures as well as individual lives. They challenged their communities, society, and nation to recognize their participation in various forms of idolatry, immorality, abuse of power, and injustice. They challenged their people to reestablish a covenantal relationship with Yahweh and to serve as a light to the nations, leading the way as God's chosen people. And they spelled out the destructive consequences of a failure to do so. Far from being popular, they were frequently threatened and at times attacked and/or killed. The danger implicit in such a prophetic stance has been understood by the church from its beginning. Accepting the kind of cross it entails requires maturity in its commitment to be the Body of Christ.

Shalom, the primary Hebrew word for peace, or *salaam,*[7] the Arabic word, frequently was used comprehensively to refer to all intrapersonal, interpersonal, and socioeconomic and political relationships. Including far more than the absence of armed conflict, it referred to the health, wholeness, and integrity of individuals, communities, and society. Thus, its meaning included the health, prosperity, moral righteousness, and security of individuals and society as a whole. All of these forms of well-being were viewed as derivative from a faithful relationship with God. This use of the word *shalom* implies, in other words, the right order of all things, personally, interpersonally, and communally. Participation in wickedness or evil negates shalom and, if it persists, contaminates the entire fabric of communal and national life.[8]

The prophetic vision of peace, then, is both a spiritual ideal and a spiritual reality and process. As a spiritual ideal, it is derivative and thus a characteristic of what Jesus called the kingdom of God—love of God and one's fellow human beings manifested in all relationships and structures of society. It is a characteristic of this whole (kingdom of God). As a spiritual reality and process, peace is a characteristic of the functional whole (kingdom of God), incomplete but actualized to whatever extent the kingdom of God is actualized. Since what is being described here is the actualizing of a process, peacemaking is a more accurate term to employ.

The whole of any system or process, whether a person, institution, society, or nation, transcends the sum of its parts, as important as those parts may be. For instance, the self is a spiritual being precisely because a person is a functional whole that is shaped by all of a person's relationships, perspectives, decisions, values, and behavior, as well as the soundness of the major parts of the organism. Whether the spirit of that self is characterized as constructive or destructive has much less to do with the absence of an arm or leg than it does the nature of the commitments that shape the functioning whole or person. Does a person who has lost a leg in an automobile accident become embittered and defeated or motivated to ski down the slope of life with one healthy leg? Does a corporation, threatened by the increasing costs of doing business, choose to cut costs in a way that is harmful to its employees or that increases pollution of the environment or that avoids what is detrimental to persons, society, and the environment? The nature of the spirit of any functional whole depends on the actualized commitments and values of that whole.

Peacemaking is first and foremost a spiritual reality and process, a characteristic of the constructive functional wholeness of individuals, institutions, and society. Constructive functional wholeness implies growth, development, and higher levels of integration and moral integrity, not perfection. It is a spiritual process, of which the direction of the movement is more important than its present level of actualization. If a politician, desirous of being elected to office in order to effect constructive change, gives in to expedience and the slow erosion of personal values in order to gain and maintain political power, the negative direction of this spiritual process leads the politician further and further away from initial commitments. The same is true for an institution or society. When the constructive purpose and values of any institution, whether family, school, government, church, or other, are eroded and depleted, the spiritual process is moving in a destructive direction that contributes to the contamination of the entire fabric of society. On the other hand, when positive goals and values are being actualized, the spiritual process of peacemaking is moving in a constructive direction that contributes to the strength and vitality of the whole.

The complexity of this spiritual process might be referred to as ontological synchronicity. This places focus on the relational nature of peace and peacemaking. In its very being or nature, peacemaking is integrally related to and inseparable from all those constructive processes promoting physical, mental, and spiritual well-being; community; justice;

and a healthy environment. Breakdowns in sustaining health, fostering morality, building community, providing sound systems of justice, or maintaining a sustainable environment impede the spiritual process of peacemaking. Destructiveness in any one or more of these processes is detrimental to the spirit of the functional whole. Peace and peacemaking cannot develop and flourish in an atmosphere of ill health, immorality, broken community, injustice, and/or ecological decay.

If shalom is rightly understood as a spiritual process integrally related to the kingdom of God, a prophetic vision of establishing worldwide peace must be shaped by the criteria for actualizing the kingdom Jesus described and lived out in ministry. What are the criteria, implicit to Jesus' understanding of the kingdom, for promoting constructive movement in the spiritual process of peacemaking worldwide? Many books have been written on Jesus' understanding of the kingdom of God. The task here is much more modest or limited: to discern the major criteria for or dynamics of this theological vision of establishing the ontological synchronicity necessary for peace and peacemaking to thrive.

The first criterion for moving toward the actualization of worldwide peace is that human commitments must be nonidolatrous. For Jesus, no form of peace is possible apart from relationship with the source of peace, the eternal spirit Jesus disclosed as agape or unconditional love. It is faith in the ultimacy of God's love alone that fosters a peacemaking identity and stance in this world. Idolatry occurs when anything displaces this ultimate reality in human commitment. When idolatry occurs, separation from a relationship with the source of peacemaking inevitably promotes destructive processes that undermine it. The kingdom of God vision, love of God and one's fellow human beings, discloses the view of Jesus that God as agape is the most powerful life-giving and peace-generating reality of the universe.

There are many examples of the destructiveness of idolatrous commitments. When the central commitment of the majority (or powerful minority) of a nation is to the ultimacy of that nation, which results in fervent nationalism, this idolatrous stance leads inevitably toward division and conflict with other nations. That which is viewed as of national interest is given priority over the interests of other countries or the world community. Love of God and all people negates any and every commitment that limits the scope of that love.

The above example suggests the second criterion: inclusiveness. All persons are beloved by God. No person or group of persons is to be excluded for any reason. Those individuals and groups that exclude themselves or others through some form of idolatry are most in need of the love implicit in peacemaking. It is the nature of peacemaking to embrace all, condemning evil, but in love confronting rather than condemning the persons engaged in destructive processes. Jesus made this abundantly clear: "Let anyone among you who is without sin be the first to throw a stone..." (John 8:7). All persons are in the same boat; all are in need of God's love and forgiveness. Peacemaking thus reaches out to all individuals and groups in need of liberation from idolatry and destructive living.

The third criterion of peacemaking is constructive humanization, that is, all that is entailed in becoming mature human beings. Promoting the well-being, health, and wholeness of human beings is essential to peacemaking. This includes the meeting of basic human needs as well as the enhancement of personal and interpersonal growth and development. When the meeting of human needs is not the highest priority or raison d'être of institutions and all human endeavors, peacemaking is weakened if not silenced. Without respect for persons and their civil rights, peacemaking becomes superficial and/or a manipulative tool in the service of dehumanizing goals.

Take, for example, the sanctioning of slavery in the South on the part of a number of churches prior to the Civil War. In an effort to maintain a profitable way of life for plantation owners, slavery was frequently given the blessing of the church, which emphasized peacemaking between slaves and slave owners. The superficiality of this form of peacemaking within such an abusive system is obvious. Enslavement, as well as its remnants of racism and segregation, negates authentic peacemaking through its divisiveness and dehumanization of people. The constructive humanization process must apply to all human beings in order to eliminate the primary enemy of peacemaking, domination systems. There is no domination system in the kingdom of God.

The fourth criterion of peacemaking is the continuity between constructive ends and means. That which is inconsistent with loving God and one's fellow human beings, whether in terms of goals or means for attaining goals, is destructive to authentic peacemaking. Jesus understood that to attempt to establish a more just society by means of a bloody revolution was to destroy the goal by employing the same means as the detested domination system. If the means are not consistent with the goal of peacemaking (i.e., nonviolent), what inevitably results is the replacement of one form of a domination system with another form.

The fifth and final criterion of peacemaking, then, is commitment to nonviolence. Violence in any form is detrimental to authentic peacemaking.[9] Even when it is viewed as necessary in the service of peacemaking, as many have held was true about fighting the Second World War to stop Nazi and Japanese aggression, violence is a destroyer that has a pervasive effect on any person, group, or nation that employs and attempts to justify its use on the basis of constructive ends. History has demonstrated that the constructive nature of the ends seems elusive once violent means have been employed.[10] In the absence of peacemaking, the only war that can end all wars is the one that destroys all but one of the world's inhabitants.

It is important to recognize that the dynamics of domination systems negate those of peacemaking. As was implicit in Jesus' major pronouncements, they form the antithesis to the kingdom of God: (1) idolatrous commitments, (2) exclusion of the nonelite, (3) distortion of the humanization process, (4) discontinuity between ends and means or continuity of destructive ends and means, and (5) violent confrontation of all that threatens domination systems.

Domination systems require commitment to the ultimacy of wealth together with political and military power employed on their behalf. The only security for those exercising these forms of power lies in maintaining control. Those in control, the elites, view all nonelite groups as threats to their power status or way of life. Thus, those who control the resources must exclude and prevent those who do not from participating fully in the humanization process because utilizing resources to provide for the basic needs, development, and rights of nonelites is viewed as empowering the enemy. The humanization process is distorted; the meaning of authentic development, wholeness, and integrity is not grasped by those who believe that they are the only ones deserving of full participation in it. Destructive ends, maintaining domination, are viewed as justification for the use of destructive means. Even when some of the ends appear to be or are constructive, they are used to justify destructive means. In either case, violence is affirmed as necessary to maintain control.

When seen in their nakedness, these dynamics of domination systems readily disclose the complex forces working against authentic peacemaking. They disclose why domination systems are secretive and antidemocratic[11] in nature. Though they may out of necessity tolerate the appearance and partial practice of democracy, they are basically against, and make use of their resources to counter, participatory government. In contrast, peacemaking promotes democratic principles with the hope that the majority will participate in moving toward and eventually establishing nonexclusive power sharing and the equitable distribution of resources.

To summarize, from a theological perspective, peacemaking is a spiritual process derived from actualization of Jesus' prophetic vision of the kingdom of God. The criteria for participation in peacemaking consist of commitments to (1) nonidolatrous living, (2) inclusion of all humanity, (3) the constructive humanization process, (4) continuity between constructive ends and means, and (5) nonviolent confrontation of all domination systems. A prophetic vision of establishing worldwide peace, then, requires communities of faith professing to be the Body of Christ to engage in the prophetic leadership role of confronting and countering the destructiveness of domination systems in whatever form, whether a Saddam Hussein style of dictatorship or a U.S. style of militarism and abusive capitalism. All socioeconomic, political, and religious structures and processes, as well as individual acts, that abuse power; demonize, dehumanize, or in other ways attempt to denigrate and/or injure individuals and groups; disregard or attack human rights, thwart justice, and tear the fabric of world community or pollute the environment form powerful forces aligned against peacemaking. On the other hand, all socioeconomic, political, and religious structures and processes, as well as individual acts, that foster the building of the kingdom of God form powerful forces contributing to peacemaking.

This prophetic vision of peacemaking recognizes that faithful living is peacemaking. To live in Christ, to be liberated and transformed by the unconditional love of God, is to be part of the authentic Body of Christ and, hence, free to participate in all forms of peacemaking. Thus, it is not that churches *should* confront all forms of destructiveness; they *must* confront all forms of destructiveness. The authentic Body of Christ, in order to be true to its very nature, can do no other. Faithful living, in short, is nonidolatrous, cares about the whole human community, affirms the potential for growth and the civil rights of all people, attempts to maintain consistency between means and ends, and employs nonviolent approaches to confronting all forms of evil.

There is no perfection in either the goal or functioning of faithful living. Rather it is a growth in functional wholeness, integrated around the center of faith or the love of God that is intended here. The liberation and transformation that result from relationship to the empowering love of God free people and communities to mature in faithful living as peacemakers. This life in Christ, though in no way perfect, empowers faithful individuals and communities to be engaged in peacemaking even under threat of imprisonment, torture, or death. It is one's strengthening, energizing, and fulfilling experience of life in the spirit that overcomes the threats posed by domination systems.

This understanding of faithful living as peacemaking clarifies the fact that, implicit to the ontological synchronicity of the prophetic peacemaking vision, there are many interrelated and different levels and dimensions of peacemaking that are interrelated. Parents relating to their children; managers relating to workers; sexes, races, religions, nationalities, and cultures relating to each other; the utilization of capital and resources; the training and deployment of armies; the interests and rights of individuals, communities, and governments defined and pursued—all contribute constructively or destructively to peacemaking. When there is a passion for peacemaking at work in an increasing number of levels and dimensions of individual and corporate living, the development of new forms of conflict resolution decreases the need for large standing armies and armament stockpiles. Once capital and resources are utilized to meet the human needs of the world's citizens, trust is gradually restored between classes, and democratic principles are strengthened at all levels of government, from local communities to the United Nations, then cooperation in the interest of world community, justice, and peace begins to replace control-oriented strategies and maneuvers in the interest of select groups. In short, once peacemaking becomes a dominant force, the components of domination systems are dismantled by nonviolent means that are consistent with the kingdom of God vision. A world at peace is the result of a world community that has matured in all forms of peacemaking, both locally and worldwide.

In order to clarify the implications of this prophetic vision of peacemaking, I will examine two forms of peacemaking in which the Body of Christ is at least partially engaged: (1) confronting the acts of the domination system in Iraq and (2) countering the domination system's attempt to limit democracy through its efforts to pass the Multilateral Agreement on Investment. While there are many forms of peacemaking that would serve my illustrative purpose here, from building houses for the poor through Habitat for Humanity or similar programs to advocating for civil rights or the meeting of other human needs, these two examples are chosen as ones more problematic for congregations and, perhaps, in the long run, more crucial to the relevance and credibility of the prophetic leadership of the Body of Christ. By now it should be abundantly clear, however, that all acts of faithful living, expressing love of God and one's fellow human beings, are contributions to peacemaking.

Not dissimilar to the domination system of ancient Rome during Jesus' lifetime, the U.S.-led domination system pursues its own interests with whatever means it deems necessary. Perhaps the only substantial difference lies in the fact that Rome had no need to justify its actions. Whether it be in Cuba, Chile, Colombia, El Salvador, the Philippines, Guatemala, Nicaragua, Indonesia, Kosovo, Iraq, or Afghanistan, to name a few, the United States has employed, directly or indirectly, violent approaches to the resolution of conflict. At times it has trained and armed military death squads to attack their own people, engineered or attempted to engineer the collapse of governments, helped dictators maintain power, implemented and enforced embargoes, and/or attacked nations. Justification for its actions have ranged from stopping the advance of Communism or promoting democracy to combating the drug trade or defending another nation, all of which are stated to be in the national interest. Whether or not there has been a measure of truth in the justifications used for intervention, and whether or not the action taken was carried out under the auspices of the United Nations, the ulterior motives of the domination system have usually, if not always, been predominant.[12]

In the case of Iraq, the United States once supported Saddam Hussein, providing him with advanced armaments and biological weapons, prior to Iraq's attack on Kuwait. As destructive as it would have been, if the United States had chosen to remove him from office and assisted the Iraqi people in establishing a democracy, most of Iraq's population would have supported and applauded the United States. Instead, assisted by the United Kingdom, the United States chose quite a different and far more destructive course.

As intimated at the beginning of this chapter, the military action in Iraq during the 1990s, an air war and siege, was a highly destructive form of state terrorism directed at the civilian population. Though the American press reported little, documentation of what took place in Iraq is provided by a number of observers in articles, books, and videos. The summary of the plight of the Iraqi people that follows fails to do justice to the reality of the magnitude of the destruction to life-sustaining systems and living conditions. All of this destructive containment was ignored as the 2003 march toward all-out war gained momentum.

The decimation of the entire infrastructure of Iraq, from destruction of the sewage treatment, water purification, and electricity generating plants to the destruction of educational and health care systems, resulted in massive suffering of civilians, over one million of whom died, among them over 500,000 children.[13] Due to severe sanctions, not only were insufficient supplies of food and medicine blocked from entering the country, but spare parts needed to restore services, provide refrigeration for the food and medicine that were received, and repair everything from hospital equipment to delivery trucks were either denied or delayed.[14] Thousands of people, especially the most vulnerable, were dying weekly of diseases that could have been readily cured had the appropriate medications been available.

Exacerbating the situation was the presence of particles of depleted uranium (DU) in the dust, water, plants, and livestock. (DU does not dissipate for, at minimum, thousands of years.) The fallout from the DU-tipped bombs that were dropped in Iraq and Kuwait, estimated to be over 300 tons, is believed to be the cause of the increased rate of cancer cases that occurred since the beginning of the Gulf War. (Since unusual amounts of DU have been measured in the urine of Gulf War veterans, it may also be a major cause of the Gulf War Syndrome.)[15] To make matters worse, more DU-tipped weapons were used during the 2003 war.

This brief description of the catastrophic conditions inside Iraq leaves no doubt that state terrorism was inflicted on the civilians of Iraq. Even William Webster, CIA director at the time, testifying before Congress in 1990, admitted that such an approach would probably not result in the overthrow of or a change of policy by Saddam Hussein.[16] Clearly it was the civilians, not Saddam Hussein, who were being severely and brutally punished. To then claim that one of the reasons for the preemptive war against Iraq was to liberate the people from the regime was indeed a brutal irony, denial, and cover-up of massive proportions. To the citizens of Iraq, the terrorism resulting from U.S. policies has been more destructive than the terrorism inflicted on them by their hated dictator.

Though an increasing number of churches spoke out against these illegal and just plain evil acts of terrorism, which resulted in destroying the lives of innocent civilians, no roaring outcry demanding the end of sanctions was heard throughout our nation during the 1990s. Those who were profiting from this destructive form of state terrorism and from the 2003 war, leaders of the political, industrial, and military sectors of the domination system,[17] must be confronted in every way possible to assure that constructive change, meeting the needs and respecting the political will of the Iraqi people, will be fundamental to the reconstruction that takes place during the postwar years. It will take a considerable period of time and testing of future U.S. policy before trust can be restored. If our government really does hold restored trust as a goal, and it is dubious that it does, it will have to make major changes in its policies that affect the entire Middle East.

Peacemaking will gain momentum when increasing numbers of congregations become engaged in informing themselves and others about the nature and scope of the evil that has occurred in Iraq through seminars, worship, and networking with informed observers and each other. Creative liturgies that include prayers, responsive readings, relevant Scriptural readings from the prophets and gospels, and portions of relevant video presentations that prepare members to write officials in Washington, D.C., and the United Nations, submit articles to local newspapers, and become involved in protests. Exposing and demanding an end to destructive policies, contacting and forming supportive relationships with Iraqi churches and mosques, finding other practical and creative ways to convey solidarity with the Iraqi people, and supporting and helping to organize massive demonstrations in Washington, D.C., London, and elsewhere will make it increasingly impossible politically to continue to wage war preemptively against other nations.

If peacemaking is to maintain momentum in countering the destructiveness of the domination system, more than what is described above is required. Gaining an understanding of the dynamics of peacemaking (as well as those of domination systems), the ontological synchronicity inherent to its theological nature, and the empowerment that can result from envisioning and becoming a just peace church[18] will help restore the church to its leadership role in peacemaking. For the destructive policies of the domination system to be curtailed, preventing future Iraqs from occurring, the church will need to mobilize all of its resources to act on its peacemaking mission as the Body of Christ.

The second form of peacemaking in which the church needs to become increasingly engaged focuses on the strengthening of democracy. Although democracy is a term used daily by politicians, close examination of the context usually discloses that it is being used as a code word for capitalism. Informed debate; participation of citizens on all sides of issues; affirmation, protection, and utilization of basic freedoms; a just system of law; and participatory elections and government are among the basic principles of a democratic society. When policies are shaped in secret, civil rights curtailed, and legislation purchased by elite groups of the powerful and claimed to be in the national interest, democracy is undermined, and, as occurred in the Weimar Republic of Germany, can be fatally wounded and destroyed.

Democracy is essential to the promotion and strengthening of peacemaking. Thus, it is imperative that the Body of Christ be aware of, vigilant about, and prophetically active in confronting all efforts to undermine democracy.

One example of how the domination system has operated in secret to establish global policies that, if enacted, would have dire consequences for all democratic local and national governments, is the proposed Multilateral Agreement on Investment. At the same time that President Clinton was seeking fast-track legislation from Congress, allowing Clinton to negotiate trade agreements without congressional or public debate, the agreement negotiations, which began in May 1995, under the sponsorship of the

Organization for Economic Cooperation and Development (OECD), were moving along at a fairly rapid pace with a target date of May 1997. While this target date was later changed to April 1998, once activists obtained a copy of the draft and placed it on the Internet in February 1997, the public began to raise questions about the scope, intent, and possible consequences of such a treaty. The negotiations were finally concluded without an agreement.[19]

It should be noted that little appeared in the American press and that even the U.S. Congress was unaware of these negotiations prior to 1997.[20]

What is the Multilateral Agreement on Investment all about? In the introduction to an analysis (by the Public Citizen Global Trade Watch) of the most recent text, which is dated April 24, 1998, the agreement is described as follows:

> The MAI was, in the words of its OECD architects, to create "state of the art" standards for the treatment and protection of foreign investment. It was also to set into motion a mechanism for the progressive liberalization of investment regimes by establishing rights for foreign investors and by constraining the power of governments to regulate the activities of foreign, and in some cases, domestic investors. Proposed MAI provisions would, for instance, significantly limit stock market safeguards, performance requirements on foreign ownership of real estate and even strategic industries, and direct controls on the movement of capital.[21]

The Multilateral Agreement on Investment is viewed by those familiar with its content as a document that is intended to build on the North American Free Trade Agreement (NAFTA). Some critics have referred to it as "corporate rights agreements" rather than "investment rights agreements."[22] It has also been referred to as "the investment chapters" of NAFTA.[23] Once peace, justice, labor, and environmental organizations began criticizing the contents of the Multilateral Agreement on Investment, the OECD released a draft in February 1998 followed by the April draft that included annexes on such issues as labor and environmental standards. However, none of the annexes were ever adopted, so the April draft, which had changed very little from earlier drafts, provided the substance of what the negotiating nations hoped to achieve.[24]

At minimum, the Multilateral Agreement on Investment grants extraordinary rights, at times beyond those given by the domestic laws of Western nations, to international investors, including, of course, international corporations. At worst, it reads like a Machiavellian wish list of international corporations. Its thrust is that nothing should infringe upon, limit, or modify the absolute rights of corporations to invest in countries signing the agreement, while at the same time shifting major liabilities to the host governments. The intent of much of its content appears to be to counter, inhibit, and/or bring to an end the regulatory and expropriation functions of government that are carried out in the public interest.[25]

That the U.S. Congress was not informed about the negotiations for the Multilateral Agreement on Investment and its early drafts is in itself alarming. In November 1998, when becoming aware of and reading one of the drafts, a group of twenty-five members of Congress wrote President Clinton, seeking answers to the following questions:

- Given the administration's recent claims that it cannot negotiate complicated, multisectoral, mutilateral agreements without fast track authority, how has the Multilateral Agreement on Investment nearly been completed, with a text as intricate as NAFTA or GAT and with provisions that would require significant limitations on U.S. laws and policy concerning federal, state, and local regulations of investment?
- How has this agreement been under negotiation since May 1995 without any congressional consultation or oversight, especially given Congress' exclusive constitutional authority to regulate international commerce?
- The Multilateral Agreement on Investment provides expansive takings, language that would allow a foreign corporation or investor to directly sue the U.S. government for damages if we take any action that would restrain enjoyment of an investment. This language is broad and vague and goes significantly beyond the limited concepts of takings provided in U.S. domestic law. Why would the United States willingly cede sovereign immunity and expose itself to liability for damages under vague language such as that concerning taking any actions with an equivalent effect of an indirect expropriation?[26]

It is clear that these members of Congress were deeply disturbed by the secrecy of the negotiations and the antidemocratic nature and implications of the agreement. In Noam Chomsky's words: "The treaty is designed to undercut democracy and rights of citizens."[27]

Although the agreement negotiations ended in failure, they served notice to all individuals, groups, and agencies concerned about strengthening democracy and humanitarian policies that the powerful forces of the domination system have a different vision of the Earth's future. This anti-Christian and antidemocratic vision is shaped by the desire of the elite to maintain a position of power, privilege, and control. Legal structures are being established that increase the potential for amassing wealth; the control of Earth's resources; and the ability to limit governmental regulations, liability, and the development of the less powerful.[28]

The forces of democracy are seen as a direct threat to the actualization of this vision. Even though defeated in their initial effort, the positions spelled out in the Multilateral Agreement on Investment will no doubt reappear, perhaps under the auspices of the World Trade Organization.[29] Churches as well as peace and justice organizations need to remain informed and vigilant to assure the strengthening of democracy amid such threats as posed by the agreement.

Fulfilling the prophetic role of the Body of Christ in identifying and confronting all forms of corruption and/or proposed policies and laws that undermine democracy is fundamental to its own integrity and concomitant peacemaking activities. Keeping informed, writing editorials or letters to the editor, raising questions of and sharing viewpoints with those in political power, and establishing peacemaking networks and action groups are all essential activities of churches desirous of celebrating and enacting the prophetic vision of peacemaking. In prayers, liturgies, sacraments, hymns, statements of faith, and sermons, the peacemaking nature of the Body of Christ may be explicated, shaped, and celebrated, all of which prepare the congregation for constructive action.

Finally, one way to initiate the above would be to establish a weekly seminar series that focuses on the way the biblical prophets and Jesus confronted the domination systems of their day, imparts information about a significant issue such as the Multilateral Agreement on Investment, and closes with a communion service gathered around tables. The liturgy might focus on disclosing the destructiveness proposed or taking place, confessing the congregation's (society's) complicity in that destructiveness (stressing linkages between our decisions and lifestyles and their consequences for the world's less privileged societies), and discerning a hopeful vision of constructive change. This could be followed by celebrating communion and taking some positive action, be it writing letters, signing petitions, and/or participating in a demonstration. As an increasing number of churches assume a leadership role through this and other forms of prophetic engagement in the peacemaking process, the prophetic vision of establishing worldwide peace is creatively broadened and advanced, gains momentum, and becomes increasingly actualized.

Notes

1: Introduction: The Prophets as Challengers of Authority

[1]Alexander Rofé, *The Prophetical Stories* (Jerusalem: Magnes Press, Hebrew University, 1988), 146.

[2]Abraham Heschel, *The Prophets* (New York: Harper, 1962), 252.

[3]Rofé, 148.

[4]Ibid., 149–50.

[5]B. S. Childs, *Biblical Theology of the Old and New Testaments* (Philadelphia: Fortress Press, 1992), 170.

[6]James L. Crenshaw, *Prophetic Conflicts: Its Effect upon Israelite Religion* (ZATW 124; Berlin: Walter de Gruyter, 1971), 110.

[7]This is impressively expanded in Isaiah 1:11–17.

[8]Samuel Sandmer, *The Hebrew Scriptures* (New York: Knopf, 1963), 61.

[9]Hans Walter Wolff, *Joel and Amos* (Philadelphia: Fortress Press, 1977), 310.

[10]Ibid., 316.

[11]Shalom M. Paul, *Amos*, trans. F. M. Cross, Jr. (Minneapolis: Augsburg/Fortress Press, 1991), 239.

[12]B. S. Childs, *Introduction to the Old Testament as Scripture* (Philadelphia: Fortress Press, 1971), 410.

[13]R. E. Clements, *Prophecy and Tradition* (Oxford: Oxford University Press, 1975), 3.

[14]See William E. Phipps, *Assertive Biblical Women* (Westport, Conn.: Greenwood, 1992).

[15]J. Lindblom, *Prophecy in Ancient Israel* (Oxford: Basil Blackwell, 1980), 203.

[16]Crenshaw, 94.

[17]T. Overbolt, in *Harper/Collins Bible Commentary* (San Francisco: Harper, 1988), 572.

[18]Crenshaw, 121.

[19]Ibid.

[20]Davie Napier, *Time of Burning* (Philadelphia: Pilgrim Press), 88, 89.

[21]Crenshaw, 123.

[22]Ibid., 93, on Zechariah 13:2–6.

[23]Leander Keck, *The Church Confident* (Nashville: Abingdon Press, 1993), 20.

[24]Ibid., 121.

2: The Failure of Community

[1]Simone Weil, *The Need for Roots* (Boston: The Beacon Press, 1952), 43.

[2]Ziauddin Sardar and Merryl Wyn Davies, *Why Do People Hate America*? (Grange Road, Duxford, Cambridge: Icon Books Ltd., 2002). In this work, the authors talk about the origins of the United States as a myth:

> The American story is myth in the precise sense of the term. Myths are stories concerned with origins or the creation of some phenomenon that is social rather than individual. The American mythic vision is a set of connected motifs; from taming the wilderness and settling the frontier, the quest for freedom, the rugged individualism and self-reliance of those who created the nation, to establishing the perfect union and enshrining self-evident truths and living out a "manifest destiny." The American narrative tradition embodies this mythic vision as morality tales in which the idea of America is pure and perfect and the American self is innocent and good (p. 141).

[3]Bill Clinton, speech at the University of California, San Diego, June 14, 1997.

[4]Benjamin E. Mays, "Response" in *American Religious Values and the Future of America,* ed. Rodger Van Allen (Philadelphia: Fortress Press, 1978), 24.

[5]Sidney E. Ahlstrom, "American Religious Values and the Future of America" in *American Religious Values and the Future of America,* ed. Rodger Van Allen (Philadelphia: Fortress Press, 1978), 21.

[6]See his extended analysis of this phenomenon in Robert Jay Lifton and Greg Mitchell, *Hiroshima in America: Fifty Years of Denial* (New York: G. P. Putnam's Sons, 1995). The last

three chapters, "American Numbing," "Futurelessness and Cultural Disarray," and "Late-Twentieth-Century Death—Renewal" offer a helpful summary of his argument.

[7]Ronald J. Herring, "International Education Week: Freedom and Terror," a statement at http://www.einaudi.cornell.edu/iew.

[8]Sardar and Davies, 11.

[9]Walter Brueggemann, *Deep Memory, Exuberant Hope: Contested Truth in a Post-Christian World* (Minneapolis: Fortress Press, 2000), 60–61.

[10]Ibid., 60.

[11]Ibid., 61.

[12]Edward W. Said, *Reflections on Exile and Other Essays* (Cambridge, Mass.: Harvard University Press, 2000), 184.

[13]Ibid., 177.

[14]Brueggemann, 60.

[15]Ibid., 59.

[16]Ibid., 61.

[17]Ibid., 64.

[18]Ibid., 64–65.

[19]Said, 181.

[20]Elie Wiesel, "Longing for Home" in *The Longing for Home*, ed. Leroy S. Rouner (Notre Dame, Ind.: University of Notre Dame Press, 1996), 28.

[21]Dorothee Soelle, *The Strength of the Weak: Toward a Feminist Christian Identity* (Philadelphia: Westminster Press, 1984), 34.

[22]Wiesel, 20.

[23]Sardar and Davies have noted that in the United States we use only our own history and ideas as yardsticks for what is normal and reasonable. This becomes problematic because it puts us in binary opposition to other cultures. They suggest that the only hope for U.S. security will be through learning and knowing ourselves and the rest of the world afresh by listening to others and placing what other people know of themselves in equal prominence with what we think we know (12–13). Furthermore, they stress that this will involve our ability to learn how others see us which will be difficult, because, "To see ourselves as we appear in the eyes of other people requires us to forget our own myths and self-perceptions" (58). This is precisely what Lifton says we have the most difficulty doing.

[24]Soelle, 34.

[25]Said, 175.

[26]Ibid., 185.

[27]Dorothee Soelle, *Suffering*, trans. Everett R. Kalin (Philadelphia: Fortress Press, 1975), 5.

[28]Brueggemann, 63.

[29]Brueggemann, 64.

[30]Mary Jo Leddy, *Reweaving Religious Life: Beyond the Liberal Model* (Mystic, Conn.: Twenty-Third Publications, 1990), 158.

[31]*Book of Common Prayer*, http://anglicansonline.org/resources/bcp.html.

[32]Brueggemann, 63.

[33]Frederick Buechner, *Longing for Home: Recollections and Reflections* (San Francisco: Harper San Francisco, 1996), 140.

3: Building Authentic Faith Communities

[1]For the classical test to examine how North Americans express ambiguity about the role of community in their lives, see Robert Bellah, et al., *The Good Society* (New York: Knopf Random House, 1991).

[2]One of the best short essays that argues for multiculturalism is that of Charles Taylor, *Multiculturalism and "The Politics of Recognition": An Essay* (Princeton: Princeton University Press, 1992). A classic argument warning about the dangers of multiculturalism is given by Arthur Schlesinger, Jr., *The Disuniting of America* (New York: W. W. Norton & Co., 1992).

[3]For a more detailed analysis of the notion of spheres, see Michael Walzer, *Spheres of Justice: A Defense of Pluralism and Equality* (New York: Basic Books, 1983). Also see Ismael Garcia, *Dignidad: Ethics through Hispanic Eyes* (Nashville: Abingdon Press, 1997).

[4]A brief but insightful analysis of political cynicism and cultural meaninglessness within our culture is provided by Cornel West in *Race Matters* (Boston: Beacon Press, 1993).

[5]One of the most creative and insightful interpretations of politics as a human enterprise is given by Hannah Arendt in *The Human Condition* (Chicago: University of Chicago Press, 1958).

[6] For one of the best depictions of the biblical notion of the covenant, see William F. May, *The Physician's Covenant: Images of the Healer in Medical Ethics* (Philadelphia: Westminster Press, 1983); also see Roger Betsworth, *Social Ethics: An Examination of American Moral Traditions* (Louisville, Ky: Westminster/John Knox Press, 1990).

[7]See James Gustafson, *Theology and Christian Ethics* (Philadelphia: Pilgrim Press, 1974).

4: A Prophetic Vision of Building Worldwide Community

[1]Ralph Della Cava, "Another World Is Possible: The World Social Forum in Pôrto Alegre," *Fellowship Magazine* 68, no. 7–8 (July/August 2000): 24.

[2]Jeremy Brecher and Tim Costello, *Global Village or Global Pillage* (Boston: South End Press, 1994).

[3]Della Cava, 24.

[4]R. Marston Speight, *God Is One: The Way of Islam* (New York: Friendship Press, 1989), 79.

[5]See Michael Parenti, *The Terrorism Trap: September 11 and Beyond* (San Francisco: City Lights Books, 2002).

[6]From a speech that Dennis Kucinich, Democratic U.S. Congressman from Ohio, gave at the University of Southern California. Rep. Kucinich is the leader of the Progressive Caucus and a longtime defender of free speech, civil liberties, and international peace. This speech made him the first member of the U.S. Congress to openly repudiate President Bush's war rationale. (http://www.alternet.org, February 25, 2002).

[7]Tareq Ismael and Jacqueline Ismael, eds., *The Gulf War and the New World Order: International Relations of the Middle East* (Gainesville: University Press of Florida, 1994), 1.

[8]Michael Hardt, *Empire* (Cambridge: Harvard University Press, 2000); Noreena Hertz, *Silent Takeover: Global Capitalism and the Death of Democracy* (New York: Free Press, 2001); William Grieder, *One World, Ready or Not: The Manic Logic of Global Capitalism* (New York: Touchstone, 1998); David Korten, *When Corporations Rule the World* (San Francisco: Berrett-Koehler Publishers, 1995).

[9]*Singing the Living Tradition*, issued by The Unitarian-Universalist Association (Boston: Beacon Press, 1993), no. 475.

[10]See Psalm 137:4, which reads: "How could we sing the LORD's song in a foreign land?"

[11]John Pilger, *The New Rulers of the World* (London: Verso, 2002), 33.

[12]Walter Wink, *Engaging the Powers: Discernment and Resistance in a World of Domination* (Minneapolis: Fortress Press, 1992).

[13]"What to the Slave Is the Fourth of July?," a speech given by abolitionist Frederick Douglass, http://www.ecapc.org/newspage_detail.asp?control=335.

[14]Carol Hunter, "Does the War System Depend on Church Support?" an article introducing "Every Church a Peace Church" July 20, 2002, http://www.ecapc.org/newspage_detail.asp?control=335.

[15]Ibid.

[16]Gustavo Gutierrez, *A Theology of Liberation* (Maryknoll, N.Y.: Orbis Books, 1973).

[17]See Martin Luther King, Jr., http://www.afsc.org/nero/pesp/dppress.htm-6k.

[18]*Singing the Living Tradition*, no. 577.

[19]Michael Parenti, 18–19.

[20]See Eli Gifford and R. Michael Cook, eds., *How Can One Sell the Air: Chief Seattle's Vision* (Summertown, Tenn.: Cook Publishing Co., 1992), 31–55.

[21]Pilger, 115–31.

[22]"Reflections" of David Potor, who works with Peaceful Tomorrows, an advocacy organization founded by family members of September Eleventh victims, http://www.ecapc.org.

[23]Nuremberg War Crime Tribunal, 1950: see *Yearbook of the International Law Commission*, 2 (1950): 374–378; also see *Report of the International Law Commission Covering Its Second Session*, Document A/1316 (June 5–July 29, 1950): 11–14.

[24]Hadith 13 of Prophet Mohammed, http://members.lycos.co.uk/AshrafS/hadith.sana.htm.

[25]A quote by an eighth grader, Marlia, in William Sloane Coffin, *A Passion for the Possible* (Louisville, Ky.: Westminster/John Knox Press, 1993), 15.

[26]See http://gos.sbc.edu/w/bwilliams.html.

[27]Parker Palmer, *In the Company of Strangers: Christians and the Renewal of America's Public Life* (New York: Crossroad Publishing, 1985).

[28]Samuel P. Huntington, "Clash of Civilizations?" *Foreign Affairs* 72, no. 3, (Summer 1993): 22–28.

[29]Sura "The Chambers," in *The Holy Quran*, text, translation and commentary by A. Yusuf Ali (Maryland: Amana, 1983), no. 49, verse 13, 1407.

[30]Edward Said, "Thoughts about America," *Al-Ahram Weekly*, 28 February 2002.

[31]"ACLU Calls Immigrant Registration Program Pretext for Mass Detentions," press release, Washington, D.C., December 19, 2002, http://www.aclu.org/SafeandFree/SafeandFree.cfm?ID=11503&c=206.

[32]See Martin Luther King, Jr., "Beyond Vietnam," an address delivered to the Clergy and Laymen Concerned about Vietnam at Riverside Church, April 4, 1967, http://www.stanford.edu/group/King/publications/speeches.Frame.htm.

[33]*Singing the Living Tradition*, no. 584.

5: Issues of Ecological Concern for the Church and Society

[1]Written by an anonymous author. See endnote 4 of the article given at the following Web site: http://image.guardian.co.uk/sysfiles/Guardian/documents/2001/08/14/intro.pdf.

[2]*World Resources 2000–2001: People and Ecosystems: The Fraying Web of Life* (Washington, D.C.: WRI, 2002).

[3]"On the Brink," *Time* 156, no. 15 (October 9, 2000): 92.

[4]Walter Brueggemann, *Using God's Resources Wisely: Isaiah and Urban Possibility* (Louisville, Ky.: Westminster/John Knox Press, 1993), 15.

[5]Ibid., 5.

[6]Ibid., 50.

[7]Larry Rasmussen, *Earth Community, Earth Ethics* (Maryknoll, N.Y.: Orbis, 1996), 188.

[8]Jürgen Moltmann, *Trinity and the Kingdom* (Minneapolis: Fortress Press, 1993), 105.

[9]Demos, Raphael, ed., *Theaetetus: Plato Selection* (New York: Charles Scribner's Sons, 1927), 305–356.

[10]Quoted in Will Durant, *The Story of Philosophy* (New York: Washington Square Press, 1961), 137.

[11]James Walsh, ed., *The Cloud of Unknowing* (Mahwah, N.J.: Paulist Press, 1981), 204.

[12]Walter Hilton, *Scale of Perfection*, trans. John Clark and Rosemary Doward (Mahwah, N.J.: Paulist Press, 1991), 245.

[13]*Julian of Norwich, Showings*, trans. Edmund Colledge and James Walsh (Mahwah, N.J.: Paulist Press, 1978), 183.

[14]Brueggemann, 38.

6: Becoming a Church for Ecology and Justice

[1]Report of the Nairobi Assembly of the World Council of Churches (Geneva: WCC Publications, 1975), 54. Also see Roger Shinn, *Forced Options: Social Decisions for the 21st Century: With Reconsiderations, 3d ed.* (Cleveland: Pilgrim Press, 1989), 249.

[2]"Creation, Technology, and Human Survival" (taped recording, reels 1 and 2, at the World Council of Churches, Fifth Assembly, Nairobi, Kenya, 1975).

[3]To sample mature Christian ethical reflection from that era, read Roger Shinn, *Forced Options: Social Decisions for the 21st Century: With Reconsiderations, 3d ed.* (Cleveland:Pilgrim Press, 1989).

[4]The Annecy Consultation Report is reprinted in an appendix to *Liberating Life*, ed. Charles Birch, William Eakin, and Jay McDaniel (Maryknoll, New York: Orbis, 1991).

[5]"*A probacion del Processus Confessionis*," http://www.warc.ch/pc/harav2-s.htm.

[6]See Wesley Granberg-Michaelson, *Redeeming the Creation* (Geneva: WCC Publications, 1992), 70–73.

[7]See Roderick Frazier Nash, "The Greening of Religion," in *The Rights of Nature: A History of Environmental Ethics* (Madison: University of Wisconsin, 1989), chapter 4.

[8]Glenn C. Stone, *A New Ethic for a New Earth* (Cincinnati, Ohio: Friendship Press, 1971).

[9]See Peter Bakken, Joan Engle, and I. Ronald Engle, *Ecology, Justice and Christian Faith: A Critical Guide to the Literature* (Westport, Conn.: Greenwood Press, 1995), as well as Dieter T. Hessel and Rosemary Radford Ruether, eds., *Christianity & Ecology: Seeking the Well-being of Earth and Humans* (Cambridge: Harvard University Center for the Study of World Religions, 2000, distributed by Harvard University Press).

[10]Toward that end, in 1992, I became the founding director of the Program on Ecology, Justice, and Faith, and codirector of Theological Education to Meet the Environmental Challenge (TEMEC). These endeavors nurture in-depth theological and ethical reflection as well as cross-disciplinary study. TEMEC also has worked intensively with "lead institutions"—i.e., seminaries and religion departments—that focus on the environmental challenge through their curriculum, institutional operations, and public engagement.

[11]See Grandberg-Michaelson, 7–8.

[12]D. Hessel, ed., *Energy Ethics: A Christian Response* (New York: Friendship Press, 1979).

[13]Amory Lovins, "Energy Strategy: The Road Not Traveled?" *Foreign Affairs* (October 1976): 77.

[14]Dinyar Godrej, *The No-Nonsense Guide to Climate Change* (London: Verso, 2001), 104.

[15]Jim Schwab, *Deeper Shades of Green* (San Francisco: Sierra Club, 1994), 441.

[16]Ibid., xxii.

[17]Earth Charter, http://earthcharterusa.org.

[18]See D. Hessel, "Active Forms of the Church," in *Social Ministry* (Louisville, Ky.: Westminster/John Knox Press, rev. 1992).

[19]Discussed in D. Hessel and L. Rasmussen, eds., "The Church Ecologically Reformed," in *Earth Habitat: Eco-Injustice and the Church's Response* (Philadelphia: Fortress Press, 2001).

[20]The prophet's vision of God breathing life into the dry bones is found in Ezekiel 37. Note the role of human prophecy and of nature's four winds in enlivening the community of faith.

[21]See "A Brief Statement of Faith, Presbyterian Church (U.S.A.)," approved by the 202d General Assembly (1990), *Book of Confessions: Study Edition* (Louisville, Ky: Geneva, 1999).

7: A Prophetic Vision of Restoring the Earth

[1]Matthew Fox, speech before the United Church of Christ Office for Church Life and Leadership Dinner at UCC General Synod, June 25–30, Cleveland, Ohio; also see James E. Kiefer, "Biographical Sketch of Memorable Christians of the Past—Julian of Norwich," in Julian of Norwich, ed., *Divine Revelation* (Penguin paperback edition, http://justus.anglican.org/resources/bio/154.html).

[2]Libby Bassett, ed., *Earth and Faith: A Book of Reflection for Action* (UN Publications, 2000), 6.

[3]His Holiness the Dalai Lama, *Ethics for the New Millennium*, read by B. D. Wong, Simon and Schuster Audio, 1999.

[4]Cousteau Society Web site, http://www.cousteausociety.org/indexmain.htm.

[5]The Dalai Lama, *Ethics for the New Millennium.*

[6]Noel Brown, ed., *Ethics and Agenda 21: Moral Implications of a Global Consensus* (New York: UN Publications, 1994), 99.

[7]Ibid., 107.

[8]Ibid., 109.

[9]Ibid., 113.

[10]Ibid. 115.

[11]Phil Lane, Jr., speaking at Asset Empowerment Training on Indian Spirituality seminar (Salt Lake City, Utah, November 15, 2002).

[12]Bassett, 75–79.

8: Issues of Injustice in the Church and Society

[1]James Baldwin, "Stranger in the Village," in *The Price of a Ticket* (New York: St. Martin's/Marek Press, 1985), 85.

[2]Note that the recent national elections in the state of Florida resulted in the disenfranchisement of many black voters on false pretences. See http://www.truthout.org/docs_02/08.29A.fl.face.2K.htm.

[3]Claud Anderson, *Black Labor, White Wealth: The Search for Power and Economic Justice* (Englewood, Colo.: Powernomics Corp. of America, 1994), 13.

[4]See http://www.census.gov/hhes/www/prevcps.html.

[5]See *Statistical Abstracts of the United States: 2001* (Washington, DC: U.S. Department of Commerce, 2001), 442, 445.

[6]"Poverty in the United States: 2000," in *U.S. Bureau of the Census, Current Population Reports* (Washington, D.C.: U.S. Government Printing Office, 2001), 6.

[7]See http://www.idanetwork.org/archives/idanetwork/aug.2001/0023.html.

[8]James Carr and Jenny Schuetz, *Financial Services in Distressed Communities: Framing the Issue, Finding Solutions* (Washington, D.C.: Fannie Mae Foundation, 2001), 10, 14.

[9]See "Dred Scott Case: The Supreme Court Decision," http://www.pbs.org/wgbh/aia/part4/4h2933.html.

[10]Forrest E. Harris, *Ministry for Social Crisis: Theology and Praxis in the Black Church Tradition* (Macon: Mercer University Press, 1993), 3.

[11]See http://www.ojp.usdoj.gov/bjs/glance/tables/drracetab.htm.

[12]Cf. Scott Harris, "Between the Lines: Severe Racial Disparities in War on Drugs," a Human Rights Watch study, July 19, 2000, http://www.alternet.org.

[13]Forrest Harris, vii.

[14]Andrew Billingsley, *Climbing Jacob's Ladder: The Enduring Legacy of African-American Families* (New York: Touchstone Books, 1992), 393.

9: Building a Justice-affirming Church

[1]Statement made by the Rev. Eugene Rivers at the Call to Renewal National Summit, February 1999.

[2]Marshall Ganz, personal correspondence with Jim Wallis.

[3]The Institute for Intercultural Studies, founded by Margaret Mead, states the following about this well-known quote: "Although the Institute has received many inquires about this famous admonition by Margaret Mead, we have been unable to locate when and where it was first cited, becoming a motto for many organizations and movements. We believe it probably came into circulation through a newspaper report of something said spontaneously and informally. We know, however, that it was firmly rooted in her professional work and that it reflected a conviction that she expressed often, in different contexts and phrasing." See http://www.mead2001.org/faq_page.htm#quote.

10: From Empire to Common Security

[1]Patrick Tyler, "In Washington, a Struggle to Define the Next Fight," *New York Times*, 2 December 2001.

[2]Martin Luther King, Jr., *Where Do We Go from Here: Chaos or Community?* (New York: Bantam Books, 1968), 217.

[3]"Voice on the Tape: 'You Will Be Bombed,'" *New York Times*, 15 November 2002.

[4]See, among others, Edward S. Herman and Noam Chomsky, *Manufacturing Consent: The Political Economy of the Mass Media* (New York: Pantheon Press, 1988). Unlike any period since World War II, the Bush administration sent officials to Hollywood to enlist its resources to mobilize the nation for its global military "crusade."

[5]My favorite artifact from this period is a flag-bedraped booklet of "patriotic" quotations titled *United We Stand* that I picked up at Logan Airport in Boston. Published by the Peter Pauper Press in White Plains, New York, it was printed in China, the country in which many of the flags that graced people's homes, places of work, and automobiles were made.

[6]Nicholas Lemann, "The Quiet Man," *The New Yorker*, 2 May 2001. See, among others, Chas. Freeman and General Wesley Clark in "What This? Why Now?" a roundtable discussion in *Rolling Stone*, 26 December 2002; and David E. Sanger and James Dao, "U.S. Is Completing Plan to Promote a Democratic Iraq," *New York Times*, 6 January 2003.

[7]Nicholas Lemann, "The Next World Order," *The New Yorker*, 1 April 2002.

[8]William Appleman Williams, *Empire as a Way of Life* (New York: Oxford University Press, 1980).

[9]Dean Rusk, interview with Dr. Howard Zinn, *The Last Empire* (Cambridge Documentary Films, Cambridge, Mass., 1985). Rusk's testimony came before a Joint Hearing of the Senate Foreign Relations and Armed Services Committees.

[10]Forty-seven members of the U.S. Senate voted against authorizing the use of force against Iraq, and on successive weekends, more than 100,000 people demonstrated in Washington, D.C. against the war.

[11]Noam Chomsky, *American Power and the New Mandarins* (New York: Vintage Books, 1967).

[12]See Zbigniew Brzezinski, *The Grand Chessboard: American Primacy and Its Geostrategic Imperatives* (New York: Basic Books, 1997); Walter Russell Mead, *Mortal Splendor* (Boston: Houghton Mifflin Co. 1987).

[13]Joseph S. Nye, Jr., *The Paradox of American Power* (New York: Oxford University Press, 2002).

[14]Muto Ichiyo, "Thoughts about the Empire, Global Power Centres, and People's Alliance," in "War and Peace, Despair and Hope: Re-positioning Asian Intellectuals After 9-11," a roundtable discussion organized by the Asian Regional Exchange for New Alternatives, Hong Kong, May 8 and 9, 2002.

[15]Ambassador Edy Korthals Altes, "Pax Maricana—Fata Morgana!," Cordoba Dialog, Cordoba, Spain, November 25, 2002.

[16]James Peck, ed., *Noam Chomsky, The Chomsky Reader* (New York: Pantheon, 1987), 318.

[17]Remarks by President Clinton to AFL-CIO Biennial Convention, Pittsburgh, September 24, 1997.

[18]*Christian Science Monitor*, 16 June 1978.

[19]Jeff Gerth, "Growing U.S. Need for Oil from the Mideast Is Forecast," *New York Times*, 26 December 2002.

[20]Daniel Yergin, *The Prize: The Epic Quest for Oil, Money & Power* (New York: Simon & Schuster, 1991); Noam Chomsky, "The Drift Towards War and the Alternatives" in Peggy Duff, ed., *War or Peace in the Middle East?* (London, Spokesman Books, 1978), 27; Saburo Ienaga, *The Pacific War: 1931–1945* (New York: Pantheon Books, 1978); Joseph Gerson, *With Hiroshima Eyes: Atomic War, Nuclear Extortion, and Moral Imagination* (Philadelphia: New Society Publishers, 1995).

[21]Transcripts, World Conference against Atomic and Hydrogen Bombs (Tokyo: Japan Council against Atomic and Hydrogen Bombs, 2002).

[22]A quotation from then General Dwight D. Eisenhower, in Gar Alperovitz, "The Hiroshima Decision: A Moral Reassessment," *Christianity and Crisis* (February 3, 1992). See also Gar Alperovitz, *The Decision to Use the Atomic Bomb* (New York: Vintage Books, 1995).

[23]Martin J. Sherwin, *A World Destroyed: The Atomic Bomb and the Grand Alliance* (New York: Vintage Books, 1975), 209. (This is the targeting criteria initially suggested by James Conant, Chairman of the Interim Committee.)

[24]William Appleman Williams, *The Tragedy of American Diplomacy* (New York: Delta Books, 1962), 254.

[25]See, among others, transcripts of the World Conference against Atomic and Hydrogen Bombs (Tokyo: Japan Council against Atomic and Hydrogen Bombs, 2002), and "Global Hibakusha Share Their Stories and Hopes," Testimonies of the Global Hibakusha Delegation to the Hague Appeal for Peace Conference (Cambridge, Mass.: American Friends Service Committee, 1999, http://www.afsc.org/nero/pesp/hibak.htm).

[26]Joseph Gerson, *With Hiroshima Eyes;* Dana Milbank, "An Implied Threat," *Washington Post National Weekly Edition*, 15–21 October 2001.

[27]Noam Chomsky, interview conducted during the production of *The Last Empire* (Cambridge, Mass.: Cambridge Documentary Films, 1985).

[28]Natural Resources Defense Council, "Faking Nuclear Restraint: The Bush Administration's Secret Plan for Strengthening U.S. Nuclear Forces," February 13, 2002, http://www.nrdc.org/media/pressreleases/020213a.asp; Michael R. Gordon, "U.S. Nuclear Plan Sees New Targets and New Weapons," *New York Times*, 10 March 2002; John H. Cushman, Jr., "Rattling New Sabers," *New York Times*, 10 March 2002.

[29]Natural Resources Defense Council study, "Faking Nuclear Restraint."

[30]Ibid. The immediately available stockpiled arsenal will include 240 warheads of Trident submarines being overhauled, 1,350 strategic missile and bomber warheads in the response force reserves, 800 nonstrategic nuclear weapons deployed on U.S./NATO dual capable aircraft, 320 nonstrategic sea-launched cruise missile warheads in the reserve force, 160 spare strategic and nonstrategic warheads, 4,900 intact warheads in the inactive reserve stockpile, and 5,000 stored primary and secondary components available for reassembly.

[31]Ezra Vogel, Wenrong Qian, Dingli Shen, Ouyang Liping, and Xia Liping, interviews in Cambridge, Mass., Beijing, China, and Shanghai, China, April and May 1998.

[32]J. William Fulbright, *The Arrogance of Power* (New York: Random House, 1967).

[33]In addition to the widely reported remarks of the German Justice Minister in the weeks before the 2002 German election, senior European diplomats have made similar comments to the author in private conversations.

[34]Karl Jaspers, *The Question of German Guilt* (New York: Capricorn Books, 1961), 32.

[35]Ibid., 76.

[36]Stella Rimington, "Terrorism Did Not Begin on September 11," *The Guardian* (4 September 2002).

[37]Before the 1991 Gulf War, quality health care was available to all Iraqis for the cost of forty cents per visit. A friend of the author's benefited from successful neurosurgery that cost forty cents.

[38]Information from, among others, the Campaign of Conscience for the Iraqi People, of the American Friends Service Committee and many other groups.

[39]See, among others, Daniel Ellsberg, "A Call to Mutiny," in *The Deadly Connection: Nuclear Weapons and the U.S. Intervention*, ed. Joseph Gerson (Boston: South End Press, 1984); McGeorge Bundy, *Danger and Survival: Choices about the Bomb in the First Fifty Years* (New York: Random House, 1988); Richard K. Betts, *Nuclear Blackmail and Nuclear Practice and Nuclear Balance* (Washington, D.C.: The Brookings Institution, 1987); Barry M. Blechman and Stephen S. Kaplan, *Force without War: U.S. Armed Forces as Political Instruments* (Washington, D.C.: The Brookings Institution, 1978); Michio Kaku and Daniel Axelrod, *To Win a Nuclear War: The Pentagon's Secret War Plans* (Boston: South End Press, 1987).

[40]John Deutch, panel on Loose Nukes at MIT, Cambridge, Mass., October 16, 1998.

[41]Quoted in speech of Ambassador Hasmy Agam, permanent representative of Malaysia to the United Nations, in his speech to the World Conference against Atomic and Hydrogen Bombs, August 9, 2001, Nagasaki, Japan. Transcripts of the 2001 World Conference against Atomic and Hydrogen Bombs (Tokyo: Gensuikyo, 2001).

[42]See, among others, Alyn Ware, *Neither Sword nor Shield: Nuclear Disarmament as the Response to Military Threats* (Tokyo: Gensuikyo, 2001).

[43]Martin Luther King, Jr., 199, 200.

[44]Ibid.

[45]In the Greek myth that is central to Western culture, Prometheus steals fire from the gods.

[46]Martin Luther King, Jr., 198–200.

[47]Independent Commission on Disarmament and Security Issues, *Common Security: A Blueprint for Survival* (New York: Simon and Schuster, 1982), 100.

[48]Ibid., 8–10.

[49]Ibid., ix, 11, 12. See also Xiong Guangkai, "New Security Concept Boosts Peace," *Washington Post National Weekly Edition*, 23 December 2002, S3.

[50]Carroll Quigley, *The Evolution of Civilizations* (New York: The Macmillan Company, 1961).

[51]Karl Jaspers, 89.

[52]Two of the many ads that dominated the Boston airwaves in December 2002.

[53]See, among others, Christopher Lasch, *Haven in a Heartless World: The Family Besieged* (New York: Basic Books Inc., 1977); Christopher Lasch, *The Culture of Narcissism: American Life in an Age of Diminishing Expectations* (New York: Warner Books, 1979).

[54]"Is Truth a Victim?" http://news.bbc.co.uk/1/hi/programmes/newsnight/1991885.stm. In a May 17, 2002, interview with the British Broadcasting Corporation, Dan Rather confessed that leading journalists feared posing the most important and challenging questions to national leaders, saying that it would be the equivalent of South African necklacing. (During the antiapartheid struggle, blacks who collaborated with the apartheid government sometimes had tires that had been soaked in gasoline placed around their neck and ignited.) At the very least, Rather explained, asking those hard questions could jeopardize a journalist's career from the lack of access that would then follow as retaliation.

[55]Ambassador Edy Korthals Altes, "Pax Maricana—Fata Morgana!," Cordoba Dialog, Cordoba, Spain, November 25, 2002.

[56]James Carroll, "Cloning, Terror and Our Humanity," *The Boston Globe*, 7 January 2003. Another insightful exploration about the relationship between individual and moral identity and democracy can be found in Patrick Smith's book, *Japan: A Reinterpretation* (New York: Pantheon Books, 1997).

[57]John Rawls, *A Theory of Justice* (Cambridge, Mass.: The Harvard University Press, 1971).

[58]Rep. Steven Lynch, Needham (Mass.) Public Library, December 17, 2002.

[59]Mark Solomon, "The Pianist," distributed by PortsideMod@netscape.net, December 28, 2002. (Solomon is Professor Emeritus of Sociology at Simmons College in Boston.)

[60]C. Wright Mills, *The Causes of World War Three* (New York: Simon and Schuster, 1958), 132, 133, 139, 140.

[61]Peck, ed., *Noam Chomsky, The Chomsky Reader*, 325.

[62]See, among others, John Dewey, *Experience & Education* (New York: Collier Books, 1963); Myles Horton and Paulo Freire, *We Make the Road by Walking* (Philadelphia: Temple University Press, 1990); Carol Gilligan, *In a Different Voice: Psychological Theory and Women's Development* (Cambridge: Harvard University Press, 1982).

[63]Kato Miki, personal conversation with Joseph Gerson.

[64]I refer here to the 2000 presidential vote in Florida that was confirmed by a Supreme Court that included members whose families were on the payroll of George W. Bush. Also referred to here is the "Peoples' Power" revolution that ousted the Marcos dictatorship and the corrupt administration of President Estrada. Remarkably, Floridians and others in the United States were willing to tolerate the continued disenfranchisement of blacks that contributed to Jeb Bush's reelection as governor in 2002.

[65]Michael Ignatieff, "The Burden," *New York Times*, 5 January 2003.

[66]Numerous models for reducing the size and cost of the U.S. military, without sacrificing U.S. security, have been made, including those of the Center for Defense Information, the Brookings Institute, and the Commonwealth Institute.

11: Issues of Peacemaking in the Church and Society

[1]Quoted in Richard Newell Myers, "A Gathering of Many Faiths," *Fellowship* 48, no. 7–8 (July/August 1982): 13.

[2]From the personal files of Richard L. Deats who was arrested at the Chinese mission while delivering this message.

[3]From charts of Business Leaders for Sensible Priorities, http://www.moveourmoney.org.

[4]Jonathan Schell, "The Growing Nuclear Peril," *The Nation* 274, no. 24 (June 24, 2002): 11–13.

[5]Jonathan Schell, "The Gift of Time," *The Nation* 266, no. 4 (February 2/9, 1998): 57.

[6]The religious leaders signing were the Rev. H. George Anderson, the Rev. John A. Buehrens, Archbishop Demetrois, the Rev. Bob Edgar, the Rev. Wesley Granbert-Michaelson, the Most Rev. Frank T. Griswold, III, the Rev. R. Burke Johnson, Shaykh Muhammad Hisham Kabbani, the Rev. Clifton Kirkpatrick, Rabbi Charles A. Krolof, Rabbi Vernon Kurtz, Bishop William B. Oden, the Rev. Judy Mills Reimer, Rabbi David Saperstein, the Rev. Robert Sawyer, Monsignor Dennis M. Schnurr, Dr. Muzammil H. Siddiqi, Metropolitan

Theodosius, the Rev. John H. Thomas, the Rev. Jim Wallis, and the Rev. Daniel E. Weiss. The military leaders (all retired) signing were Lt. Gen. Julius Becton, Brig. Gen. Homer Boushey, Brig. Gen. Dallas Brown, Jr., Maj. Gen. William F. Burns, Rear Adm. Eugene J. Carroll, Jr., Lt. Gen. John H. Cushman, Lt. Gen. Robert G. Gard, Adm. Noel Gayler, Gen. Chas. A. Horner, Rear Adm. Robert G. James, Chaplain (Maj. Gen.) Kermit D. Johnson, Maj. Gen. Jack Kidd, Gen. Robert C. Kingston, Rear Adm. Eugene LaRocque, Adm. Stephen T. Quigley, Vice Adm. John J. Shanahan, Adm. Stanisfield Turner, and Vice Adm. James B. Wilson. From Joint Nuclear Reduction/Disarmament Statement, June 2000, http://www.cathedral.org/cathedral/nuclear.

[7]"In the Name of God, Let Us Abolish Nuclear Weapons Now," brochure issued by the Fellowship of Reconciliation, the New Call to Peacemaking, Pax Christi USA, Sojourners, World Peacemakers, and Kirkridge Retreat Center (1998).

[8]Center for Global Development/Center on Budget and Policy Priorities, http://www.centeronbudget.org.

[9]SOA Watch, *School of Assassins* (Washington, D.C., 1999).

[10]SOA Memorial Service leaflet (November 22, 1998), 2.

[11]Nunca Mas! Never Again! Tenth Anniversary Commemoration Program (November 21, 1999).

[12]*Fellowship* 65, no. 5–6 (May–June 1999): 4–6.

[13]*Ecumenical News International Daily News Service*, 05 February 2001.

12: Building a Peacemaking Church

[1]National Conference of Catholic Bishops, *The Challenge of Peace: God's Promise and Our Response, A Pastoral Letter on War and Peace* (Washington, D.C.: U.S. Catholic Conference, 1983).

[2]Susan Thistlethwaite, *A Just Peace Church* (New York: United Church Press, 1986).

[3]United Methodist Council of Bishops, *In Defense of Creation: The Nuclear Crisis and a Just Peace* (Nashville: Graded Press, 1986), 33.

[4]For example, see V. Bernat, "Teaching Peace," *Young Children* 48, no. 3: 36–39; N. Carlsson-Paige and D. Levin, *Helping Young Children Understand Peace, War, and the Nuclear Threat* (Washington, D.C.: National Association for the Education of Young Children, 1985); M. Montessori, *Education for Peace* (Washington, D.C.: Regnery, 1972); J. Guliano, "A Peer Education Program to Promote the Use of Conflict Resolution Skills among At-risk School Age Males," *Public Health Reports*, no. 109 (March 1994): 158–61; Judy Hoffein, ed., *Resolving Conflict Creatively: A Collection of Activities for Elementary and Middle School Students* (Houston: Houston Area Committee for Youth and Nonmilitary Opportunities, 2000). Also see the curriculums published by all of the major Protestant denominations.

[5]Roland Bainton, *Christian Attitudes toward War and Peace* (New York, Abingdon Press, 1960).

[6]Carol Cory, Jay Lintner, and Lowell Livezey, *Peace Futuring* (a curriculum; New York: Office for Church in Society, United Church of Christ, 1981).

13: A Prophetic Vision of Establishing Worldwide Peace

[1]See Anthony Arnove, ed., *Iraq under Siege* (Cambridge: South End Press, 2000), 10, 60–64. Also note that Denis Halliday, former UN humanitarian coordinator in Baghdad, labels what was taking place in Iraq in the 1990s under U.S. leadership "genocide"—see *Iraq under Siege*, 44–45.

[2]Ibid., 164.

[3]"US struggles to limit the reach of a global court," *Christian Science Monitor*, 3 July 2000, 10.

[4]See the *New York Times International*, 7 May 2002, 11.

[5]For a convincing exposition of the nature of domination systems, see Walter Wink, *Engaging the Powers: Discernment and Resistance in a World of Domination* (Minneapolis: Augsburg, 1992), 39–43, 66–85. Given the policies of the U.S.-controlled International Monetary Fund and World Bank—requiring undeveloped nations in need of loans to withdraw funding from education, medical care, welfare, etc.—and the exploitation of cheap labor by international corporations, one might argue convincingly that the United

States is utilizing its superpower status to maintain a modern form of the feudal system in which undeveloped nations fulfill the role of indentured serfs.

[6]See Noam Chomsky, *Profit over People* (New York: Seven Stories, 1999), 21–25.

[7]Salaam is frequently used in the Koran to refer to salvation in this world as well as the next. In this world, it refers to the "interdependence and solidarity" of all humans with one another and with Allah. "There can be no permanent system in human life until this integration and unification has taken place. This step is a prerequisite for true and complete human life, so that the rule of force may be done away once and for all, and so that those who have wandered from the true path may be brought back to it." S. N. K. Singh, *Social Justice and Human Rights in Islam* (New Delhi: Gyan, 1998), 83.

[8]Cf. E. M. Good, "Shalom," in *The Interpreter's Dictionary of the Bible*, ed. by George Buttrick (Nashville: Abingdon Press, 1962), 704–706.

[9]Though most U.S. newspapers made no mention of it, more than 200 leaders of the world's major religions met at Assisi, Italy, on January 24, 2002, and reached agreement on the following "Decalogue of Assisi for Peace":

1. We commit ourselves to proclaiming our firm conviction that violence and terrorism are incompatible with the authentic spirit of religion, and, as we condemn every recourse to violence and war in the name of God or of religion, we commit ourselves to doing everything possible to eliminate the root causes of terrorism.
2. We commit ourselves to educating people to mutual respect and esteem, in order to help bring about a peaceful and fraternal coexistence between people of different ethnic groups, cultures and religions.
3. We commit ourselves to fostering the culture of dialogue, so that there will be an increase of understanding and mutual trust between individuals and among peoples, for these are the premise of authentic peace.
4. We commit ourselves to defending the right of everyone to live a decent life in accordance with their own cultural identity, and to form freely a family of his own.
5. We commit ourselves to frank and patient dialogue, refusing to consider our differences as an insurmountable barrier, but recognizing instead that to encounter the diversity of others can become an opportunity for greater reciprocal understanding.
6. We commit ourselves to forgiving one another for past and present errors and prejudices, and to supporting one another in common effort both to overcome selfishness and arrogance, hatred and violence, and to learn from the past that peace without justice is no true peace.
7. We commit ourselves to taking the side of the poor and the helpless, to speaking out for those who have no voice and to working effectively to change these situations out of the conviction that no one can be happy alone.
8. We commit ourselves to taking up the cry of those who refuse to be resigned to violence and evil, and we desire to make every effort possible to offer the men and women of our time real hope for justice and peace.
9. We commit ourselves to encouraging all efforts to promote friendship between peoples, for we are convinced that, in the absence of solidarity and understanding between peoples, technological progress exposes the world to a growing risk of destruction and death.
10. We commit ourselves to urging leaders of nations to make every effort to create and consolidate, on the national and international levels, a world of solidarity and peace based on justice.

See www.vatican.va/special/assisi_20020124_en.html.

[10]Cf. Wink, 195–207.

[11]Cf. Chomsky, 9–11.

[12]Cf. Peter Mitchell and John Schoeffel, eds., *Understanding Power: The Indispensable Chomsky* (New York: New Press, 2002), 1–12, 64–67.

[13]*Iraq under Siege*, 67.

[14]Ibid., 26, 60, and 71.

[15]Ibid., 93–103.

[16]Ibid., 152.

[17]Cf. Ibid., 50–55.

[18]See Susan Thistlethwaite, *A Just Peace Church* (New York: United Church, 1986), 86.

[19]Cf. Chomsky, 185–86.

[20]Ibid., 140 and 142.

[21]"MAI Provisions and Proposals: An Analysis of the April 1998 Text," Public Citizen Global Trade Watch, 1998, 1.

[22]Chomsky, 147–48.

[23]MAI Provisions and Proposals, 1.

[24]Ibid., 1–2.

[25]Cf. Ibid., 3–6.

[26]Chomsky, 140–41.

[27]Ibid., 145.

[28]With increasing awareness of the serious ethical issues implicit within international trade and investment negotiations, a number of organizations, church bodies, and other institutions have endorsed the following five principles:

1. International trade and investment systems should respect and support the dignity of the human person, the integrity of creation, and our common humanity.
2. International trade and investment activities should advance the common good and be evaluated in the light of their impact on those who are most vulnerable.
3. International trade and investment policies and decisions should be transparent and should involve the meaningful participation of the most vulnerable stakeholders.
4. International trade and investment systems should respect the legitimate role of government, in collaboration with civil society, to set policies regarding the development and welfare of its people.
5. International trade and investment systems should safeguard the global commons and respect the right of local communities to protect and sustainably develop their natural resources.

For further elaboration on these five principles, see "An Interfaith Statement on International Trade and Investment," www.iwg@coc.org.

[29]Since these words were written, early reports about the private negotiations on the Free Trade Area of the Americas (FTAA) indicate that much of the content of the Multilateral Agreement on Investment will be included in this attempted hemispheric expansion of NAFTA scheduled for completion and implementation in 2005. See "Unveiling NAFTA for the Americas," Public Citizen Global Trade Watch, January 6, 2001, 1–2.

Printed in the United States
21550LVS00005B/1-66